THEY KNEW LINCOLN

THEY KNEW LINCOLN

JOHN E. WASHINGTON

with a new introduction by Kate Masur

OXFORD
UNIVERSITY PRESS

OXFORD
UNIVERSITY PRESS

Oxford University Press is a department of the University of Oxford. It furthers
the University's objective of excellence in research, scholarship, and education
by publishing worldwide. Oxford is a registered trade mark of Oxford University
Press in the UK and certain other countries.

Published in the United States of America by Oxford University Press
198 Madison Avenue, New York, NY 10016, United States of America.

© Oxford University Press 2018

Original text first published by E.P. Dutton & Co., Inc., New York, in 1942

Library of Congress Cataloging-in-Publication Data
Names: Washington, John E., author. | Masur, Kate.
Title: They knew Lincoln / John E. Washington ; with a new
introduction by Kate Masur.
Description: New York, NY : Oxford University Press, 2018. | Originally published
in 1942 and now reprinted for the first time, with new introduction.
Identifiers: LCCN 2017026385 (print) | LCCN 2017026698 (ebook) |
ISBN 9780190270971 (Updf) | ISBN 9780190270988 (Epub) |
ISBN 9780190270964 (hardback)
Subjects: LCSH: Lincoln, Abraham, 1809–1865—Anecdotes. | Lincoln, Abraham,
1809–1865—Friends and associates—Attitudes—Anecdotes. | Lincoln, Abraham,
1809–1865—Employees—Attitudes—Anecdotes. | Lincoln, Abraham,
1809–1865—Relations with African Americans—Anecdotes. |
African Americans—Attitudes—History—19th century—Anecdotes. |
African Americans—Washington (D.C.)—History—19th century—Anecdotes. |
Presidents—United States—Biography—Anecdotes. |
BISAC: HISTORY / United States / 19th Century. |
HISTORY / United States / General.
Classification: LCC E457.15 (ebook) | LCC E457.15 .W32 2018 (print) |
DDC 973.7092—dc23
LC record available at https://lccn.loc.gov/2017026385

1 3 5 7 9 8 6 4 2
Printed by Sheridan Books, Inc., United States of America

CONTENTS

ACKNOWLEDGMENTS

My research on the life of John E. Washington and the publication of *They Knew Lincoln* has spanned a decade, and many people have assisted and inspired me along the way. Tom Schwartz, then state historian of Illinois and now director of the Herbert Hoover Presidential Library and Museum, offered crucial early advice and encouragement. Historian Catherine Clinton nudged at a moment when I was doubtful. Archivists and librarians at Howard University have scoured their records looking for relevant materials. For their time and patient guidance, I thank Celia Daniel, Joellen El Bashir, Clifford Muse, and Arthuree Wright. I'm particularly grateful to Sonja Woods of the Moorland-Spingarn Research Center at Howard for unearthing sources that surprised me. At the Library of Congress, Clark Evans, Jeffrey Flannery, and Michelle Krowl were invaluable guides and supporters. Kimberly Springle, executive director of the Charles Sumner School Museum and Archives, went to great lengths to help me trace John E. Washington's history as a teacher in the District of Columbia Public Schools.

Martha S. Jones has supported this project all along and encouraged me to present my research at the 2014 conference, *Black Historians and the Writing of History,* at Université Paris Diderot. I am grateful to the organizers, especially Claire Parfait and Marie-Jeanne Rossignol, for including me and for creating an occasion in which scholars with allied interests could exchange ideas. Thanks also to Jean-Christophe Cloutier for pointers about Claude McKay; James Cornelius, curator at the Abraham Lincoln Presidential Library; and Derek Gray at the District of Columbia Public Library. For valuable conversations and advice I also thank Terry Alford, Marc Fisher, John Sellers, David Von Drehle, and Douglas Wilson. Toward the end of the project, David McKenzie and Matthew Gilmore helped me with key details about John E. Washington's family and the Ford's Theatre neighborhood. The office of digital curation at the Northwestern University Library scanned the images from *They Knew Lincoln* and made them available to Oxford University Press. Susan Ferber, my editor at Oxford, immediately saw merit in republishing this book, and I'm grateful for her support. The press sent my draft introduction to four expert readers, including Clare Corbould, and I benefited enormously from their feedback. For astute readings of the penultimate version, I thank Henry Binford, Melanie Chambliss, Clare Corbould, Leslie Harris, Jonathan Holloway, and Peter Slevin. All remaining errors of fact or interpretation are of course my own.

They Knew Lincoln sold out quickly and was never reprinted, a fact that frustrated John E. Washington. I like to imagine that he would appreciate his book's republication and be pleased that the field of African American history is flourishing and that our collective curiosity about Abraham Lincoln and the era of the Civil War continues.

INTRODUCTION

John E. Washington and They Knew Lincoln

KATE MASUR

Elizabeth Keckly's 1868 memoir, *Behind the Scenes, or, Thirty Years a Slave, and Four Years in the White House,* suddenly reentered national consciousness in the mid-1930s, when journalist and Democratic political operative David Rankin Barbee claimed that Keckly had not written the book and, remarkably, had never existed.[1] Barbee's bold assertions, widely circulated by the Associated Press, caused special consternation in Washington, DC, where many African Americans personally remembered Keckly, the black woman who had created many of Mary Todd Lincoln's famous gowns and had been the First Lady's trusted confidante. The day after the AP story was published, Barbee's "phone rang all day" as black Washingtonians sought to disabuse him of his wrongheaded ideas.[2]

Perhaps the most determined person to stand up for Keckly was a public school teacher named John E. Washington. In a lengthy letter to the *Washington Star,* Washington rebutted Barbee's charge that Keckly had never lived while conceding that questions remained concerning who, if anyone, might have helped her write the book that bore her name. Noting that the Library of Congress's curator of rare books had suggested that Barbee's allegations were plausible, Washington said it was "fortunate" that the controversy was occurring "at this time because these gentlemen can easily obtain all facts pertaining to Mrs. Keckley from persons who knew her best."[3]

John E. Washington's encounter with popular skepticism about Keckly and *Behind the Scenes* changed his life and led him to write a remarkable book of his own—*They Knew Lincoln*. Already a collector of Lincoln-related materials, Washington plunged into research on Keckly, determined to publish a pamphlet explaining who she was and how *Behind the Scenes* came into existence. But his project expanded as he became increasingly interested in the largely unknown lives of the African American domestic workers the Lincolns had known in Springfield, Illinois, and Washington, DC. He conducted research in collections across the Southeast and Midwest. He interviewed elderly African Americans in Washington, Maryland, Virginia, and Illinois. And he reached out to the foremost Lincoln scholars and collectors of his era, hoping for leads and new information. This would be a book on the "colored side of Lincolniana," he told a friend. *They Knew Lincoln* was published by E. P. Dutton in January 1942, with a strong endorsement by the famed poet and Lincoln biographer Carl Sandburg.

Part memoir, part history, part argument for the historical significance of common people, *They Knew Lincoln* was the first book to focus exclusively on Lincoln's relationship to African Americans. By contrast, William Herndon, the prominent early Lincoln biographer, had collected interviews and letters from hundreds of Lincoln's friends and acquaintances but ignored the many black people whose lives had intersected with Lincoln's. Characteristic of Herndon's approach was his description of Lincoln's revulsion on witnessing a slave auction in New Orleans, a vignette that was central to early accounts of Lincoln's opposition to slavery. Unlike Herndon, John E. Washington knew from childhood that African Americans had not been merely objects of Lincoln's attention or sympathy but important figures in his daily life. "Lincoln's views on the injustices of slavery did not all come from his visit to the slave markets in New Orleans," Washington wrote. "They were strengthened by his observation of the colored people who served him."[4] *They Knew Lincoln* revealed that African Americans, from the obscure folk preacher known as Uncle Ben to the much more prominent Elizabeth Keckly, had shaped Lincoln's life, and it demonstrated that their stories were worth knowing.

The book proceeds from the local to the general, connecting the lives of black men and women of Lincoln's time to John E. Washington's own, largely twentieth-century existence and, by the end, offering a unique compilation of sources and stories. The first section consists of vignettes from Washington's early life and stories told by the men and women of his grandmother's circle, many of whom had crossed paths with Lincoln. In the second section, Washington takes up the histories of black people who worked in the Lincoln White House or otherwise knew the Lincolns. In the final parts of the book, Washington describes episodes in the lives of more prominent figures, including William de Fleurville, Lincoln's barber and legal client in Springfield, Illinois, and Elizabeth Keckly herself. Wherever practical, including in a lengthy appendix, he included transcriptions or photographs of documents meant to authenticate his work and make his sources available to others.

Across the country, newspapers and magazines reviewed *They Knew Lincoln,* and most critics acclaimed the work as an important new contribution in the crowded field of Lincolniana. Many noted the unprecedented nature of Washington's collection of African American perspectives on Lincoln. Prominent actors dramatized portions of the book in a Harlem radio show, and the editors of an anthology of African American literature printed an excerpt. The book's initial print runs sold out almost immediately. Yet Dutton never republished it, and copies became exceedingly hard to find. This Oxford University Press reprint edition makes *They Knew Lincoln* newly available to twenty-first-century readers. The book is a pioneering work of history, and the story of its author and original publication is told here for the first time.

* * * * * * *

In *They Knew Lincoln,* John E. Washington wove together narratives of his own experience with the stories of African Americans who had encountered Lincoln. The son and grandson of slaves, Washington was born in Annapolis, Maryland, in 1880 and orphaned as a small boy. His grandmother raised him in Washington, DC, and he spent his early years in the boarding house she managed near Ford's Theatre. Influenced by stories he heard from elderly people in his community, he developed a lifelong fascination with Abraham Lincoln and the era of the Civil War. Washington came of age in a period when the nation's capital was a center of for black education and intellectual life. He was a part of that world, earning three degrees at Howard University and gaining access to some of the city's most elite black institutions while working as a dentist and, later, a teacher at Cardozo High School. Barbee's assault on Keckly's credibility pushed Washington to intensify his research on black people's connections with Lincoln, and in the process he reached out to the largely white world of Lincoln scholars and collectors. Cultivating allies and drawing on deep wells of determination, he was able to overcome hurdles that might have hobbled someone else. His book was his proudest achievement.

They Knew Lincoln begins on a personal note. "My earliest recollections are those of a little boy playing on E Street near Ford's Theater," he wrote. Fifteen years before he was born, John Wilkes Booth assassinated Abraham Lincoln in that theatre, which stood just around the corner from the boarding house where he lived with his grandmother, Caroline Washington. His life was shaped by his experiences there, "sitting up nights and listening to ghost stories of the neighborhood as told by the old colored people who worked and lived there, and hearing wonderful stories about Lincoln, his family, and Booth, from the mouths of some who had really seen them, and from others who claimed they had seen their ghosts."[5]

Caroline Washington spent her early life enslaved in Maryland, and she envisioned upward mobility and education for her descendants. Her grandson wrote admiringly of the values she instilled. She read the newspaper every day. She advised him to live in a "home," not an apartment; to avoid alcohol and nightclubs; and to be faithful to God. And she had strong ideas about family lineage. Their family had "blue blood" in its veins, she told John, and some of their ancestors were Native American.[6] Caroline rejected what she saw as the superstitious beliefs and practices of many of her friends and neighbors. She saved money to send a granddaughter to college and made sure John had access to a big shelf of books. The granddaughter—John's cousin Annie—worked as a teacher and contributed books to his collection. That was how Washington first learned of Elizabeth Keckly's *Behind the Scenes*. The volume had become difficult to find soon after its publication, but somehow Annie procured one and brought it home to E Street.

Even as Caroline urged her offspring to have high expectations for themselves and to set themselves apart from others in their milieu, she fostered a sense of community and shared destiny with her neighbors. She was "her own boss and really ran the [boarding] house," her grandson wrote.[7] Unlike many in her community who lived in the homes of their employers, his grandmother had her own space, and she put it to good use. "All of the boarders and roomers were white," Washington recalled, but his grandmother made the basement kitchen and sitting room hospitable places where her black friends and neighbors could gather and speak freely, reminisce about their lives, and observe holidays.[8] Among her friends were tellers of ghost stories, singers of spirituals, and practitioners of folk medicine. Most had been born in slavery, and many had never learned to read or write. As those women and men passed away, John felt himself "the sole survivor of a once great storytelling group."[9]

Born a decade and a half after the Thirteenth Amendment abolished slavery in the United States, Washington attended school from early boyhood, pursued advanced degrees, and worked as a teacher and a dentist. As an adult he owned a home in Washington's LeDroit Park neighborhood and a vacation residence in Highland Beach, Maryland. Perhaps it was his understanding of the opportunities he had been able to enjoy that made him so interested in the increasingly distant world of his grandmother and her friends. Raised in what seemed a wholly different place and time, they had lived as slaves and experienced the drama and displacement of the Civil War. Washington determined that their stories and experiences must not be lost to history, and in *They Knew Lincoln* he described them respectfully and without apology, recounting not only their stories but his own perspectives as a child who was sometimes scared and confused by things his elders said.

The sketches Washington offered of his grandmother's friends and their milieu should not be understood as accurate in every detail. They are Washington's recollections of stories told by elderly people whose own memories had likely shifted and faded over time. He evidently committed many of the stories to paper decades after he heard them, and his choices were shaped by his views of what would be important and interesting for his readers in 1942. Most of the details cannot be independently corroborated for precisely the reason that Washington was so committed to preserving them—because they were not documented or saved in other ways.

Yet the narratives capture something of how the Civil War transformed the lives of African Americans in Washington, DC, and the surrounding region. From the beginning of the war, the US Army made the capital a training ground and assembly point for troops and war materiel. The military presence rendered the city a beacon for freedom-seeking slaves from surrounding areas of Maryland and Virginia. In fact, even before the war, the District of Columbia was known as a refuge for runaways. Aunt Mary Dines, one of Caroline Washington's closest friends, had escaped from slavery in Charles County, Maryland, shortly before the war and, drawing on support from "friendly slaves" in the countryside, made her way to Washington. She arrived at a reputed Underground Railroad stop on Capitol Hill, but she didn't need to keep running north to live as a free woman because it was widely known that "in Washington when once an ex-slave was put with a colored family he lived as a free man."[10]

The outbreak of the Civil War in summer 1861 only intensified the capital's possibilities as a place where escaping slaves, including many who would become members of Caroline Washington's social circle, could find employment and relative safety. Aunt Phoebe Bias left her home in Virginia when General Benjamin Butler's forces arrived in 1861. She traveled to Washington on a government ship and obtained work in the household of a northern family.[11] Uncle Sandy, unlike the others, was from "way deep-down South." But he too had "worked his way up North with the army."[12] As Washington put it, "nearly every colored servant was from a different part of the South," but "all were sisters, brothers, aunts, and cousins to each other, and could tell great stories."[13]

The elderly people whom Washington knew as a child saw the capital city as a special place and their neighborhood as a sacred part of it. Events of national importance transpired in the capital, and mundane activities could bring common people into contact with the nation's most powerful. Aunt Phoebe Bias recalled hearing that "important white and colored men would speak about President Lincoln and the Emancipation Proclamation" at the December 31, 1862, Watch-Night meeting at her church, Union Bethel AME. Before the formal service began, "the brothers and sisters sang, prayed and spoke of their earthly experiences, just as they had done in class meetings." The pastor opened the service with a sermon about

"God, old Satan, Lincoln and the coming day of eternal freedom." Then came "a white man," who talked about "freedom,
and the war, and then read every word in the Emancipation
Proclamation from a copy which he had brought in his pocket
and told them just how Lincoln had fought for it." Singing and
celebration ensued, and the "very roof of the church seemed
to be tumbling down."[14]

During the Civil War, American politicians, often with
visiting dignitaries in tow, regularly toured the capital's
government-run refugee camps (known as contraband camps)
or attended services in black churches. Many were fasci-
nated that the war seemed to have unleashed an unquench-
able desire for freedom among enslaved people, and they
observed freedpeople's behavior with an eye toward the future
of government policy and of the nation itself. Many historical sources describe dignitaries' views on contraband camps
and the people they saw there, but *They Knew Lincoln* reveals
something of how it felt to be watched and expected to perform. Aunt Mary Dines recalled two visits Lincoln made to a
refugee camp that may have been on his route between down-
town Washington and the Soldiers' Home, where he often
stayed in the summer. Dines was a prominent person in her
camp—a teacher and letter writer with a strong soprano voice.
She recalled how nervous she was when she and others were
told that the president planned to visit. Dressed in "their best
clothes," including cast-off soldiers' uniforms, the camp's residents delivered a powerful performance for the president.[15]
Mary Dines's friend, Uncle Ben, preached a sermon. Lincoln
brushed away tears as the camp residents sang spirituals, and
then he joined in a rendition of "John Brown's Body." Lincoln
soon returned to the camp for a second visit, Dines recalled,

seeking solace from Uncle Ben and the singers and once again joining in.[16]

Dines's account of Lincoln at the contraband camp resonated with other stories and parables offered by members of Caroline Washington's circle. Her friends identified with Lincoln's upbringing in rural poverty. They believed he was a hard worker and a humane man who had great sympathy for the poor because of his own modest background. Aunt Eliza, a widely admired woman who prescribed folk remedies to residents of the neighborhood, kept a portrait of Lincoln at the foot of her bed. Washington wrote that she cared for her employers' children with reference to Lincoln—that is, "by making them suck fat meat at meals, rubbed them down with goose grease when sick with colds, and bathed their limbs with pot-liquor, just, as she said, she bet Abe Lincoln's mother did when he was a baby."[17]

Lincoln's violent death left a lasting mark on African American residents of the Ford's Theatre neighborhood and played an important role in Washington's childhood. Many of his grandmother's friends believed the theater was haunted. After the assassination "it was a common thing at nights to see lights in the Old Ford's Theater and to hear heavy iron chains rattling across its floors, and other strange noises," one explained.[18] Others described hearing ghostly shots, screams, and sounds of Booth making his escape. As a child, Washington was deeply affected by such stories. In his mind, Booth became a monster of frightening proportion. Artistically inclined, Washington painted a grotesque picture of the assassin and then tore it apart, perhaps hoping to lay the ghost to rest. He felt relieved when he and his family moved out of the neighborhood and away from the ghosts. His fear returned, however, when he learned that one of his new neighbors, a black woman from southern Maryland who had known some of Booth's co-conspirators, had seen apparitions associated with the Lincoln assassination and was sure there were ghosts nearby.[19]

In his accounts of his grandmother's friends and of their belief in spirits, Washington not only recalled his own childhood but also established himself as a collector of folklore. Across classes and cultures, many nineteenth-century Americans believed that the boundary between life and afterlife was permeable and that communication with the dead was possible. Mary Todd Lincoln herself at one point had turned to "spiritualism" to connect with her dead sons and husband. Yet some versions of supernatural belief were considered more respectable than others. White Americans often wrote condescendingly about freedpeople's primitive and uncivilized "superstitions," which they considered a manifestation of ignorance or racial inferiority. In the years after the Civil War, many black intellectuals likewise accepted the idea that superstition, as opposed to more conventional religion, was an artifact of slavery that would fall by the wayside as freedpeople became increasingly educated. The cultural winds shifted in the early twentieth century, however, as intellectuals came to see supposedly premodern belief systems, particularly among rural people, as valuable and worth preserving—perhaps even as an antidote to the ills of modernity. The work of James Weldon Johnson and Zora Neale Hurston, on slave spirituals and folk culture among rural African Americans, reflected that trend among African American writers.[20]

Growing up with his grandmother, Washington was well aware of the differences in class and culture that characterized

African American life. Caroline Washington had been a "great 'race' woman," he wrote, who went out of her way "to patronize some sister or brother who was running a store or making clothes."[21] He recognized that her work as a boarding house proprietor had given her unusual independence from white employers and that her emphasis on formal schooling and rejection of superstition had helped prepare him for upward mobility. As a child, John had opportunities to know members of long-standing free black families. He played with the children of John H. Brooks, the former steward to Navy Admiral John Dahlgren, and he was acquainted with Katherine Slade, a teacher and daughter of free-born William Slade, the lead servant in Lincoln's White House.[22] Washington's pedigree was different from theirs, at least insofar as his parents had been slaves. But he imbibed from his grandmother and others an ethic of self-help and an aspiration toward refinement and "civilization," and as an adult he moved decisively into the ranks of the black elite. Like many other black intellectuals of his era—and like many ethnographers and folklorists of the 1920s and 1930s—John E. Washington saw himself as a sympathetic nonbeliever, a modern man committed to collecting and compiling the disappearing cultures of rural folk.

Yet the stories he heard as a boy stayed with him. Uncle Ben, the elderly preacher, said God had created Lincoln to answers slaves' prayers for liberation and had arranged "his education in a manner that his language could be understood by all whom he was to lead." God's earthly messenger "had to be unlettered and uncultured in the beginning," Ben said, so he could understand the people he would someday free. God then placed this latter-day Moses "where he could know the abilities and ideas of men of a different race and color and

brought him up in it."[23] Indeed, Ben said that God had provided Lincoln with an African American mentor, "someone to
teach his chosen prophet, Lincoln, by example all that a Negro
could attain with freedom and equal opportunity." Someday,
Ben said, that black teacher of Lincoln "would be found."[24]

Uncle Ben's words instilled in Washington a persistent
question: How had African Americans themselves shaped
Lincoln's views on emancipation and racial equality? This is a
question many subsequent historians have asked. Rather than
assume that Lincoln's views emerged fully formed from his
own head, or that they were shaped exclusively by his interactions with other white people or by the changing trajectory of
the Civil War, the question asks us to consider how the dynamic
give-and-take of Lincoln's experiences with black people may
have affected him, including how African Americans may
have intentionally sought to help Lincoln see the world in a
more racially egalitarian way. Washington, spurred on by the
people he knew and the stories they told, would continue to
track these questions as he sought information about the black
people who had known or encountered Lincoln. How had the
president and his family shaped their lives? How had they
shaped his?

* * * * * * *

As *They Knew Lincoln* unfolds, it takes up increasingly
broad themes concerning the work experiences of African
Americans in the capital during Lincoln's era, particularly
those employed in the White House. Washington sought to
lift up and commemorate the otherwise-forgotten lives of people who did their best under difficult circumstances. He well

understood that Abraham Lincoln and his family had always attracted intense interest from historians and hobbyists but that virtually no one had thought to consider the Lincolns' relationship to people they saw almost every day—those who cooked their meals, watched their children, tidied their house, and thus knew a great deal of their most intimate business. Historians, he said, "have neglected to study the lowly companions of great men, the servants, who served their masters from morn till night, who thought of their welfare every moment and who could observe them in their home, where the cares and restraints of official life are laid aside."[25] Lincoln biographer William Herndon had the benefit of soliciting information immediately after Lincoln's death. Decades later, Washington faced far greater research challenges. Yet he gathered oral histories and unearthed archival documents that provided an entirely unprecedented account of the people who staffed the Lincoln White House.[26]

Servants in the White House, as in any other big house, did the often tedious and unappreciated work that made the household function. The Lincolns' hired help included not just fancy dressmakers like Elizabeth Keckly but everyday seamstresses like Rosetta Wells, a friend of Washington's grandmother, who darned the family's socks and mended linens. The staff included a cook who designed menus and labored over meals large and small, a variety of waiters, and temporary workers for special occasions. All employees were overseen by the person whom Washington referred to as "the butler or steward," who kept the keys to the house and managed accounts. In the Lincoln White House, that person was William Slade. Slade was new to the White House in 1861, but he was a long-standing member of Washington's black elite, having worked as a porter in a fancy hotel before moving with his family to Cleveland in the turbulent 1850s.[27] Most of the White House staff kept their jobs as presidents came and went, and in fact Slade remained in his position when Andrew Johnson took office. Washington wrote that members of the long-term staff tended to be light in complexion and to consider themselves the best of local black society. By the time of Lincoln's presidency, they were a rather insular group—doubtful about newcomers and proud of their own stature. When Lincoln arrived in Washington, the existing staff resisted working with William Johnson, a darker-skinned man who had accompanied the president from Springfield.[28]

They Knew Lincoln is unusual for providing a glimpse of domestic work from the perspective of workers rather than employers. With his grandmother's relative independence as a point of comparison, Washington observed that in the early post–Civil War days, most African American servants "generally lived where they worked, not so much because the wages were low, but mainly because of great difficulties in getting to work in the mornings." It was only later that domestic workers began to "live out," residing in their own homes and commuting to and from work each day.[29] Many nineteenth-century writings on domestic work and household management described the "servant problem"—that is, the complaints of wealthy people that it was difficult to find and keep good household help. John E. Washington was not averse to representing black domestic workers in stereotypical ways, as docile and eager to please their employers, but *They Knew Lincoln* also revealed aspects of what might be considered the "employer problem."[30] Black domestic workers were vulnerable to inconsiderate employers who, he noted, might "bring servants to strange cities and then dispense with their services and leave them stranded in a strange place without home or employment."[31] By contrast, he said the Lincolns were scrupulous employers. Drawing on documents kept by the Treasury Department, Washington showed that Lincoln helped William Johnson find a job after the White House servants rejected him, and Lincoln continued to aid Johnson when he became ill with smallpox and eventually died in 1864.[32] Washington had "heard it said that the Lincolns were so freehearted that there was a fear that when their days in the White House were over, they would leave as poor as they went in."[33] Although Mary Lincoln was reputed to have been a difficult person, Washington maintained that she was an empathic boss and, among African Americans, "beloved as no other white woman in public life."[34]

As he wrote about black working-class life in the nation's capital, Washington also shed light on African Americans' early employment in the federal government. Using Treasury Department records, he described the career of Solomon Johnson (no relation to William Johnson), who had worked for the Quartermaster's department in Ohio as the war began. He soon moved to Washington with a military company destined to provide security for Lincoln. In 1864, Lincoln helped Johnson get work at the Treasury Department run by Salmon Chase, an anti-slavery politician from Ohio who hired numerous African Americans during the war. Johnson kept working at Treasury and was eventually recognized as the first black man to be employed as a federal clerk—that is, to occupy a white-collar position.[35] His story was not unique. Many black men and a few black women began working in clerical jobs for the federal government after the Civil War. Although Congress could be unpredictable and government supervisors could be patronizing, government jobs like those Johnson held were critical to making Washington, DC, a hub for members of the nation's black elite.[36]

The world of African Americans and government work described in *They Knew Lincoln* was a hierarchical one, in which connections to powerful white people often mattered a great deal. Black government workers might enjoy greater job security and better wages than their counterparts in the private sector, but they also had to remain in the good graces of their white patrons. Nor was the work easy. After discussing how Solomon Johnson kept up a barbering business even while working as a government clerk, Washington explained: "Most of the colored men then in Government services as laborers and messengers depended on outside work to help them in supporting their families. Nearly everyone not only did the work required by the Government, but also served as house servants and valets for their chief without extra compensation. They served him faithfully at his home, before Government time and often into the night at dinners and receptions."[37] Government work could be a sort of elaboration of traditional forms of domestic employment, with labor extending from elite white people's homes to government buildings and back again.

In focusing on working people who had been neglected by historians and on understanding how federal government records could help tell their story, Washington took a creative approach to history. He assembled and published in *They Knew Lincoln* Treasury Department personnel documents that illuminated the careers of William Johnson and Solomon Johnson and Pension Bureau documents showing Elizabeth Keckly's efforts to get a veteran's pension after her son died in the Civil War. As Washington recognized, government files could provide biographical information about people whose lives had otherwise gone largely undocumented. The Treasury records showed something of how African Americans used connections to powerful whites to obtain positions and push for promotions. Keckly's pension file, in turn, contained a sworn affidavit in which she offered the rudiments of her own story—where she was from, to whom she was related, and how she came to live in the nation's capital. Those details helped corroborate some stories in her published autobiography, *Behind the Scenes*. And here was another advantage to living in Washington, DC: John E. Washington could pay regular visits to the Treasury Department and the National Archives, hobnob with archivists, and follow up to clarify details when necessary. Since the 1960s, historians interested in the lives of everyday people have embraced the kinds of sources Washington used—pension and employment files, as well as the voluminous records of the armed forces and the Freedmen's Bureau—finding them invaluable for writing about the lives of everyday African Americans. In this respect, Washington was a historian ahead of his time.

* * * * * * *

John E. Washington's life story attested to the unusual opportunities available to a subset of African Americans in Washington, DC, in the late nineteenth and early twentieth centuries. The city was widely known as a hub for the nation's black elite. Strong public schools, jobs in the federal government, and Howard University attracted upwardly mobile and aspiring African Americans from all over the country.

Figure I.1 John E. Washington sent this portrait to correspondents during the period when he was working on *They Knew Lincoln*. From the Lincoln Financial Foundation Collection, courtesy of the Indiana State Museum and Allen County Public Library.

Washington had begun his formal education at a Catholic school in the Ford's Theatre neighborhood and transferred into the capital's "colored" public school system when his family moved to the north side of the city. The District of Columbia's black public schools were established by Congress during the Civil War, at the behest of a Republican-controlled Congress that supported public education for all and believed schooling was a crucial step toward full citizenship for African Americans. Politicians and educators envisioned a complete educational system for African Americans in the capital, in which the most talented students would have the opportunity to attend a preparatory high school and then Howard

University, chartered by Congress in 1867 as the national cap-
stone of black education. From the beginning, the capital's
black public schools attracted highly trained teachers, including graduates of Oberlin College and the few other northern
institutions that had accepted black students before the Civil
War. It was often the daughters and sons of the black elite—
people like William Slade's daughter Katherine—who taught
in those schools, and many migrated from distant places for
such jobs. By the late nineteenth century, when Washington
was a teenager, some of the nation's foremost black intellectuals sought work as teachers and administrators in the capital's
black public schools.[38]

Washington appreciated the remarkable educational
climate in which he grew up. As a student, he took field
trips to the US Capitol building, the Smithsonian, and the
Emancipation statue on Capitol Hill, and he observed the
collections of historical materials in the homes of his friends.
All this piqued his interest in Lincoln and the era of the Civil
War.[39] Washington attended the "M Street School," the city's
elite preparatory high school for black students, where he
studied liberal arts. He was heavily involved in the school's
popular cadet program, in which students trained in militia
units and competed against other schools. As an adjutant
cadet, Washington served as an usher in the 1898 funeral of
Blanche K. Bruce, one of two black men to serve in the US
Senate during Reconstruction. After his term ended, Bruce
had remained in Washington, DC, holding appointments
under Republican presidents as register of the US treasury
and recorder of deeds for the District of Columbia. He and
his wife Josephine had been widely admired and socially
prominent members of the black elite.[40]

After high school Washington embarked on a career in both teaching and dentistry, pursuing three post-secondary degrees from Howard University in the process. His first Howard degree, awarded in 1901, enabled him to begin teaching in the black public schools. He soon began attending Howard's dental school at night and earned his DDS in 1904.[41] Washington was a pioneer of black dentistry, involved in an early black dentists' association and recognized as the first African American to pass the District of Columbia's dental boards.[42] He wanted to teach school while practicing dentistry on the side, but in 1910, the school board denied his request for permission to do so. In a decision that was surely disappointing, the board admonished him that he already made a "good salary and that the sixth grade is a particularly important one, demanding the full time of teachers."[43] By the early 1920s the school board reversed course, however, and from that time forward he maintained an off-hours dental practice, presumably in his home.[44]

Washington lived in a prime location for the city's increasingly numerous and accomplished black elite. In 1908, he married Carolyn Virginia Ross and purchased a house at 463 Florida Avenue, in the fashionable LeDroit Park neighborhood.[45] Founded as an exclusive suburban subdivision and settled by white homeowners in the 1870s, LeDroit Park was located just east of Howard University. Upwardly mobile African Americans began moving there during the 1890s, attracted by the fine housing and proximity to Howard and the busy 7th Street corridor. Some of the city's most prominent African Americans were among the earliest black settlers, including the educator and activist Mary Church Terrell and her husband, Robert Terrell, a municipal judge; poet Paul

Laurence Dunbar; and Christian Fleetwood, a Civil War medal of honor winner, and his wife Sarah, the first African American superintendent of nurses at nearby Freedmen's Hospital. By the early twentieth century when the Washingtons moved in, LeDroit Park was filled with African American teachers and other professionals, including Garnet Wilkerson, the highest-ranking official in the capital's black public schools.[46] The Washingtons witnessed the rise of LeDroit Park as a black professional enclave, the development of the "U Street" corridor, and the area's heyday as a center of black cultural and intellectual life.

John E. Washington cultivated his teaching career at a time when black cultural institutions and the arts were thriving in the capital. New York City was the place most associated with the "New Negro" movement, but Washington, DC, had its own version, particularly in the 1920s when such writers as Langston Hughes, Alice Dunbar Nelson, Jean Toomer, and Georgia Douglas Johnson made the capital their home. Washington's sensibilities were far more conservative than those that characterized the black literary avant-garde.[47] He was, however, involved in a burgeoning black art scene developed by teachers at Dunbar High School (formerly the M Street School). They called their organization the Tanner Art Students Society and in 1919 declared their desire to "promote co-operation and encourage the further development of art among our workers and stimulate in the general public that sense of refinement and high citizenship that the study of the beautiful inspires." Washington, who had been painting since childhood, served on the jury of the organization's first exhibit.[48] He remained an officer, and at the 1922 show he exhibited paintings titled "Eventide" and "Over the Hill." Although no visual evidence of those paintings has been discovered, the paintings' titles suggest that in his visual art, as in his writing, he was concerned with themes of aging and the passage of time.[49]

Washington returned to school in the early 1920s, perhaps in an effort to improve his chances of a promotion within the public school system. He had already earned a degree from the International Correspondence Schools of Scranton, Pennsylvania, which offered business and technical education to millions of people in the first decades of the twentieth century. John and Virginia Washington seem to have decided to resume their education together. Like her husband, Virginia had a professional degree from Howard but no bachelor's. The pair had attended the M Street School together in the late 1890s, and she had graduated from Howard's pharmacy school in 1911. In the early 1920s they both pursued bachelor's degrees in liberal arts, with John graduating in 1924 and Virginia in 1925. The aphorism associated with his yearbook entry was "Labor has sure reward."[50]

The bachelor's degree, together with his teaching experiences and personal connections, likely helped Washington land a position at a new public high school for black students. Francis L. Cardozo High School, founded in 1928, was designed to train students for careers in business and industry. The school's namesake was a Reconstruction black educator and political leader from South Carolina who had held statewide offices as secretary of state and then state treasurer. Cardozo was forced from office amid the Democrats' violent takeover of the state in 1877 and, like many other high-level southern black politicians of the era, moved to Washington, DC, and found work in the federal government—in Cardozo's case as a clerk in the Treasury Department. In 1884 Cardozo had become principal of the preparatory high school for black students (the progenitor of the M Street School), where he promoted business education. Cardozo died in 1903 and twenty-five years later became the namesake for the city's new business-oriented high school for black students.[51]

Washington had an ambitious vision for his job as a teacher of commercial art at Cardozo High School. According to a 1938 commemorative yearbook, under Washington's leadership, the commercial art department offered "courses based on the practical needs of the community," including "practical courses in drawing, lettering, poster-making, air-brushing, silk screening and window-displaying." Washington and his students "assist[ed] many worthy enterprises held throughout the District of Columbia, namely by making toys for poor children, making posters for crippled children, and making displays for the United States Federal Housing Administration." They demonstrated advanced techniques in screen-process posters for "instructors in private schools" and sent their air-brush displays to nationwide exhibitions.[52]

All the while, Washington was pursuing his interest in African American history and Lincolniana. There is no evidence that Washington was in direct contact with the era's leading figure in black history—Carter G. Woodson—but he was certainly part of the milieu in which Woodson established himself. Woodson was born in Virginia in 1875, and like Washington he was the child of former slaves. After earning a degree from Berea College and teaching for several years, in 1903 Woodson took the federal civil service exam and was hired as a government teacher in the Philippines. After traveling the world and earning a master's degree in history at the University of Chicago, he enrolled in the history PhD program at Harvard. While a doctoral student, Woodson began teaching in the Washington, DC, black public schools, where he spent ten years, eventually becoming a high school principal. In 1915, Woodson garnered praise from the superintendent of those schools, who declared that black history "gives our children and youth a sense of pride in the stock from which they sprang, an honorable self-confidence, [and] a faith in the future and its possibilities." Woodson founded the Association for the Study of Negro Life and History (ASNLH) in Chicago, but in 1922 he moved the association's headquarters to Washington, where they remain to this day. In the pages of the ASNLH's *Journal of Negro History,* Woodson often published heretofore obscure documents in an effort to promote the study of African American history in general and of slavery in particular. In fact, in the summer of 1935, just a few months before the controversy over Keckly and *Behind the Scenes,* the journal published an article arguing for the use of ex-slaves' testimonies as a source for understanding slavery.[53] In *They Knew Lincoln,* John E. Washington attributed his interest in history to his childhood experiences, but the broader context was also significant. He lived in a place and time in which appreciation of African American history ran high, where the project of writing about the black past was strongly associated with racial progress and uplift.

Washington was not one of the capital's most famous black intellectuals or artists, yet in adulthood he made a place for himself among the city's famed (and at times infamous) African American elite. His light complexion, evident in photos, likely helped in his quest for elevated status. The city's black elite valued light skin tones and straight hair as markers of status and refinement. He worshipped at St. Luke's Episcopal, a black church strongly associated with its prominent founder, Alexander Crummell.[54] But Washington's status is perhaps best revealed through the leading role he played in Highland Beach, an exclusive black vacation community on the Chesapeake Bay in Maryland. The community was founded in 1891 by Frederick Douglass's son, Charles. The earliest investors included prominent Reconstruction-era politicians who had fled the South, including Blanche Bruce of Mississippi and P. B. S. Pinchback of Louisiana, the first two black men to serve in the US Senate. At first Charles Douglass had difficulty finding buyers for his planned resort, but development blossomed in the prosperous 1920s. The community officially incorporated as a town in 1922, making it, in the words of historian Andrew Kahrl, "the first independent black vacation resort town in the nation."[55] As it grew, Highland Beach became a refuge for the region's black upper class, a place where its members could enjoy the beach and a sense of community, separate from whites who were drawing the color line ever more rigidly, particularly in leisure activities.[56]

Washington was a relatively early investor in the community, and over time he emerged as a local leader and advocate of the town. Charles Douglass's son, Haley Douglass, became town mayor in the early 1920s, and Washington, who once called Haley his "best friend," soon became town clerk. In 1939, the *Chicago Defender* characterized Washington's Highland Beach home as "a sort of town hall" and Washington as particularly influential "in municipal affairs."[57] By then the town had grown controversial among African Americans nationwide. From the beginning, Highland Beach homeowners had tried to ensure that only the "right" sort of people vacationed there. They put up fences, stymied commercial ventures, impeded road construction, and otherwise tried to maintain control over their vacation paradise. Washington was among the defenders of that exclusive vision of the community. He publicly championed what he saw as the town's traditional values, at one point arguing against critics of the residents' elitism and obstructionism that the town "will always stand on its present high ground—long for law and order, equal rights and protection to all of its citizens, true to its noble traditions, the race and native land."[58]

Washington and other members of the capital's black elite sometimes held themselves apart from African Americans of more modest means, but all were caught in a web of encroaching segregation and white supremacy. In 1913, Woodrow Wilson, the first southern-born president since the Civil War, took decisive measures to segregate the federal government, a move that stymied or ended the careers of many black civil servants in Washington. In July 1919, white soldiers, sailors, and civilians attacked black residents and neighborhoods in an uprising that was characteristic of that summer's widespread racial conflagrations. And in the early 1920s, under Republican president Warren Harding, the federal superintendent of public buildings demanded segregated picnic areas at Rock Creek Park, prohibited African Americans from using recreational spaces near the Tidal Basin, and arranged for segregated seating at the opening of the Lincoln Memorial. The 1920s also witnessed serious conflicts over race and housing in the capital, as white residents violently resisted African American incursions and the US Supreme Court in 1926 upheld the use of racially restrictive covenants to bar African Americans from buying homes. Yet black Washingtonians—relatively well-off and well educated, and boasting strong civic organizations, including an active branch of the National Association for the Advancement of Colored People (NAACP)—were well equipped to fight back. That peculiar combination of oppression and opportunity was a defining feature of elite black life in the nation's capital.[59]

✿ ✿ ✿ ✿ ✿ ✿ ✿

A part-time dentist and full-time art teacher, owner of two homes, history buff, and married man with no children, in fall 1935 John E. Washington thrust himself into a sort of prominence when he contested David Rankin Barbee's scandalous assertion that Elizabeth Keckly could not possibly have written *Behind the Scenes*. Barbee made that claim to an Associated Press reporter named Bess Furman, who was all too ready to believe him. An up-and-coming Washington journalist who spent much of her time covering Eleanor Roosevelt, Furman was interested in the history of women newspaper correspondents in Washington and had sought Barbee's expertise on Jane Grey Swisshelm, a Civil War–era correspondent from Minnesota. When Barbee told her that Swisshelm was the true author of *Behind the Scenes*, Furman believed him. Upon filing her story on this supposed new discovery, Furman jotted in her daily diary that the work revealed "Madame Keckley the Negro seamstress . . . being really Jane Swisshelm, the best darned newspaper woman out blazing trails."[60]

Furman's piece ran in the *Washington Star* on Saturday, November 11. Four days later the paper published John E. Washington's refutation.[61] Washington established his authority by stating "that for over 30 years, I too, have been a close student of Lincoln" and that he possessed "some of the rarest items pertaining to the assassination period." From there, Washington insisted that Keckly had indeed lived and that, while others might have helped her write the book, Keckly had taken "full responsibility" for it. Barbee quickly countered with his own letter to the editor a few days later, claiming he had never denied Keckly's existence but, instead, had argued that "no such person" had written *Behind the Scenes*. He maintained that position, reiterating that

Swisshelm was the real author and that *Behind the Scenes* was a work of fiction.[62]

Barbee, born in Tennessee in 1874, was a gadfly who regularly sought to explicate and defend the white South to outsiders. In the mid-1930s, he was working on a book about the Lincoln assassination and became interested in Swisshelm, who had also written about Lincoln's murder.[63] Barbee's claim that Swisshelm wrote *Behind the Scenes* rested on the thinnest of evidence—one line of a satirical news item written in 1868 that had noted "Swizzlem" in the gallery of the Senate and nonsensically identifed her as "the colored authoress of Mrs. Keckley's book."[64] But that tiny clipping was probably far less important to Barbee than his deeply held beliefs about race and gender. No one, he told a friend in private correspondence, could "find in all the United States of 1869 [*sic*] one negro woman who had enough culture to have written such a book."[65] Meanwhile, he insisted, Mary Lincoln "was not the type of woman who would gossip before servants. No well-bred Southern woman would do that."[66] He also claimed (incorrectly) that Mrs. Lincoln bought all her dresses in New York and Paris and had no need of a fine seamstress.[67]

Barbee's condescension toward African Americans knew few limits. In a letter to a white Lincoln aficionado, Barbee called the *Washington Star* the "Negroes' newspaper Bible."[68] He told Louis Warren, whose newsletter, *Lincoln Lore*, had cited an early twentieth-century interview with Keckly to challenge Barbee's assertions, that Keckly was evidently the "patron saint" of Washington's African Americans and warned: "Had you, like myself, grown up among Negroes in the South—we had a family of them under our roof for many years, and educated them—you would be skeptical about what any old colored woman eighty years old might say." He insisted to Warren that there was no evidence "acceptable in the court of history" that Keckly had ever worked for Mrs. Lincoln or Varina Davis, as stated in *Behind the Scenes*.[69] Over and over again he told acquaintances that black people's memories were faulty and that John E. Washington's research was poor.

On learning of black Washingtonians' strong objections to Barbee's claims, Bess Furman decided to investigate further. "Someone who knew Madame Keckley turned up," she recorded in her calendar a few days after the initial story ran.[70] She headed to the home of Francis Grimké, Keckly's former pastor, who had a photo of Keckly and talked extensively about having known her and preaching her 1907 funeral service. Soon Furman was at John E. Washington's Florida Avenue home, interviewing him about Keckly and taking down the names and addresses of other black Washingtonians who could attest to her existence. Furman's new story, which she privately called a "correction," went over the AP wire and appeared in the *Washington Star* on December 1. Barbee's assertions had "brought Negro leaders forward in spirited defense of Elizabeth Keckley as an author," Furman wrote. "In old albums they found photographs of her to prove her a decidedly dressy and intelligent person."

> They cited as living witnesses to various phases of her long existence the pastor who preached her funeral sermon here in 1907; a namesake in whose family she lived as far back as 1864; the daughter of a man who almost married her in North Carolina, before she ever came to Washington; a pupil in her domestic science class in Wilberforce University for Colored at Xenia, Ohio; a teacher in the public schools, who

recalled her extreme old age here as a matron of a home for colored children.

The "staunchest" defender of Keckly, she said, was John E. Washington, a high school art teacher and Lincoln hobbyist.[71] At that point, Washington thought it possible that Swisshelm had persuaded Keckly to tell her story and that Swisshelm might even have "rearrange[d] the matter in good form and English for the publishers."[72] He was certain, however, that the stories contained in the book were true and that Keckly had been Mrs. Lincoln's confidante.

The outpouring occasioned by Barbee's assault on Keckly's reputation and on her very existence confirmed something Washington had observed as a boy: African Americans harbored, in their homes and in their memories, great quantities of meaningful history, untapped and at risk of being forgotten or even destroyed.[73] His long-standing interests in both Lincoln and African American history converged as he envisioned further research and a pamphlet that would vindicate Keckly. By 1938 he was deeply engaged in collecting further information about her, conducting interviews with local people and taking a summer trip to the Midwest for more digging.[74] He had launched a new phrase of his multifaceted life.

* * * * * * *

Seeking information on Keckly and *Behind the Scenes*— and hoping to get his research published—Washington began to make inroads into the white Lincoln establishment. A culture of Lincoln fandom had flourished in the wake of Lincoln's

100th birthday in 1909, as Americans hunted for new stories about the man many considered the nation's greatest president. Amid jokes about the quantities of Lincoln books published and whether anything remained to say or discover, hobbyists searched out autographed Lincoln documents and debated the minutiae of his life. Interest in Lincoln grew in subsequent decades and reached its twentieth-century apex during the Depression, when Americans of varying political stripes lauded him as a representative of perseverance through hard times and the dignity of common people. The world of Lincoln buffs and collectors was diffuse, with local "roundtable" organizations operating relatively autonomously. Yet a measure of centralization existed through organizations such as the American Lincoln Association, based in Springfield, Illinois, and the Abraham Lincoln National Life Insurance Company in Fort Wayne, Indiana, where Louis Warren directed the Lincoln Library Museum and published a weekly newsletter, *Lincoln Lore*.[75]

John E. Washington's path into that world began with Valta Parma, the curator of the Library of Congress's Rare Books Collection who, early on, had affirmed Barbee's thesis that Swisshelm had written *Behind the Scenes*. Parma was receptive to Washington's research on Keckly and encouraged him to keep digging. Washington, in turn, used Parma's name freely as he reached out to leading Lincoln aficionados. Louis Warren was particularly helpful, encouraging Washington's wide-ranging interests and recommending that in addition to writing a pamphlet on Keckly, he should author a separate short work "on colored people who were closely associated with Lincoln." "You could give us a very excellent story about Lincoln's appreciation for his colored associates," he wrote Washington.[76] Washington was already thinking along similar lines and responded enthusiastically that he too was interested in "the colored side of Lincolniana."[77] By the summer of 1939, as he neared his 60th birthday, his "colored Lincolniana" project commanded his full attention, and he decided to organize his materials as a narrative of his search for information about the African Americans who had known the Lincolns.[78] That vision for the book acknowledged the challenge of researching people who had left behind few written records of their lives. The project required not just reading and interpreting documents but also dedication, creativity, and a willingness to travel to new places and talk to living people.

Washington took pleasure in the quest. As he wrote in a private letter, he wanted to get out of the city, to find places "where colored people are found in primitive conditions."[79] Sister Payne, an elderly woman he knew from boyhood, advised him to speak to an old acquaintance, Aunt Vina. Washington recounted his trip to southern Maryland with Sister Payne as a kind of time travel. They were going to places "so far off the main highway" that residents "had never seen an automobile, nor an electric light and didn't care to do so."[80] Driving a team of horses, Washington and Payne traveled hours to Aunt Vina's remote and tidy home. "Unscrupulous relic hunters" had already been in the neighborhood and had "beaten" people like Aunt Vina "out of some of their most cherished objects." Aunt Vina therefore talked about her experiences only after Payne assured her that Washington was an honest man. Then she told of her experiences during the war: how her children had left to find work elsewhere but stayed in touch by mail; how she and her friends had traveled to the capital to witness Lincoln's second inauguration; and how she had been among the mourners at Lincoln's funeral.[81]

In southern Maryland and Caroline County, Virginia, Washington also gathered African Americans' perspectives on the Lincoln assassination, a topic of perennial interest. Immediately after the assassination, General Winfield Hancock had published a circular letter calling on black Americans to help capture Booth and his co-conspirators. Booth had fled to southern Maryland, and several local white families—people with surnames like Mudd and Surratt—were widely known as sympathizers. In Caroline County, Washington interviewed John Henry Coghill, an elderly man who said he had witnessed Booth's demise on a Virginia farm at the hands of US soldiers.[82] Coghill's account of the capture and killing of Booth may have added little of substance to what people already knew of the incident, but Washington believed it important to publish Coghill's verbatim testimony and his photo in *They Knew Lincoln*, giving him a voice and a place in history he would never otherwise have had.

Washington also included in *They Knew Lincoln* interviews with two white men who he believed had something new to say about the assassination. One was Tom Gardiner, a dental patient of Washington's who had been a close associate of the conspirators. The other, William Ferguson, was an actor who claimed to have been the only person who actually saw Booth shoot Lincoln—a vantage he had because of where he stood on the stage that night. Washington, always interested in art work and illustrations, had rare pictures of Ford's Theatre and a diagram of the stage and seating. On the images, Ferguson made marks showing where he was standing and where the other actors were positioned. Washington, with a sense of duty to the historical record, published the picture with Ferguson's annotations drawn in.

In the main, however, it was African Americans' perspectives that Washington sought to emphasize in his nascent book. The dignity and possibility of black history stood at the center of his endeavor. "I hope to produce a book with the soul of a disappearing people in it, and I think we have the material to do so," Washington told one of the white Lincoln experts with whom he was in touch.[83] His emphasis on the validity and significance of African Americans' testimony about their own experiences and the nation's history stood in stark contrast to contemporaneous efforts to discredit *Behind the Scenes* and diminish Elizabeth Keckly. Washington filled his book with an accumulation of black voices, demonstrating convincingly that African Americans had a great deal to say about the past and that their perspectives mattered.[84]

As he began to write, Washington started with the chapter that would lead off the book: an account of his own childhood spent near Ford's Theatre. That draft chapter captured the imagination of James G. Randall, a professor at the University of Illinois and the era's foremost university-based historian of Lincoln.[85] Randall had done his doctoral work at the University of Chicago and wrote his dissertation and first book on Lincoln and the Constitution.[86] In the wide and eclectic world of Lincoln collectors and fans, Randall styled himself the consummate professional historian. In a 1934 address that received national attention, Randall declared that despite the ridiculous quantity of writing about Lincoln, the "Lincoln theme" was not "exhausted." Rather, it was time for "trained specialists" to take over.[87]

Randall's commitment to professional history writing did not prevent him from becoming a genuine supporter of Washington and his book project. The two men met while working at the Library of Congress and remained in regular contact after Randall read Washington's first chapter.[88] Randall consistently encouraged Washington to make his own life story part of the project and considered the book more folklore than history. He called Washington's work "unhistorical legend," but he liked it nevertheless for "such intangible things as quaintness, flavor, half-articulate race memories, and a quality which some would call unliterary, but which amounts to expressive eloquence." His attitude toward Washington, at least in letters to others, was notably paternalistic, his views resting on assumptions about the different innate characteristics of different "races" of people. Yet Randall also wrote Washington supportive letters, at one point assuring him, "Except for your efforts, the story of the colored people who knew Lincoln is lost." Washington seemed to value the encouragement. Appealing to Randall's empiricist commitments, Washington promised that every fact in the book "is historically true" and that in telling about Lincoln's "servants," the book "would serve to supply very valuable missing links in the biographies of Lincoln."[89]

As an African American, amateur historian, and outsider to the largely white world of Lincoln scholarship and collecting, Washington faced steep challenges in getting his book published. He hired Valta Parma, of the Library of Congress's Rare Books Collection, as his editor and literary agent, and Parma began to pursue a publisher in New York in spring 1939.[90] Parma tried Simon and Schuster but made no headway, and in the meantime he lost his job at the Library of Congress. When Washington finished the manuscript in spring 1940, Parma and his wife, Pallas, took charge of editing it. By the fall, Parma had succeeded in securing a contract with E. P. Dutton.[91] Just as publication seemed imminent, however, things began to go awry. Dutton had hired the well-known Jamaican writer Claude McKay to edit the manuscript. Best known for his poetry and fiction, McKay had worked for the Federal Writers' Project in the 1930s, and in 1940, Dutton had published his non-fiction book, *Harlem: Negro Metropolis*. McKay made extensive alterations to Washington's manuscript that winter, and then an anonymous "expert" reviewer—said to be a Lincoln scholar—panned the manuscript as valueless both as Lincoln scholarship and as folklore.[92] The Parmas were horrified at demands to overhaul the book and went directly to the president of Dutton, John Macrae, insisting that *They Knew Lincoln* could be printed only if the "integrity" of the original manuscript were preserved. As Parma wrote to Randall, the "publishers' literary authorities . . . would have destroyed the very atmosphere of the book by too much editing." He wanted to ensure that "the book in its final shape will preserve the folklore and warmth of color that Dr. Washington gave to it."[93]

Parma enlisted Randall's support at this crucial juncture, and Randall agreed wholeheartedly that the book's original tone must be preserved. Its "essence" was in its "quaintness, naivete, and folk-lore quality," Randall assured Parma. But Randall also acknowledged the significance of Washington's effort to unearth a history that had almost been lost: "I cannot restrain a certain poignant feeling concerning Dr. Washington's story—especially the intensity of his devotion to the subjects that it partakes almost of the quality of a Negro spiritual, and the pathetic inability to recover more than mere fragments of what, if fully told, would be a most moving narrative."[94] Randall seemed to admire Washington's tenacity as a researcher and to appreciate the difficulty of the task. And yet, by comparing the

book to "a Negro spiritual," he also resorted to racial essential-
ism, implying that Washington had song coursing through his
veins rather than recognizing his formal education, elite standing, and seriousness of purpose.

Dutton allowed the book to proceed as Randall and the
Parmas thought best. Soon Randall, Louis Warren, and Carl
Sandburg, the beloved Lincoln biographer, all pledged public endorsements. Dutton had wanted a prominent Lincoln
scholar to write a "preview" to lead off the book, and Sandburg's
assent instantly raised the book's profile and credibility.[95] As
They Knew Lincoln went into production in fall 1941, Randall
and others agreed to write blurbs for advance publicity, and
Warren and his colleagues in Fort Wayne promised to advertise it to their mailing list of 5,400 Lincoln fans.[96] Washington
was pleased with how the book had emerged from the spring's
crisis, writing Randall that although the Parmas had reorga-
nized the manuscript, "my words are not changed."[97] Still, the
stable of white endorsers and the introduction by Sandburg
echoed the practice of opening nineteenth-century slave
narratives with testimonials from white abolitionists. The
endorsements suggested the publisher's concerns about the
book's marketability and the difficulty of establishing a black
writer's authority, particularly in the world of Lincoln scholarship and collecting.

＊ ＊ ＊ ＊ ＊ ＊ ＊

With blurbs from key players in the world of Lincoln scholarship and fandom, Dutton marketed the book as an essen-
tial new piece of Lincolniana, downplaying its significance
as African American history. Publication was scheduled for

January 26, 1942, to encourage reviews in time for Lincoln's birthday, February 12. Months before the release, the *New York Times* announced that Dutton would publish "a book of Negro stories, legends and memories of Lincoln" with an introduction by Carl Sandburg.[98] Three weeks out, the newspaper identified the book as one of Dutton's "leading titles" and described it as "a portrait gathered from out-of-the-way persons who had memories of Lincoln."[99] The noteworthy shift away from the racial term "Negro" to "out-of-the-way persons" probably reflects the press's decision to market the book to the largely white world of Lincoln collectors. Dutton's full-page advertisement in the *New York Herald Tribune*'s February 1 book review touted *They Knew Lincoln* as "almost an entirely new volume of unrevealed Lincolniana!" The ad's only reference to the book's African American content was its acknowledgment that the author was "a distinguished member of the race Lincoln served so well." More to the point, Dutton announced, *They Knew Lincoln* had been endorsed by Sandburg and was "indispensable to the student of Lincolniana" and "fascinating reading for all who enjoy historical narrative told in colorful, swift-moving prose."[100]

Dutton's publicity operation proved effective. Reviews in the *New York Times*, the *Herald Tribune,* and the *Washington Post* appeared immediately, and by Lincoln's birthday the book had been noticed in papers across the country.[101] The *Herald Tribune*'s daily book columnist, Lewis Gannett—who several years earlier had called W. E. B. Du Bois's *Black Reconstruction* "an impassioned attack upon slave-minded historians"—was one of the few to grasp some of the methodological and interpretive stakes of Washington's work. "Historians had neglected the testimony of the servants in

Lincoln's house," Gannett wrote, recognizing that Herndon's disregard for African Americans had left a giant hole in the historical record that John E. Washington was attempting to fill. Decades after Lincoln's death, Washington had to settle for interviewing descendants—a step removed, perhaps, but this was an important project. The result was "uneven," Gannett commented, but worthy.[102]

Reviews in white periodicals across the country tended to emphasize that the book was original and interesting, if a little syrupy. The Chicago *Tribune* framed *They Knew Lincoln* amid the welter of books on Lincoln and the popular suspicion that there was "little left to write," especially after Sandburg's 1939 biography. But Washington's book, the reviewer concluded, "actually does say something that nobody else has said and adds to the legend if not to the facts of the Lincoln picture." Washington, he wrote, had set down the "recollections of Lincoln and Lincoln tales" told by "ancient men and women of his race." The result was "almost as much autobiography as it is Lincolniana."[103] The Catholic magazine *America* was more exuberant, heralding *They Knew Lincoln* as a "literary marvel." Echoing Randall's statement that the book had "both the lilt and the deep pathos of a Negro spiritual," *America* commented: "As you read the pages you seem to live with these people, and Dr. Washington's simple, unadorned style has much of the quality of a Negro spiritual." The book was not really a work of history, the reviewer concluded. Still, "it matters not whether the stories these people tell are in strict accord with historical verity. What is of interest and, at times, of importance, is what they thought about Lincoln."[104]

Not all reviews struck such positive chords. *They Knew Lincoln* made the *Herald Tribune*'s (rather long) list of "important spring books," but Lincoln scholar Paul Angle's essay in the spring book issue was dismissive. Angle sniffed that the "durable parts" of the book were "hardly of sufficient importance to make up for its general lack of substance," and he criticized Washington's quaint and folkloric tone. The *Abraham Lincoln Quarterly*, which Angle edited, also condemned the book's "many aimless pages."[105] In the Chicago *Sun*, reviewer Otto Eisenschiml, the author of a controversial—and highly speculative—book on the Lincoln assassination, praised *They Knew Lincoln*'s concept and the research on Keckly. But he called the writing "almost painfully amateurish" and condemned Washington for not distinguishing sufficiently between fact and legend.[106]

Although Dutton marketed the book mainly to the largely white world of Lincolniana collectors, African American journalists, historians, and educators took note. A columnist for the Atlanta *Daily World* lauded recent publications by contemporary writers Alain Locke, Langston Hughes, and Richard Wright and added that *They Knew Lincoln* was "a recent 'find'" and a "current Dutton's best seller."[107] In its annual report on "Books by Negro Authors," the NAACP's *Crisis* captured the book's heterogeneity, describing it as an "interesting collection of history, biography, reminiscences and folk lore" that presented "in a fascinating manner a human picture of the Negroes who were in intimate contact with Abraham Lincoln."[108] A Howard University publication compared John E. Washington to two towering figures in American culture: "Washington is wise enough in understanding and shrewd enough in intellect to preserve the customs and superstitions of his people during his boyhood in the nation's capital precisely as Mark Twain recorded those of his boyhood in the river town of Hannibal. And he writes this down as living language, a contribution to Negro culture as sincere and inevitable and inspiring as a spiritual sung by Marian Anderson." A few years later, a columnist in the Chicago *Defender* called *They Knew Lincoln* "one of the most interesting books on Lincoln's life written from the Negro's interest."[109]

In Washington's home community, black institutions publicized and feted the book. His colleagues from Cardozo honored him with a banquet that featured a skit, music, and toasts. Howard University hosted Washington for a lecture and what he called "a big entertainment," and Carter Woodson's ASNLH honored the book at its 1942 annual meeting.[110] William H. Brewer, director of history programming in the District of Columbia's black high schools, reviewed the book for the ASNLH's *Journal of Negro History,* hailing it as a "refreshing volume bristling with irresistible human interest because it reveals something new" and "the first account of those who were closest physically and spiritually to [Lincoln]."[111] Washington gave radio interviews in New York and Washington.[112] Three years later, a prominent Harlem radio show, *New World A Comin',* converted the material on William de Fleurville, William Slade, and Elizabeth Thomas of Fort Stevens into a radio play that featured the prominent actors Georgia Burke and Canada Lee.[113]

For his own part, Washington was exuberant about his book's popularity and the accolades that accompanied it. He employed a clipping service to keep him apprised of reviews as they were published, and he wrote his correspondents in a triumphant mood. He enjoyed hearing from far-flung readers, including prisoners in a penitentiary who had read reviews but could not get a copy of the book. He was also delighted that the work seemed to be making a difference in Washington.

In particular, he noted that Mordecai Johnson, president of Howard University, had been amazed to learn that the school stood on or near land once occupied by a contraband camp and had spoken of erecting a statue of Lincoln in the place where "the Great Emancipator . . . became a man of the people not <u>too big</u> to join with the most humble in prayer."[114]

* * * * * * *

In the book's final chapters, Washington provided robust accounts of several relatively well-known individuals. Among them, his research on Lincoln's Haitian-born barber, William de Fleurville, garnered particular acclaim. Fleurville had been born in Haiti around 1806, migrated to Baltimore in the early 1820s, and then made his way to Illinois in 1831. He established a barbering practice in Springfield and became a prominent figure in the community, publishing whimsical advertisements for his barbershop in the local newspaper, accumulating wealth through real estate investment, and contributing generously to local institutions. Documents showed that Lincoln was Fleurville's real estate lawyer. Oral tradition among local African Americans held that Fleurville's shop was "the 'club house' of Springfield," where men gathered to swap stories. It was "Lincoln's second home," they said, and the two men were close friends. Fleurville—sometimes spelled Florville—was profiled in early histories of Sangamon County, Illinois, but Lincoln's early biographers had largely written him out of Lincoln's life, as they had the entire black community of Springfield.[115]

In the summer of 1938, Washington traveled to Illinois, stopping in Springfield and Chicago and meeting with some of Fleurville's descendants.[116] He listened to Lincoln stories told by Springfield African Americans, and he saw the mirror from Fleurville's barbershop and imagined Lincoln inspecting his face in the reflection.[117] Washington's interest in Fleurville and Haiti grew in 1940, when he met the Haitian minister to the United States, Élie Lescot, at a meeting of the Mu-So-Lit Club, a long-standing African American literary society. The club was hosting its annual February celebration of Abraham Lincoln and Frederick Douglass, and Lescot was the guest of honor. The two men spoke at length, and Lescot offered to learn what he could about Fleurville's life in Haiti. The results were disappointing, however. The records in Fleurville's birthplace, Cap-Haïtien, had been destroyed by fire, so Lescot was able to assist with only broad details about the history of Haiti, the world's first independent black republic.[118]

Still, when *They Knew Lincoln* was published, Lescot—who had recently become president of Haiti—was pleased with how Washington represented Fleurville and awarded Washington a diploma from the Haitian government, recognizing him for "honor and merit." The Port-au-Prince *Haiti-Journal* ran a front-page story featuring the only known photo of Fleurville, which Washington had worked to restore. It also published a picture of Lescot, Washington, and others sharing a meal, probably at the Mu-so-Lit Club meeting. The story touted the positive reception in the United States of *They Knew Lincoln* and praised the book for recounting the heretofore unknown story of Fleurville and his relationship to Lincoln.[119] Black newspapers across the United States covered Haiti's recognition of Washington, and the chapter on Fleurville was selected for inclusion in the Modern Library's 1944 *Anthology of American Negro Literature*.[120]

Washington had come to believe that William de Fleurville played a special role in history. Harkening to Uncle Ben and his assertion that God had sent a black "teacher" to educate Lincoln, Washington told a colleague that Lincoln and Fleurville had come together as "part of a Divine plan for Lincoln to meet a free negro of education who could not only tell him about the possibilities of colored people who governed themselves," but also "be a constant acquaintance" who "would help him in understanding the colored man."[121] In *They Knew Lincoln,* Washington wrote that Fleurville taught Lincoln "by example all that a Negro could attain with freedom and equal opportunity."[122] In a private letter Washington was even more direct about what he believed Lincoln had learned from Fleurville and the example of Haiti, an independent republic governed by people of African descent since 1804. "What Haytians could do in their own colony, undoubtedly Lincoln thought other colored people who had seen the benefits of American civilization, even if gained the hard ways of slavery, could do," he wrote.[123]

Washington was certain that everyday interactions with African Americans had shaped Lincoln's views on slavery and race, and he threaded that argument throughout his book. Reviewing the book for the *Journal of Negro History,* William Brewer was persuaded. "How much the warmth of servant-inspiration gave to the flowing of freedom in Lincoln's imagination may be clearly estimated from many facts cited," he wrote.[124] Robert Mattingly, the principal of Cardozo, agreed, praising the book for "lifting the Negro from the position as a mere recipient of emancipation at the hands of Lincoln to a higher plain of recognition as a racial group which played an important and a heretofore unrevealed part in the development of Lincoln's personality."[125] At a time when few people thought to ask how African Americans might have influenced Lincoln's outlook and decisions, Washington asked the question and began to answer it. Subsequent historians have followed his lead, plumbing additional sources and approaching the question from a variety of angles.[126] They continue to return to Washington's book because, as reviewers recognized at the time, much of what Washington recorded, particularly his interviews with people who had encountered the Lincolns, was unique and could never be replicated or confirmed.

* * * * * * *

By 1942, when *They Knew Lincoln* was published, the furor over Elizabeth Keckly and the authorship of *Behind the Scenes* had quieted down. Yet many Lincoln buffs noticed that Washington offered a significant new theory about the identity of the person who had helped Keckly put her words to paper. Washington believed that person was James Redpath, a white abolitionist and editor. The evidence came from an interview with Hannah Frances Brooks, who was well into her nineties and a member of a prominent African American family. Brooks, born in 1842, told Washington that she had stayed at the same New York City boarding house as Keckly while Keckly was working on her book. That boarding house was a common meeting place for members of the era's black political elite, and its proprietor, Mary Bell, was an aunt of Hannah Brooks. In fact, Mary Bell had raised Hannah after Hannah's mother had died, and Hannah had married John H. Brooks in New York in 1861, with Henry Highland Garnet, a prominent black minister, officiating.[127]

Washington conducted several interviews with Mrs. Brooks in her old age, with her daughter Mary always present. Mrs. Brooks recalled that Keckly often stayed at Mrs. Bell's house when she was in New York and that she had seen Redpath sit for hours with Keckly. She told Washington, "Everybody in the house knew that Mrs. Keckley was writing a book on Mrs. Lincoln and that Mr. Redpath was helping her compile it."[128] Washington found Brooks's account persuasive. Redpath had been a radical anti-slavery journalist, with fingers in many different pots. He was well connected in the New York publishing world and could certainly have taken down Keckly's oral account of her life or advised her as she wrote her own story.

Washington knew his account of Redpath's connection would draw attention, and he provided as much authenticating material as he could. He published a full transcript of the interview with Hannah Brooks, written by Brooks's daughter, Mary. Mary also wrote a memo attesting to her mother's sound mind and memory. Given the scrupulousness with which Washington approached his research, it is very likely that his account of the interview itself is accurate. But did Mrs. Brooks remember correctly? Her detailed recollections and the broader historical context suggest that her account could well have been accurate, but we cannot know for certain.

Here, as in Washington's other descriptions of interviews with elderly survivors of the Civil War era or their children, readers must consider the many challenges of researching and publishing *They Knew Lincoln*. People's memories are fallible and shifting, and the stories they told were likely influenced by subsequent events in their lives and by processes of forgetting and retelling. Washington then made choices about which vignettes to include in his original manuscript, and the text was further shaped by editors who pruned and tweaked. Washington's papers have apparently been lost, so there are no original interview transcripts to examine. Washington tried, wherever he could, to find written documents that verified, or at least connected to, the oral testimonies he described. But, as historians have long understood, many aspects of the lives of poor and working-class people are never recorded in writing. Mundane interactions between Lincoln and his servants—or the arrangements made to publish the memoir of an African American woman—are the kinds of incidents that often go undocumented. No scholar has found documentary evidence that Redpath helped get *Behind the Scenes* into print, nor has anyone advanced a more plausible theory than Washington's for who connected Keckly with her publisher and put the wheels in motion for the controversial printing of Mary Lincoln's personal letters to Elizabeth Keckly.[129]

In recent decades, students and scholars have found in *Behind the Scenes* a trove of invaluable information. They have mined the book as an ex-slave narrative and as a unique source on the lives of Abraham and Mary Lincoln. But they have rarely considered what the book's publication cost Keckly herself. Whoever was Keckly's co-author or amanuensis was likely also the person who did her the great disservice of publishing her personal correspondence with Mary Lincoln. In those letters, Mary Lincoln had revealed her vulnerability and desperation after her husband's murder, as well as her reliance on the advice and wherewithal of her African American confidante, Elizabeth Keckly. Although the book's revelations about life inside the Lincoln White House were controversial, what rankled people most was seeing that correspondence in print. Their publication, which Keckly evidently did not expect, ruined her relationship with Mary Lincoln and imposed on her years of grief and regret. The people who knew Elizabeth Keckly in her old age recalled what a striking figure she cut—her sense of fashion, her erect stature, and the elegance of her speech. But they also remembered her deep sadness. She did not like to talk about the book that had made her famous. Her friend Anna Eliza Williams, who worked at the Home for Destitute Women and Children, where Keckly lived in her old age, told Washington that Keckly said "the book caused her much sorrow and loss of friends," and that she had "never thought of injuring such a loyal friend" as Mary Lincoln.[130]

✿ ✿ ✿ ✿ ✿ ✿ ✿

They Knew Lincoln made a strong claim that African Americans had held Abraham and Mary Lincoln in high esteem to the point of seeing them as almost god-like. In a letter to Paul Angle, Washington promised that his book would reveal "a NEW ABRAHAM and MARY LINCOLN . . . the one the old colored slave loved and admired so much and which I heard so many stories about when I was a little child and in my present interviews." Many elderly freedpeople hung prints of Lincoln's assassination and deathbed scene in their homes, he wrote, and they saw Mary Lincoln as "the Holy Mother of their race because her picture with Lincoln was in every hut and hovel where the poor occupant could get a quarter to get one."[131]

Washington believed Lincoln was a true humanitarian who had always intended to find a way to end slavery, and those views inform the book's overall sensibility. Living amid ferment over the meanings and legacies of Lincoln, Washington was some-what extreme in his own regard for Lincoln and in his asser-tion of freedpeople's unmitigated admiration. Two decades earlier, W. E. B. Du Bois had insisted that African Americans should not revere Lincoln as a flawless hero but, rather, appre-ciate him for his "contradictions and inconsistencies" on issues of slavery and race. In 1931, NAACP field secretary William Pickens emphasized that Lincoln "was no friend to colored people in particular."[132] Likewise, former slaves interviewed by the Works Progress Administration (WPA) in the 1930s some-times criticized Lincoln for not having done enough to secure slaves' freedom and protection from former owners.

And yet *They Knew Lincoln* captures something important about the significance of Abraham and Mary Lincoln for many southern African Americans who lived through the Civil War. Most elderly former slaves who spoke to WPA interviewers about Lincoln voiced a high opinion of the wartime president, and some of the perspectives that emerge in both *They Knew Lincoln* and the WPA narratives—particularly on Lincoln as a larger-than-life or Christ-like figure—resonate with accounts from the Civil War itself and its immediate aftermath. Many enslaved people who lived through the Civil War interpreted the crisis of war and emancipation through biblical stories of Exodus and salvation, and they hoped and imagined that Lincoln would come among them and deliver them from slav-ery. Washington's assertion of an earlier generation's universal admiration does not tell a complete story, but it does reveal a crucial thread of African American thought, both during the Civil War and in the several decades that followed.[133]

That said, Washington's motives and frame of reference were complicated. *They Knew Lincoln* began with the words

"This book is dedicated to my race." Washington wanted his book to inform readers about the role of African Americans in the Lincolns' lives but also to remind them of values and loyalties he believed were too quickly being abandoned. Like many of his counterparts among the capital's black elite, Washington worried about demeaning representations of African Americans in mainstream culture and wanted to ensure that "clean" literature was available to black readers. As a teacher, he worried that African American youth were morally adrift and believed he could help by writing a book that conveyed what he saw as the simple, old-fashioned values of a heroic generation.[134] He told a reporter for the *Evening Star* that *They Knew Lincoln* was an attempt to get "back to normalcy against the jazz age—to portray the good old life with religious background." Once that book was finished, he promised a new one, titled *They Loved Lincoln*, that would present a "moving panorama" of African American life during the Civil War and Reconstruction.[135] He told Louis Warren it would be "folk lore and a continuous unbroken story of devoted people trying to keep alive the love of Lincoln in these modern days of doubt about everything."[136]

Washington imagined that his second book would be more explicitly political than *They Knew Lincoln*. He had been researching and writing amid a wholesale shift in African Americans' orientation toward the nation's two main political parties. Before the 1930s, African Americans, where they were permitted to vote, generally voted Republican, in no small measure because the party was strongly identified with Lincoln and emancipation. Yet it had been a long time since either major party had respected African Americans as constituents or attempted to address problems of racial inequality and oppression. Among African Americans, doubts about the Republicans grew in the early years of the Great Depression, and in December 1931 approximately three hundred black leaders met in Washington to discuss the political crisis. Gradually—as the administration of Franklin D. Roosevelt took steps to curtail racial discrimination in government contracting and to create employment that was accessible to African Americans as well as whites—black voters began to cast their lot with Roosevelt and the Democrats.[137]

Yet Washington was among the relatively better-off and older African Americans who, historian Nancy Weiss has shown, were less likely to tilt Democratic than younger and more working-class people.[138] He remained an active Republican in the early 1930s, supporting Herbert Hoover's campaign for reelection in 1932 and serving as assistant sergeant at arms at that year's Republican National Convention.[139] In 1941, the year before *They Knew Lincoln* was published, Washington linked African Americans' declining reverence for Lincoln to their diminishing support for the Republicans, adding a dash of resentment about the growing diversity of the black population: "You don't know just how much vicious politicians have tried to kill the <u>love</u> that old colored people had for Lincoln," he told Harry Pratt of the Abraham Lincoln Association. "The West Indian Democrats in big cities who sold out to the Democrats took the lead."[140] Washington had kept party politics out of *They Knew Lincoln,* but he still had plenty of material in his files and hoped to put it to the service of teaching African Americans about traditional Christian values and loyalty to the Republicans and their standard-bearer, Abraham Lincoln. His second book, he told Pratt, would be "the greatest argument ever written by a colored man in defense of Lincoln's actions," a work that could be "used by Lincoln lovers everywhere, in politics, on the forum and in debate."[141]

As far as the Lincoln establishment was concerned, however, Washington's window of opportunity—briefly open—had now closed. It seems Louis Warren and James G. Randall had time and space in their heads for one book of "negro folklore" on Lincoln but no more. Washington reached out to both men in the two years following publication of *They Knew Lincoln,* offering a plethora of ideas about his new book and its potential audience. He got nowhere. Both men informed him that they were too busy to read draft chapters or help him find a publisher for his new work.[142] Yet they did not abandon Washington entirely. Late in 1944, Washington asked them to help nominate him for the NAACP's Spingarn Medal, awarded annually to an African American for outstanding achievements. Warren and Randall wrote letters of support, as did the Cardozo principal and many others.[143] The gambit was unsuccessful, however. The NAACP's choice that year was no less a figure than labor organizer and civil rights activist A. Philip Randolph.[144]

In the years between publication of *They Knew Lincoln* in 1942 and his death in 1964, John E. Washington made a place for himself in the largely white world of Lincoln enthusiasts. He was the only African American to speak at the opening of the Robert Lincoln collection of Lincoln papers at the Library of Congress in 1947, and he was active in the DC Lincoln Society, the Gettysburg Lincoln Group, the Illinois Lincoln Society, and the Lincoln Sesquicentennial Committee.[145] It

Figure I.2 John E. Washington at his home in 1961. From *The Potomac Magazine*, December 3, 1961.

was surely not easy being a black man in such a white world. A glimpse of the difficulty is evident in a 1955 *Washington Star* report that Washington had resigned from the Lincoln Group of the District of Columbia in protest that "the services of Negro troops in the Civil War" were not given "sufficient attention in writings and memorials."[146] According to the report, Washington was soon persuaded to withdraw his resignation.

However much Washington had sought white audiences with *They Knew Lincoln* and relished positive attention from the white-dominated Lincoln world, he always cared about attracting African American readers and emphasizing black history. He

Figure I.3 Washington with parts of his Lincolniana collection in 1961. *The Potomac Magazine*, December 3, 1961.

took great pleasure in knowing that the US government had distributed his book to African American soldiers stationed overseas during World War II. Cardozo students who had been drafted, he told Randall, had returned with stories of how Lincoln's message of emancipation and racial equality had resonated among the many "people of color" they had encountered during their service. Washington exhibited parts of his Lincolniana collection at Howard University in 1952 and received honors from the National Dental Association, the professional association of African American dentists, in 1947 and 1952. He retired from Cardozo sometime before 1952, and in 1957 the LeDroit Park neighborhood association honored him for his service to the community.[147] When he was eighty-one years old, a reporter from the *Washington Post*'s Sunday magazine visited his Florida Avenue home, where he had lived with his wife Virginia for almost five decades, and wrote a story about his trove of Lincolniana and the art collection that filled his walls.[148]

Yet Washington remained frustrated with multiple rejections of his second book and with the fact that *They Knew Lincoln* had gone out of print. He had no literary representation and no publisher. Washington and Parma had argued over the terms of the contract with Dutton. Then, shortly before the book was published, Parma had died suddenly of a heart attack, leaving his wife Pallas as Washington's literary agent and Washington unable to extricate himself from what he considered a poisoned relationship with her. At his request, a few white men he knew through Lincoln circles pitched the second book to publishers, but to no avail.[149] Meanwhile, Washington reported that Dutton was in financial straits and could not consider reprinting *They Knew Lincoln.* In 1950, he told an NAACP organizer in Chicago, "My book . . . was sold out in the beginning and I don't know where a copy can be found. I have none for myself."[150]

✷ ✷ ✷ ✷ ✷ ✷ ✷

There are good reasons to pay attention to *They Knew Lincoln* as a source of information on African American history, Lincoln, and the Civil War era, and as a reflection of important strands of black intellectual life in the first half of the twentieth century. Given Washington's birth in 1880 and his cultural conservatism, it is appropriate to consider him part of a longer history of black intellectuals in Washington, DC, who, as the historian Wilson Moses argued, drew inspiration from abolitionism and Christian evangelicalism and worried that the distinctively modern black cultures of jazz and primitivism were threats to racial progress. As Moses put it, their "literary awareness was still largely informed by the apocalyptic moral struggles of the Civil War and Reconstruction." Washington's veneration of Abraham Lincoln and the African Americans of his grandmother's generation, and his concerns about the degradation of African American culture, place him squarely in that often-neglected tradition. *They Knew Lincoln* might also be considered conventional in its approach to African American history. Its pastiche style has less in common with that of the generation of black professional historians that emerged in the 1940s and 1950s than with earlier black writers of history, such as George Washington Williams, who approached their subjects with greater methodological eclecticism.[151]

At the same time, however, *They Knew Lincoln* was a forward-looking book. Washington's compilation of former slaves' views of Lincoln and his concern for the lives of everyday people, particularly as workers, represented an innovation not only in Lincoln circles but in the study of African American history. During the 1930s, researchers increasingly turned their attention toward elderly former slaves, whose memories and perspectives they valued in new ways and sought to record. The most famous example of that impulse is the *Slave Narratives* project of the Works Project Administration, but African American scholars like Washington led the way.[152] Moreover, through its national distribution by a major publishing house, *They Knew Lincoln* became the first book to bring black perspectives on Lincoln directly into the homes and collections of white Lincoln fans and the white reading public. The book's very existence challenged people's tendency to exclude or diminish the testimony of African Americans, and it broke new ground by arguing that African Americans were not simply passive recipients of Lincoln's benevolence, but shaped his attitudes. John E. Washington gave us a landmark in the field of Lincolniana. His book remains a decisive reminder of the centrality of African American history to the nation's past.

NOTES

Abbreviations

ALA	Abraham Lincoln Association Papers, Manuscript Division, Abraham Lincoln Presidential Library, Springfield, IL
DRBP	David Rankin Barbee Papers, Booth Family Center for Special Collections, Georgetown University, Washington, DC
EPD	Dr. John E. Washington file, E. P. Dutton & Company, Inc. Records, Special Collections Research Center, Syracuse University Libraries, Syracuse, NY
JGR	James G. Randall Papers, Manuscript Division, Library of Congress, Washington, DC
LC	Library of Congress, Washington, DC
LMP	John E. Washington Author File, The Lincoln Museum, Fort Wayne, IN
MSR	Manuscripts Division, Moorland-Spingarn Research Center, Howard University, Washington, DC
WCDCPL	Washingtoniana Collection, District of Columbia Public Library, Washington, DC

1. Associated Press, "Bizarre Lincoln Story Is Traced," *Washington Evening Star*, Nov. 11, 1935, A10. The book is Elizabeth Keckly, *Behind the Scenes, or, Thirty Years a Slave, and Four Years in the White House* (New York: G. W. Carlton, 1868). Although the conventional spelling is Keckley, I have used Keckly throughout this essay because Jennifer Fleischner has convincingly demonstrated that Elizabeth Keckly herself spelled her surname without a second e. See Jennifer Fleischner, Mrs. Lincoln and Mrs. Keckly: The Remarkable Story of a Friendship between a First Lady and a Former Slave (New York: Broadway Books, 2003), 7.

2. David Rankin Barbee to Otto Eisenschiml, Feb. 17, 1942, Box 12, Folder 671, DRBP.

3. That line was in Washington's original letter but not published by the *Star*. For the original, see J. E. Washington to the editor of the *Evening Star*, Nov. 12, 1935, Subject file, Rare Books Collection, LC; the published version is "Ample Proof of Reality of Elizabeth Keckley," letter of J. E. Washington, *Washington Evening Star*, Nov. 15, 1935, A12.

4. William H. Herndon and Jesse W. Weik, *Herndon's Lincoln*, eds. Douglas L. Wilson and Rodney O. Davis (Urbana, IL: University of Illinois Press, 2006), 60; John E. Washington, *They Knew Lincoln* (New York: E. P. Dutton, 1942), 101. The story of Lincoln witnessing the slave auction is widely considered not credible. Historian Orville Vernon Burton has noted that "the reliability of sources is probably nowhere more contested than in Lincoln studies" but that "sources from African Americans, such as [John E.] Washington's collection, have too often been suspected of being 'more suspect' by white historians." Orville Vernon Burton, "Lincoln at Two Hundred: Have We Finally Reached Randall's Point of Exhaustion," in Thomas A. Horrocks, Harold Holzer, and Frank J. Williams, eds., *The Living Lincoln* (Carbondale: Southern Illinois University Press, 2011), 209. For the likely inaccuracy of the New Orleans vignette, see Don E. Fehrenbacher and Virginia Fehrenbacher, compilers, *Recollected Words of Abraham Lincoln* (Stanford: Stanford University Press, 1996), 198.

5. Washington, *They Knew Lincoln*, 28. Washington never used his grandmother's name in the book, but her identity was discovered through their link in the 1900 United States census. See entry for Mary Curtis, Washington, DC Census, Enumeration district 64, sheet 9. The census indicated that Caroline was born in Maryland in 1833. Her death was reported in the *Washington Post* on April 9, 1918. My thanks to Mathew Gilmore for help finding the Washington/Curtis family in the census and elsewhere.

6. Washington, *They Knew Lincoln*, 53.

7. Washington, *They Knew Lincoln*, 29.

8. Washington, *They Knew Lincoln*, 29.

9. Washington, *They Knew Lincoln*, 42.

10. For the story of Dines fleeing to Washington as told to Washington by her grandson, see *They Knew Lincoln*, 83. For another mention of Washington as a destination for people fleeing slavery, see 122. More generally, for the District of Columbia as a refuge for African Americans in the antebellum period, see Letitia Woods Brown, *Free Negroes in the District of Columbia, 1790–1846* (New York: Oxford University Press, 1972); and Katherine Chilton, "City of Refuge: Urban Labor,

Gender, and Family Formation during Slavery and the Transition to Freedom in the District of Columbia, 1820–1875" (PhD Dissertation, Carnegie Mellon University, 2009). For a survey of race and politics in the history of Washington, see Chris Myers Asch and George Derek Musgrove, *Chocolate City: A History of Race and Democracy in the Nation's Capital* (Chapel Hill: University of North Carolina Press, 2017).

11. Washington, *They Knew Lincoln*, 89–90.

12. Washington, *They Knew Lincoln*, 93.

13. Washington, *They Knew Lincoln*, 33. In a different section of the book, Aunt Vina's story also delineates the role of Washington, DC, in the region during the Civil War. On the migration of African Americans into Washington during the Civil War, see, for example, Kate Masur, *An Example for All the Land: Emancipation and the Struggle over Equality in Washington* (Chapel Hill: University of North Carolina Press, 2010).

14. Washington, *They Knew Lincoln*, 90.

15. Washington, *They Knew Lincoln*, 85.

16. Washington, *They Knew Lincoln*, 86–7. Washington said Mary Dines herself had given him the rare photo of the "contraband" singers and that Dines recalled the photo having been taken by Matthew Brady as camp residents awaited the president's initial visit to the camp. Although her stories of Lincoln's visits have not been confirmed in other sources, they are plausible, as Lincoln traveled frequently between the White House and the Soldier's Home and could have stopped at the camp en route. Drawing on the letters of a soldier who helped guard Lincoln, historian Mathew Pinsker confirmed that Mary Dines also worked as a cook at the Soldier's Home in the summer of 1862. See Pinsker, *Lincoln's Sanctuary: Abraham Lincoln and the Soldiers' Home* (New York: Oxford University Press, 2003), 81–1, 88, 94, 179. According to Washington, Dines was at a camp "off 7th Street, near where Howard University now stands" (*They Knew Lincoln*, 83–4). That would have been the site of Campbell Hospital, which was one of the city's many camps for newly arrived fugitives from slavery. Masur, *Example for All the Land*, 69; Thomas C. Holt, Cassandra Smith-Parker, and Rosalyn Terborg-Penn, *A Special Mission: The Story of the Freedmen's Hospital, 1862–1962* (Washington: Academic Affairs Division, Howard University, 1975), 8.

17. Washington, *They Knew Lincoln*, 71. Other vignettes similarly humanize Lincoln and emphasize his humble origins, including a story of the president feeding a man who had heard there were "provisions" in the Constitution and Peter Brown's description of Lincoln as "a poor man who learned to work hard as a boy. He knew all about life and the struggles of the unfortunate. That was why he sympathized with us colored folks, and we loved him." *They Knew Lincoln*, 118, 125.

18. Washington, *They Knew Lincoln*, 28.

19. Washington, *They Knew Lincoln*, 146–7.

20. For black intellectuals' orientation toward narratives of progress and civilization in the years after the Civil War, see Stephen G. Hall, *A Faithful Account of the Race: African American Historical Writing in Nineteenth-Century America* (Chapel Hill: University of North Carolina Press, 2009); for the growth of the study of folklore and the role of black folklorists, see Lee D. Baker, *From*

Savage to Negro: Anthropology and the Construction of Race, 1896–1954 (Berkeley: University of California Press, 1998), esp. 138–67; for an overview of changing approaches to the customs and traditions of formerly enslaved people, see Lawrence W. Levine, *Black Culture and Black Consciousness: Afro-American Folk Thought from Slavery to Freedom* (New York: Oxford University Press, 2007; first published 1977), 136–89; and for Mary Todd Lincoln and spiritualism, see Jean H. Baker, *Mary Todd Lincoln: A Biography* (New York; W. W. Norton, 1987), esp. 217–22; and Catherine Clinton, *Mrs. Lincoln: A Life* (New York: Harper Collins, 2009), 182–88.

21. Washington, *They Knew Lincoln*, 45.
22. John H. Brooks and William Slade had both married free black women from well-connected families. Josephine Lewis Parke Slade was a daughter of Rachael Braham, a slave of the Washington family at Mount Vernon, and Hannah Bruce Brooks was a cousin of William Slade and a member of a longstanding free black family from northern Virginia. For Brooks, see Henry S. Robinson, "Descendants of Daniel and Hannah Brooks," *Negro History Bulletin*, Nov. 1, 1960, 37; *They Knew Lincoln*, 110. For Slade, see *They Knew Lincoln*, esp. 115; "The Late William Slade," *Elevator*, May 1, 1868; July Wilbur Big Diary, entry of June 13, 1868, Julia Wilbur Papers, Haverford College Special Collections; Natalie Sweet, "A Representative 'of Our People': The Agency of William Slade, Leader in the African American Community and Usher to Abraham Lincoln," *Journal of the Abraham Lincoln Association* 34, no. 2 (2013): 21–41.
23. Washington, *They Knew Lincoln*, 61–2.
24. Washington, *They Knew Lincoln*, 62.
25. Washington, *They Knew Lincoln*, 100.
26. Apart from Washington's book, historians have discovered little specific information on the identities and lives of members of the White House staff during Lincoln's presidency. See William Seale, *The President's House: A History*, 2 vols., 2nd ed. (Baltimore: Johns Hopkins University Press, 1986), 1, 395; Ronald D. Rietveldt, "The Lincoln White House Community," *Journal of the Abraham Lincoln Association* 20, no. 2 (1999): 17–48. Many historians draw heavily on Washington himself, for example, Benjamin Quarles, *Lincoln and the Negro* (New York: Oxford University Press, 1962), 199–200, 261; Kenneth J. Winkle, *Abraham and Mary Lincoln* (Carbondale: Southern Illinois University Press, 2011), 85–6, 89; Clinton, *Mrs. Lincoln*, 158–61.
27. Washington, *They Knew Lincoln*, 107. For Slade, see note 22 above.
28. White House servants' longevity is described in Seale, *President's House*, vol. 1, and in Washington, *They Knew Lincoln*, 100, 107, 128.
29. Washington, *They Knew Lincoln*, 33. For more on domestic work in the capital, see Elizabeth Clark-Lewis, *Living In, Living Out: African American Domestics in Washington, D.C., 1910–1940* (Washington, DC: Smithsonian Institution Press, 1994).
30. Washington, *They Knew Lincoln*, 115.
31. Washington, *They Knew Lincoln*, 132.
32. Washington, *They Knew Lincoln*, 129–32.
33. Washington, *They Knew Lincoln*, 132.

34. Washington, *They Knew Lincoln,* 244.

35. Washington, *They Knew Lincoln,* 135–40.

36. For patronizing chiefs, see *They Knew Lincoln,* 140. For more on African Americans and federal employment in this period, see Kate Masur, "Patronage and Protest in Kate Brown's Washington," *Journal of American History* 99 (March 2013): 1047–71; Eric S. Yellin, *Racism in the Nation's Service: Government Workers and the Color Line in Woodrow Wilson's America* (Chapel Hill: University of North Carolina Press, 2013).

37. Washington, *They Knew Lincoln,* 140–1.

38. Washington attended St. Augustine's, the school associated with the city's preeminent black Catholic church of the era. See Paul L. Blakely, "Memories of Marse Abe," *America,* Feb. 14, 1942, clipping in LMP. For origins of the capital's black public schools, see Masur, *Example for All the Land,* esp. 77–85.

39. Washington, *They Knew Lincoln,* 148.

40. "Blanche K. Bruce No More! The Greatest American Politician Gone to Rest-Eloquent Orations, and Excellent Music," *Washington Bee,* March 26, 1898, 4. For the high school's cadet program, see Robert N. Mattingly, *Autobiographic Memories 1897–1954, M Street-Dunbar High School* (Washington, DC: Self-published, 1974), 6–8, Vertical files, WCDCPL. See also Sandra Fitzpatrick and Maria R. Goodwin, *The Guide to Black Washington* (New York: Hippocrene Books, 1993), 88–91. For Bruce, see William J. Simmons, *Men of Mark: Eminent, Progressive and Rising* (Cleveland: Geo. M. Rewell, 1887), 699–703; Willard B. Gatewood, *Aristocrats of Color: The Black Elite, 1880–1920* (Bloomington: Indiana University Press, 1990), 4–6, 35–36. For Washington, DC, as a haven for black politicians from the South, see Yellin, *Racism in the Nation's Service,* 48–51.

41. For his education, see "Dr. John Edwin Washington," O.G. 729, MSR. See also "Haiti Honors Dr. John E. Washington, Author of 'They Knew Lincoln,'" *Howard University Bulletin* 22, no. 15 (April 1, 1943); Frederick D. Wilkinson, ed., *Directory of Graduates, Howard University, 1870–1963* (Washington, DC: The University, 1965), 386. Many African American dentists went directly from high school to dental school, bypassing college. Carter Godwin Woodson, *The Negro Professional Man and the Community, with Special Emphasis on the Physician and the Lawyer* (reprint New York: New Universities Press, 1969; originally published 1934), 167–8.

42. For Washington as the first African American to pass the dental boards in the capital, see "Dr. John Edwin Washington"; Clifton Orrin Dummett, *The Growth and Development of the Negro in Dentistry in the United States* (Chicago: Stanek Press, 1952), 10. Howard University was a major educator of black dentists in the early twentieth century. The university's dentistry program launched in 1882, and black dentists in the District of Columbia organized their own professional association in 1900. Members of that early group, including Washington himself, soon founded a regional association known as the Tri-State Dental Association, and that group, in turn, became the kernel of the nation's association of African American dentists, the National Dental Association, founded in 1932. Dummett, *The Growth and Development of the Negro in Dentistry,* 16–18, 34.

43. "Work Out of Hours," *Washington Evening Star*, Oct. 20, 1910, 22.

44. For the board granting him permission to practice dentistry, see minutes of Oct. 18, 1922, Oct. 5, 1927, Oct. 3, 1928, and others in Minutes of the District of Columbia Board of Education, Charles Sumner School Archive, Washington, DC. According to a history of LeDroit Park, many black physicians and pharmacists lived along Florida Avenue and practiced out of their homes. Although that article did not mention dentists, one might surmise that Washington did the same. See "LeDroit Park" [1975], LeDroit Park vertical file, WCDCPL.

45. Square 3094, lot 56, 1908-09 Real Estate Assessment, "Real Estate Assessments and Related Plats, Maps, and Directories for Washington, D.C., to 1934," WCDCPL. For the year of his marriage, "Dr. John Edwin Washington."

46. "LeDroit Park"; Ronald M. Johnson, "Those Who Stayed: Washington Black Writers of the 1920s," *Records of the Columbia Historical Society* 50 (1980): 484–99; Fitzpatrick and Gooding, *Guide to Black Washington*, 97–126; Jonathan Scott Holloway, *Confronting the Veil: Abram Harris Jr., E. Franklin Frazier, and Ralph Bunch, 1919–1941* (Chapel Hill: University of North Carolina Press, 2002), 35–50.

47. James A. Miller, "Black Washington and the New Negro Renaissance," in John J. Czaplicka and Blair A. Ruble, eds., *Composing Urban History and the Constitution of Civic Identities* (Washington, DC: Woodrow Wilson Center Press, 2003); Johnson, "Those Who Stayed."

48. "First Annual Exhibition of Painting and Sculpture by Colored Art Students of America," Feb. 14, 1919, to March 7, 1919, catalog, William D. Nixon Papers, Box 2, Folder 3, MSR. See also "Art Exhibition," *Washington Bee*, Feb. 22, 1919, 4.

49. "Catalogue of the Third Annual Exhibition of the Tanner Art League" (1922), William D. Nixon Papers, Box 1, Folder 2. Washington also exhibited work at the annual meeting of the American Negro Academy in 1920, although he was not a member of the academy. Alfred A. Moss, Jr., *The American Negro Academy: Voice of the Talented Tenth* (Baton Rouge: Louisiana State University Press, 1981), 273.

50. For the pair's Howard degrees, see Wilkinson, ed., *Directory of Graduates*, 386, 387. She is listed as Carolyn Virginia Ross, and they graduated in the same high school class. See copy of 1898 graduation program in Robert N. Mattingly, *Birth of M Street High School* (Washington, DC: self-published, 1976), Vertical files, WCDCPL. For Washington's degree from the International Correspondence Schools, see *The Bison* (Howard University Yearbook), 1924, Howard University Archives, Moorland-Spingarn Research Center, Howard University, Washington DC. For the International Correspondence Schools, see James D. Watkinson, " 'Education for Success': The International Correspondence Schools of Scranton, Pennsylvania," *Pennsylvania Magazine of History and Biography* 120, no. 4 (Oct. 1996): 343–69.

51. Francis Cardozo's biography is sketched in Simmons, *Men of Mark*, 428–31. See also Timothy P. McCarthy, "Cardozo, Francis Louis," *American National Biography* Online, accessed Feb. 13, 2017. For more on the history of black secondary schools in Washington, see Lillian G. Dabney, *The History of Schools for Negroes in the District of Columbia, 1807–1947* (Washington: Catholic University of America Press, 1949), 137–42; Gatewood, *Aristocrats of Color*, 260–63.

52. *The Purple Wave, Nineteen Hundred and Thirty-Eight* (10th anniversary year-book), Charles Sumner School Archive; clipping from *Journal of the Columbian Education Association*, 1924–25, William D. Nixon Papers, Box 1, Folder 2; "Dr. John Edwin Washington." In 1949, a historian of black education in the capital remarked that Cardozo High School was the only high school in the country that offered "exclusively business education for colored youth." Dabney, *History of Schools for Negroes*, 148.

53. "Report of the Assistant Superintendent in Charge of Colored Schools," July 1, 1915, *Annual Report of the Commissioners of the District of Columbia*, vol. IV, *Report of the Board of Education* (Washington, 1915), 249; On Woodson in Washington, see Jacqueline Goggin, *Carter G. Woodson: A Life in Black History* (Baton Rouge: Louisiana State University Press, 1993), 12–23, 29–31, 43–55, 66–8; Pero G. Dagbovie, "'Most Honorable Mention . . . belongs to Washington, D.C.': The Carter G. Woodson Home and the Early Black History Movement in the Nation's Capital," *Journal of African American History* 96, no. 3 (Summer 2011): 295–324; and Moss, *American Negro Academy*. On Woodson and attention to ex-slaves' testimonies, see Brenda E. Stevenson, "'Out of the Mouths of Ex-Slaves': Carter G. Woodson's *Journal of Negro History* 'Invents' the Study of Slavery," *Journal of African American History* 100, no. 4 (Fall 2015): 698–705. On the dynamism of black history in the 1930s in particular, see James O. Young, *Black Writers of the Thirties* (Baton Rouge: Louisiana State University Press, 1973), 106–32.

54. For the church's association with Washington's black elite, see Gatewood, *Aristocrats of Color*, 46, 281, 299, and for the black Protestant Episcopal church more generally as a haven of the elite, see 275–83.

55. Andrew Kahrl, *The Land Was Ours: African American Beaches from Jim Crow to the Sunbelt South* (Cambridge, MA: Harvard University Press, 2012), 96. I thank Andrew Kahrl for sharing his notes on Highland Beach. For skin color and status in this era, see, for example, Asch and Musgrove, *Chocolate City*, 241–42.

56. Kahrl, *The Land Was Ours*, 88–97; Constance M. Green, *The Secret City: A History of Race Relations in the Nation's Capital* (Princeton: Princeton University Press, 1967), esp. 155–214.

57. John E. Washington to Harry Pratt, July 1, 1941, Box 23, ALA; Florence Murray, "Trees Become Issue at Highland Beach," *Chicago Defender*, Sept. 30, 1939, 19. Washington evidently purchased the house shortly after his friend Haley Douglass took over management of the properties. See "John E. Washington House," April 1982, Maryland Historical Trust, Inventory Form for State Historic Sites Survey, http://mht.maryland.gov; Kahrl, *The Land Was Ours*, 95, 96–103. According to one source, Washington took up a leadership role in the town in 1928. See "New Writer: John E. Washington," n.d., EPD.

58. Letter of John R. Francis and J. E. Washington, *Baltimore Afro-American*, Sept. 24, 1932, 9. In 1930, Washington fought against the building of a county road. See "Residents of Highland and Venice Beaches Protest County Road," *Baltimore Afro-American*, Aug. 23, 1930, 10. Washington's home was badly burned in the fire, likely an arson, that destroyed Ware's Hotel in winter 1930. See "Highland

Beach, Md., Hotel, Burned, to Be Rebuilt," *New York Amsterdam News,* Feb. 5, 1930, 6; Kahrl, *The Land Was Ours,* 104–6.

59. Yellin, *Racism in the Nation's Service;* Green, *Secret City,* esp. 155–214; Asch and Musgrove, *Chocolate City,* 217–48.

60. Entry of Nov. 2–3, 1935, Diaries, Box 1, Papers of Bess Furman, Manuscript Division, LC.

61. Barbee to Eisenschiml, Feb. 17, 1942.

62. "Ample Proof of Reality of Elizabeth Keckley," Letter of J. E. Washington, *Washington Evening Star,* Nov. 15, 1935, A12. The *Star* published only parts of Barbee's original letter. The original is Barbee to the Editor of the *Star,* Nov. 18, 1935, Box 1, Folder 59, DRBP. The published version is "Writer Explains Error in Case of Mrs. Keckley," David Rankin Barbee to the Editor, Washington *Evening Star,* Nov. 26, 1935. In his letter, Barbee claimed that a New York publisher had approached him about editing a new edition of Keckly's book. The book had been quietly republished in 1931, with a brief and laudatory foreword by James H. Stansil. See Frances Smith Foster, "Historical Introduction" in *Behind the Scenes, or Thirty Years a Slave and Four Years in the White House* (Chicago: R. R. Donnelley & Sons, 1998), lxxiv.

63. Finding aid, DRBP, http://findingaids.library.georgetown.edu/repositories/15/resources/10043. On Barbee as a southerner who opposed the veneration of Lincoln and advocated telling "the truth about the South's side of the War of the 60s," see John McKee Barr, *Loathing Lincoln: An American Tradition from the Civil War to the Present* (Baton Rouge: Louisiana State University Press, 2014), 174–79, quotation from Barbee on 175. Barbee's assassination book was never published.

64. Untitled, *Cincinnati Commercial,* May 4, 1868, 8. Evidently the author was journalist George Alfred Townsend, as the vignette was published three years later in his *Washington, Outside and Inside: A Picture and a Narrative of the Origin, Growth, Excellences, Abuses, Beauties, and Personages of Our Governing City* (Hartford, CT: James Betts, 1873), 192.

65. David Rankin Barbee to Allen C. Clark, Nov. 13, 1935, Box 1, Folder 59, DRBP.

66. David Rankin Barbee to Ralph C. Busbey, Dec. 5, 1935, Box 1, Folder 59, DRBP. Barbee was wrong about Mary Lincoln's clothing and about her relationship with Keckly, as modern scholars have shown. The definitive book on their relationship is Fleischner, *Mrs. Lincoln and Mrs. Keckly.* See also letters and commentary in Justin G. Turner and Linda Levitt Turner, *Mary Todd Lincoln: Her Life and Letters* (New York: A. A. Knopf, 1972).

67. David Rankin Barbee to Ralph C. Busbey, Dec. 5, 1935.

68. David Rankin Barbee to Otto Eisenschiml, Feb. 17, 1942.

69. David Rankin Barbee to Louis Warren, March 30, 1936, Box 1, Folder 59, DRBP; "Behind the Scenes," *Lincoln Lore,* March 23, 1936, 1. The letter to Warren is Barbee's most elaborate statement on why he believed Swisshelm wrote the book.

70. Entry for Nov. 13, 1935, 1935 Calendar, Miscellany, Box 118, Papers of Bess Furman.

71. "Mary T. Lincoln Book Stirs Row," *Washington Star*, Dec. 1, 1935. For "correction" see Notebook 41, Notebooks 1935, Speeches & Writings, Papers of Bess Furman. Grimké spoke to Furman about Keckly and soon excerpted a portion of his diary and allowed it to be published in the *Journal of Negro History*. See "Communications," *Journal of Negro History* 21, no. 1 (Jan. 1936): 56–7.

72. "Ample Proof of Reality of Elizabeth Keckley."

73. Washington, *They Knew Lincoln*, 147–9.

74. Some of his interviews occurred in 1938, and that is also the year that he traveled to the Midwest in search of additional information. See esp. *They Knew Lincoln*, 220, 237. In 1961, Washington affirmed that the 1935 Keckly scandal had been a prime impetus for his own study. See "A Rare Look at Lincoln Seen through the Eyes of Men Set Free," *Potomac Magazine*, Dec. 3, 1961, 26–27.

75. On the world of Lincoln collectors and buffs in the first four decades of the twentieth century, see Merrill D. Peterson, *Lincoln in American Memory* (New York: Oxford University Press, 1994), esp. chs. 4–6. For a contemporary discussion, see R. Gerald McMurtry, "Why Collect Lincolniana?" *Lincoln Herald* 49, no. 1 (Feb. 1947): 2–9. On Lincoln's popularity during the Depression and World War II, see Nina Silber, "Abraham Lincoln and the Political Culture of New Deal America," *Journal of the Civil War Era* 5, no. 3 (Sept. 2015): 348–71.

76. Louis Warren to John E. Washington, Nov. 8, 1938, LMP.

77. John E. Washington to Louis Warren, Nov. 19, 1938, LMP.

78. John E. Washington to Louis Warren, Oct. 29, 1939, LMP.

79. John E. Washington to Paul Angle, July 28, 1939, Box 19, ALA.

80. Washington, *They Knew Lincoln*, 150.

81. Washington, *They Knew Lincoln*, 153, 157–8.

82. Washington, *They Knew Lincoln*, 169–73. The Hancock circular is published in the appendix.

83. John E. Washington to Harry Pratt, Oct. 20, 1939, Box 19, ALA.

84. The white public's intrinsic skepticism about black testimony had dogged Keckly's book upon its release as well. See, for example, Foster, "Historical Introduction," lxix.

85. Washington reported that on their first meeting, Randall had told him, "The colored side [of Lincoln] is a good one to work out." John E. Washington to Harry Pratt, Jan. 7, 1939, Box 19, ALA. On Randall, see Robert W. Johannsen, "Lincoln, the Civil War, and Professor James G. Randall," in Lillian Hoddeson, ed., *No Boundaries: University of Illinois Vignettes* (Urbana: University of Illinois Press, 2004).

86. James G. Randall, *Constitutional Problems under Lincoln* (New York: D. Appleton, 1926).

87. Randall quoted in Johannsen, "Lincoln, the Civil War, and Professor James G. Randall," 107, 108. James Randall's wife, the historian Ruth Randall, advised Washington about who was a historian and who was not. James G., her husband,

should be identified as a historian, she wrote, but Philip Van Doren Stern was "a literary man." Ruth Randall to John E. Washington, March 11, 1940, EPD.

88. John E. Washington to Harry Pratt, Jan. 7, 1939, Box 19, ALA. Pratt helped in fall 1939 by urging Randall to read Washington's first draft chapter. He told Randall of Washington's hunt for Keckly materials and of his trip to Springfield, writing of Washington, "If he makes a good negro story for negroes then he will have done something worth while. It can't be based on written documents because few of the old people he has contacted can write but if he gets the spirit of it I will enjoy reading it." Harry Pratt to James G. Randall, Oct. 23, 1939, JGR.

89. James G. Randall to Valta Parma, May 10, 1941, JGR; James G. Randall to John E. Washington, Nov. 6, 1939, EPD; John E. Washington to James G. Randall, Nov. 1, 1939, Box 11, JGR. Randall's views resembled the "romantic racialism" of nineteenth-century northern reformers described in George M. Fredrickson, *The Black Image in the White Mind: The Debate on Afro-American Character and Destiny, 1817–1914* (New York: Harper & Row, 1971), 97–129.Washington assured another white Lincoln expert that *They Knew Lincoln* would be "a source book of facts never before gathered" and "a contribution to Lincoln knowledge." John E. Washington to Harry Pratt, Feb. 28, 1939, Box 19, ALA.

90. John E. Washington to Louis Warren, March 9, 1939, LMP

91. John E. Washington to Harry Pratt, Aug. 9, 1940, Box 21, ALA; John E. Washington to James J. Randall, Sept. 29, 1940, JGR

92. For the reader's report, see [Valta Parma] to [Randall], undated [reader's report dated March 13, 1941], JGR. For McKay's role, see John Macrae to V. Valta Parma, Feb. 7, 1941, McBlain Books Catalog 167, transcript in author's possession. Macrae wrote that Dutton had sent the manuscript to McKay on the "idea that McKay, being a Negro, would have the scholarship, the feeling and the sympathy to put the book in shape for its public."

93. V. Valta Parma to James G. Randall, April 29, 1941, JGR. For "integrity," see V. Valta Parma to Louis Warren, April 29, 1941, LMP. See also V. Valta Parma to James G. Randall, undated, Randall Papers.

94. James G. Randall to Valta Parma, May 1, 1941, LMP.

95. John E. Washington to Harry Pratt, April 21, 1941, Box 23, ALA; Carl Sandburg to John E. Washington, Sept. 6, 1941 (copy), JGR.

96. For Randall agreeing to blurb the book, see James G. Randall to Pallas Parma, Oct. 13, 1941, JGR. For Warren's operation, see Louis Warren to John E. Washington, Nov. 18, 1941, EPD; Maurice A. Cook to Elizabeth Wright, Dec. 8, 1941, LMP.

97. John E. Washington to James G. Randall, June 6, 1941, JGR. The tumultuous editing process and the powerful influence of prominent white people suggest some of the dynamics described in Jonathan Scott Holloway, "The Black Intellectual and the 'Crisis Canon' in the Twentieth Century," *Black Scholar* 31, no. 1 (Spring 2001): 2–13.

98. "Books—Authors," *New York Times*, Nov. 28, 1941, 21. For broader context, see Silber, "Abraham Lincoln."

99. "Notes on Books and Authors," *New York Times,* Jan. 7, 1942, 17.

100. Display Ad, *New York Herald Tribune*, Feb. 1, 1942, H9. See also advertising copy in EPD.

101. "Lincoln Lore Still Grows," *Milwaukee Journal*, Feb. 12, 1942, 18; James Totman, "New Lincoln Is Revealed," *Pittsburgh Press*, Feb. 1, 1942, 8; Irving Dillard, "Three New Books on Lincoln Mark His 133rd Anniversary," *St. Louis Post*, Feb. 12, 1942, clipping in LMP.

102. Lewis Gannett, "Books and Things," *New York Herald Tribune*, Jan. 27, 1942, 19. Gannett on Du Bois, quoted in David Levering Lewis, "Introduction," *Black Reconstruction in America* by W. E. B. Du Bois (New York: Athenaeum, 1992, originally published 1935), xi. Gannett also recognized that Washington's portrayal of Mary Lincoln diverged from the mainstream, "Sandburg-Angle" version.

103. F. B., "Something New in a Book about Lincoln," *Chicago Daily Tribune*, Feb. 11, 1942, 19.

104. Blakely, "Memories of Marse Abe." For Randall's blurb, see Dutton catalog, 2–3, in EPD. The *Washington Post's* reviewer called the book a "deep heavily-minored song of admiration of the Negro for his emancipation" and joined Sandburg in judging it an "important human narrative." Scott Hart, "The Negro's Lincoln," *Washington Post*, Feb. 8, 1942, L10.

105. "A Selected List of Important Spring Books," *New York Herald Tribune*, March 1, 1942, G7; Paul Angle, "Their Hero," *New York Herald Tribune*, March 1, 1942, G27; Review of *They Knew Lincoln*, *Abraham Lincoln Quarterly* 2, no. 1 (March 1942): 31.

106. Otto Eisenschiml, "Abraham Lincoln as Seen by the Negroes Who Knew Him Best," *Chicago Sun*, Feb. 7, 1942, clipping in JGR.

107. Claude Milton Dixon, "The Book Shelf," *Atlanta Daily World*, Apr. 19, 1942, 4. The major African American newspapers of the era published few book reviews but did take occasional note of Washington's successes. In early January, for example, the *Pittsburgh Courier* announced the book's forthcoming publication. *Pittsburgh Courier*, Jan. 3, 1942, 14.

108. Arthur B. Spingarn, "Books by Negro Authors in 1942," *Crisis: A Record of the Darker Races* 50, no. 2 (Feb. 1943): 46.

109. "Haiti Honors Dr. John E. Washington"; Lucius C. Harper, "Dustin' Off the News," *Chicago Defender*, Nov. 15, 1947, 1.

110. "Faculty Banquet Honors Dr. John E. Washington, *Baltimore Afro-American*, March 21, 1942; John E. Washington to Louis Warren, May 10, 1942, LMP; "What's Going On and Where," *Washington Post*, May 13, 1942; "Negro Demand to Fight Held Aid to Status," *Washington Post*, Nov. 2, 1942; "Washington Social Notes," *Chicago Defender*, March 28, 1942, 17. The banquet was at Harrison's, an elegant black-run restaurant. John DeFerrari, *Historic Restaurants of Washington, D.C.: Capital Eats* (Charleston, SC: History Press, 2013), 103–4. Generally speaking, the ASNLH covered Washington's book favorably, but no evidence has come to light that Washington was close to the organization's founder, Carter G. Woodson.

111. W. M. Brewer, Review, *Journal of Negro History* 27, no. 2 (Apr. 1942): 226. It bears noting that Washington had expressed gratitude to Brewer in the acknowledgments to *They Knew Lincoln*, 27.

112. John E. Washington to Louis Warren, May 10, 1942; John E. Washington to Mrs. Bowers, Nov. 22, 1942, EPD.

113. Barbara Dianne Savage provides background for *New World A' Coming* in *Broadcasting Freedom: War, Radio, and the Politics of Race, 1938–1948* (Chapel Hill: University of North Carolina Press, 1999), 248–57.

114. John E. Washington to James G. Randall, Dec. 27, 1942, JGR.

115. Washington, *They Knew Lincoln*, 190. Twenty years after *They Knew Lincoln*, Benjamin Quarles helped restore Fleurville and Springfield's black community to Lincoln's story. Quarles, *Lincoln and the Negro*, 25–28. See also Richard E. Hart, "Springfield's African Americans as a Part of the Lincoln Community," *Journal of the Abraham Lincoln Association* 20, no. 1 (Winter 1999): 35–54; Kenneth J. Winkle, " 'Paradox Though It May Seem': Lincoln on Antislavery, Race, and Union, 1837–1860," in Brian R. Dirck, ed., *Lincoln Emancipated: The President and the Politics of Race* (Dekalb: Southern Illinois University Press, 2007).

116. John E. Washington to Louis Warren, Oct. 4, 1938, LMP; Washington to Warren, Nov. 19, 1938.

117. John E. Washington to Louis Warren, Aug. 8, 1938, LMP. On that summer 1938 trip he also visited Chicago and various Civil War and Lincoln collections, and spent an evening with Otto Eisenschiml. From there he traveled to New York. Washington to Warren, Oct. 4, 1938, LMP.

118. John E. Washington to Harry Pratt, Feb. 27, 1940, Box 21, ALA; John E. Washington to Harry Pratt, March 29, 1940, ALA, box 21; John E. Washington to Harry Pratt, April 16, 1940, Box 21, ALA; "Club Tribute to Be Paid Lincoln and Douglass," *Washington Star*, Feb. 15, 1940, B-8.

119. "Diplome," July 27, 1942, EPD; "Autour d'un livre sur Abraham Lincoln," July 22, 1942, *Haiti-Journal*, 1, LMP. A copy of the honorary degree and the clipping from the *Haiti-Journal* are also contained in EPD. Washington thanked Lescot and his assistant in the acknowledgments of *They Knew Lincoln*.

120. "Haiti Honors Author of 'They Knew Lincoln,' " *New York Amsterdam Star-News*, Jan. 30, 1943, 6; "D.C. Dentist Honored by Haiti for Lincoln Book," *Chicago Defender*, Jan. 23, 1934, 22; "Haiti Honors Race Author," *Pittsburg Courier*, Jan. 23, 1943, 7; "Haiti Honors Dr. John E. Washington."

121. John E. Washington to Harry Pratt, April 16, 1940.

122. Washington, *They Knew Lincoln*, 62.

123. John E. Washington to Harry Pratt, July 1, 1941. Washington's thinking was not unique. Amid a growing movement to see African American history in the context of decolonization struggles elsewhere, many African American intellectuals of his era were interested in Haiti's world historical significance. See, for example, Jason C. Parker, " 'Made-in-America Revolutions'? The 'Black University' and the American Role in the Decolonization of the Black Atlantic," *Journal of American History* 96, no. 3 (Dec. 2009): 727–50.

124. W. M. Brewer, Review, *Journal of Negro History* 27, no. 2 (Apr. 1942): 225.

125. R. N. Mattingly to National office of NAACP, Dec. 26, 1944, John E. Washington folder, Box A 90, Series II, Papers of the National Association for the Advancement of Colored People, LC.

126. In addition to sources cited in note 115, see, for example, Fleischner, *Mrs. Lincoln and Mrs. Keckly*; Nell Irvin Painter, *Sojourner Truth: A Life, a Symbol* (New York: Norton, 1996); Eric Foner, *The Fiery Trial: Abraham Lincoln and American Slavery* (New York: Norton, 2010); Kate Masur, "The African American Delegation to Abraham Lincoln: A Reappraisal," *Civil War History* 56, no. 2 (June 2010): 117–44; Kate Masur, "'Color Was a Bar to the Entrance': African American Activism and the Question of Social Equality in Lincoln's White House," *American Quarterly* 69, no. 1 (March 2017): 1–22; Sweet, "A Representative 'of Our People,'" 21–41.

127. Hannah Brooks also gave birth to her first child, Ursuline Virginia, in New York. Robinson, "Descendants of Daniel and Hannah Bruce," 37.

128. Washington, *They Knew Lincoln*, 235–36, 238.

129. Many recent scholars accept Brooks's account or at least give it considerable credit while indicating that much remains unknown about who helped Keckly bring her book to publication. See, for example, John R. McKivigan, *Forgotten Firebrand: James Redpath and the Making of Nineteenth-Century America* (Ithaca: Cornell University Press, 2008), 116; Foster, *Behind the Scenes*, lx–lxii; Fleischner, *Mrs. Lincoln and Mrs. Keckly*, 316.

130. Washington, *They Knew Lincoln*, 221. Keckly had told a reporter in 1901 that she felt exploited by the "newspaper men" to whom she told her story. She had made no money from the book, and its publication had "made some enemies for me who should have always been my friends." Smith D. Fry, "Lincoln Liked Her," *Minneapolis Register,* July 5, 1901. For Keckly late in life, see "Mrs. Elizabeth Keckley," Francis J. Grimké Papers, Box 40-8, folder 378, MSR; Carrie Syphax Watson to Rev. Grimké, Carter Woodson, ed., *The Works of Francis J. Grimké*, 4 vols. (Washington: Associated Publishers, 1942), 4, 548–9; Fleischner, *Mrs. Lincoln and Mrs. Keckly*, 323–4.

131. John E. Washington to Paul Angle, July 28, 1939, Box 19, ALA. He added, "It would take a poet to describe some of the interviews and to see the tears even yet in these people's eyes, many of whom were over ninety years of age, and still they would straighten up and become young again as they described the past as if it were but yesterday. Yes, the name of Lincoln is next to that of the Holy Savior to these old people."

132. W. E. B. Du Bois, "Abraham Lincoln" and "Again, Lincoln," in Nathan Huggins, ed., *W. E. B. Du Bois: Writings* (New York: Library of America, 1986), 1196–99, quotation on 1198; Pickins quoted in Silber, "Abraham Lincoln," 357.

133. David Silkenat and John Barr, "'Serving the Lord and Abe Lincoln's Spirit': Lincoln and Memory in the WPA Narratives," *Lincoln Herald* 115, no. 2 (2013): 75–97; Steven Hahn, "'Extravagant Expectations' of Freedom: Rumour, Political Struggle, and the Christmas Insurrection Scare of 1865 in the American South," *Past and Present* 157 (Nov. 1997), esp. 135–8; Levine, *Black Culture, Black Consciousness,* 136–8.

134. John E. Washington to James G. Randall, June 6, 1941.

135. John E. Washington to Louis Warren, Dec. 26, 1942, LMP. In that letter Washington also wrote, "So great has been the demand for clean books on my race that I am now well on the way toward a companion book on the Lincoln

theme." A month earlier he had mentioned in a letter to a contact at Dutton that he was scheduled to speak to the local NAACP branch and that Walter White was about to deliver an address in Washington "protesting against the present types of negro characters selected by Moving Pictures, and the publication of recent books showing the worst and dirty side of Negro life. Reference to Deity and profanity and immorality especially are to be banned nation wide." John E. Washington to Mrs. Bowers, Nov. 22, 1942, EPD.

136. "D. C. Teacher's Book on Lincoln Will Be Published this Month," *Evening Star,* Jan. 11, 1942, clipping in O.G. 729, MSR; John E. Washington to Louis Warren, Dec. 3, 1944, LMP.

137. Nancy J. Weiss, *Farewell to the Party of Lincoln: Black Politics in the Age of FDR* (Princeton: Princeton University Press, 1983), 209–35; Terry H. Anderson, *The Pursuit of Fairness: A History of Affirmative Action* (New York: Oxford University Press, 2004), 11–3; Leah Wright Rigueur, *The Loneliness of the Black Republican: Pragmatic Politics and the Pursuit of Power* (Princeton: Princeton University Press, 2015), 13–25. For African Americans' earlier dissatisfaction with the Republican Party, see Richard B. Sherman, *The Republican Party and Black America from McKinley to Hoover, 1896–1933* (Charlottesville: University of Virginia Press, 1973), 232–59; Harvard Sitkoff, *A New Deal for Blacks: The Emergence of Civil Rights as a National Issue* (New York: Oxford University Press, 1978); Yellin, *Racism in the Nation's Service.* On debates about social policy among prominent Howard University professors in this period, see Holloway, *Confronting the Veil.*

138. Weiss, *Farewell to the Party of Lincoln,* 217–18, 229–32.

139. "Dr. John Edwin Washington." For the convention in Washington, see Henry Lewis Suggs, "The Washingtonian Legacy: A History of Black Political Conservatism in America, 1915–1944," in Peter R. Eisenstadt, ed., *Black Conservatism: Essays in Intellectual and Political History* (New York: Garland, 1999), 92.

140. John E. Washington to Harry Pratt, June 23, 1941, Box 23, ALA.

141. Washington to Pratt, June 23, 1941.

142. Louis Warren to John E. Washington, Dec. 29, 1942, LMP. See also James G. Randall to John E. Washington, Jan. 5, 1943, JGR.

143. The principal's letter, along with the rest of the nominations, are in the John E. Washington folder in Box A 90, Series II, NAACP Papers, LC.

144. For Spingarn nomination, see Louis Warren to National Office of the NAACP, Jan. 22, 1945, LMP. Washington was still trying to get the second book published in the late 1940s. See also John E. Washington to Thomas Sloane, Aug. 4, 1948, in O.G. 729, MSR.

145. "Dr. Washington Dead; Dentist, Lincoln Expert," *Washington Post,* Dec. 9, 1964.

146. "Lincoln Group Told Lee 'Was Lucky' at Antietam," *Washington Star,* Sept. 18, 1955, A-12.

147. John E. Washington to James G. Randall, March 28, 1948, JGR; "Dr. Washington Dead"; "The Lincoln Group of the District of Columbia," *Lincoln Herald* 51, no. 3 (Oct. 1949): 29; "Rendezvous at Midnight," *Lincoln Herald* 49, no. 3 (Oct. 1947): 33; "Lincoln Items on Exhibition," *Washington Post,* April 11,

1952; "Dr. John Edwin Washington"; "Civic Association Honors Two Men," *Washington Post and Times Herald,* March 31, 1957.

148. "A Rare Look at Lincoln." John and Virginia Ross Washington were married fifty-six years. The pair died just three months apart, she of cancer at age eighty-three, and he of pneumonia at eighty-four. "Virginia R. Washington, Pharmacist, Dies at 83," *Washington Post,* Sept. 22, 1964.

149. Washington described the situation in John E. Washington to Louis Warren, Dec. 26, 1942, and he provided additional details to Randall a few years later. John E. Washington to James G. Randall, March 28, 1948. See also Washington to Sloane, Aug. 4, 1948. For Parma's death, see "V. Valta Parma Dies; Former Rare Book Division Curator," *Washington Post,* Sept. 1, 1941, JGR.

150. For Dutton's financial difficulties, see John E. Washington to Faith Rich, Oct. 17, 1950, Box C 52, Part II, Illinois State Conference, 1951, Branch File, Geographical File, NAACP Papers, LC.

151. Wilson J. Moses, "The Lost World of the Negro, 1895–1919: Black Literary and Intellectual Life before the 'Renaissance,'" *Black American Literature Forum* 21, no. 1–2 (Spring–Summer 1987): 71. For the growing number of African American historians with PhDs in the 1930s and 1940s, see August Meier and Elliott Rudwick, *Black Historians and the Historical Profession, 1915–1980* (Urbana: University of Illinois Press, 1986), 98–100. When the ASNLH noted Carl Sandburg's death in 1967, it emphasized his role in promoting *They Knew Lincoln*: "Sandburg's encouragement contributed very much to the success of this book which portrayed colored people in Lincoln's time who were on the staff of helpers at the White House." The book "brought its author considerable publicity and praise although he was not a trained historical scholar." "Historical News," *Journal of Negro History* 52, no. 4 (Oct. 1967): 323.

152. When *They Knew Lincoln* was released in January 1942, transcripts and analysis of the WPA narratives had yet to be published. On the history of twentieth-century interviews with former slaves, see, for example, John B. Cade, "Out of the Mouths of Ex-Slaves," *Journal of Negro History* 20, no. 3 (July 1935): 294–337; Meier and Rudwick, *Black Historians,* 234; Stevenson, "Out of the Mouths of Ex-Slaves," 698–705; Norman R. Yetman, "The Background of the Slave Narrative Collection," *American Quarterly* 19, no. 3 (Autumn 1967): 540–42.

THEY KNEW LINCOLN

BY JOHN E. WASHINGTON

THE SHERIDAN LINCOLN PORTRAIT

The frontispiece is a production of an oil painting by Clague,* painted from life in the White House in 1865, and given to Major General Philip Sheridan by President Lincoln.

General Sheridan gave it later, during the last part of his life, to his faithful colorful orderly and servant, Richard Jones, because of his great love for the man who served him on the battlefield and in his home.

The painting was nearly life-size. The colors had so mellowed from age that it resembled the treatment of a Gilbert Stuart. The background was an olive green in the highlights and darkened toward the edges. When the light fell upon the hair and beard, little patches of dark brown color could be seen. It really seemed to live, and Jones stated that General Sheridan often spoke of how lifelike the picture was.

Richard Jones permitted me to photograph it in 1917 and often stated that he wanted me to have it for my collection after his death.

After the death of Richard Jones, his widow, thinking that tears around the edge of the canvas and stretcher had ruined it and I would not want it, destroyed it. The original negative, however, is still preserved in my collection of Lincoln items and the photograph is reproduced here for the first time.

---

* CLAGUE, RICHARD. Painter. Born in Louisiana in 1816; died in New Orleans, 1878. He studied with Ernest Hebert and at École des Beaux Arts, Paris.

The Sheridan Lincoln Portrait

THEY KNEW LINCOLN

by

JOHN E. WASHINGTON

With an Introduction by Carl Sandburg
Illustrated with Photographs,
Facsimiles and Endpapers

1942

NEW YORK

E. P. DUTTON & CO., INC.

OXFORD
UNIVERSITY PRESS

THIS BOOK IS DEDICATED TO MY RACE

If I am indebted to the wise and learned scholars who
have rendered so much valuable assistance, I feel
equally so toward these poor old souls who were willing
to tell all that they knew and heard about the man who
had broken their chains and made them free:

Those Who Knew Lincoln and Served Him

TABLE OF CONTENTS

LIST OF ILLUSTRATIONS

Also see Appendix

*Original items or photographs, the source of which is not
otherwise specified, are in the author's private
collection of Lincoln material.*

FOREWORD BY THE AUTHOR

From childhood I had always tried to get a true picture of Lincoln as he appeared to the ignorant slave and his offspring. To do this, hundreds of visits and interviews were held in backwoods sections of various parts of the land. A series of questions were asked and recorded, and from the opinions expressed by those questioned, and by others with whom I came in contact, I have written for them this short record of the man they knew and loved, with a love that went with them to the grave.

The life of Abraham Lincoln, in dates and facts, is well known to even the smallest child, but the emotional standpoint of the slaves, those who knew him and loved him best, is not known.

His life to these humble people was a miracle, and his memory has become a benediction. To the deeply emotional and religious slave, Lincoln was an earthly incarnation of the Savior of mankind. To them he was the Son of God, sent to deliver them from bondage. They adored Lincoln as their earthly Lord and Master. Was he not also a carpenter's son, born in a humble log cabin? Was he not a worker in the field, unlettered and unsung? Was he not despised and rejected by men, and did he not know by experience their sorrow? Did he not yearn for the day when he might learn to read and write, and enjoy the pleasures of life for himself and his children?

Upon whom could he depend in his hour of need but the Almighty God, for comfort and guidance? Did he not triumph over his foes? Was he not inaugurated as President amidst the waving of flags and the sounds of trumpets, only to be martyred, as Christ was, because of his services for the lowly?

Regardless of everything he did in saving this nation his undying fame was gained as the Emancipator of an enslaved race that he learned to love, and for whom he gave his last full measure of devotion, that that race under God, should have a new birth of freedom, and not perish from the earth.

I had read every book about Lincoln which I could get in the last thirty years, scanned newspapers published in Lincoln's time in Illinois, Washington and wherever I thought could be found reliable information and was convinced that it would be necessary to seek clues from the people of my own race. Hundreds of interviews were had with the old ex-slaves and their children. I wanted their stories of Lincoln, their opinions of him and his family. Only from them could I get a different picture from that found in the printed records. Books on Lincoln have hitherto been factual, differing only in the manner of treatment. To me, Lincoln was a man who had a heart and a soul; a jolly-go-lucky individual, who lived with the determination to do the right, as God had given him the light to see the right. At no time in his life was he so downhearted that he couldn't see or tell a joke. This was his life. He could laugh when he was saddest and when he was hurt the most, for he was too proud to cry. We are told that when Lincoln wanted to make some particular point he would put it in the form of a joke or quaint story.

I have attempted to tell a new story of Lincoln in the simplest language and the simplest way as told by the people who lived and worked by his side, day and night and who knew him best—his negro servants, and the lives of simple people in the land where Lincoln lived and died. I found, by their conversation, a new man—a man who though once greatly scorned because of his lifelong interest and determination to break the shackles of slavery from a despised race, today is the personification of all that is good in the true American.

These old negro saints of my childhood never doubted Lincoln's immortality. They believed in him and prayed, as millions did, for his success, and mourned, as a race, when their champion fell under the assassin's bullet.

My childhood resolution has been the cause of much travel on my part in every part of the country where Lincoln lived. Here and there I found abundant material for this humble attempt to present to the world the real Soul of the Black Folks, in its relation to their earthly benefactor.

I saw city folks, country folks, plantation folks, ignorant folks, field hands, "big house servants." Many of these, like old Sis Eliza, were too feeble to work and were inmates of charitable institutions, or pensioners of wealthy families. I wrote down their stories and opinions, and although dead and forgotten (nearly all rest in unknown graves), these souls are resurrected in the picture I have tried to make of the man who was all to them, and whom they loved to talk about, when they felt that you thought as they did.

I received wonderful aid. Some could tell about Peter Brown who was a waiter for Lincoln. But nobody knew about William Johnson, only a few had heard about him. All knew Mrs. Lincoln. A few said that they had heard from the white folks that she was crazy—but they didn't believe it, and they would talk you deaf and dumb about the day when they heard about the Emancipation.

I went from place to place, looking in the wrinkling faces, hearing the cracked voices, observing the feeble movements of these friends of Lincoln. Once, when an old neighbor died, and my grandmother took me to the funeral at the "Harmony Cemetery," the old graveyard sexton pointed out to her the places where older residents were buried. Next to the old vault, we saw the graves of William Slade who was Lincoln's messenger, and of Elizabeth Keckley who was Mrs. Lincoln's friend, and many other people of our race who knew Lincoln and served him. The Wormleys and the Grays, who catered sometimes at the large suppers in the White House, had big tombstones and large plots, beautifully decorated.

I have had a happy task, if for no other reason than that I have spent many pleasant hours listening to old tales of the past and the hopes of these old people for a reunion with their great earthly master, in the life to come, in Glory!

They knew nothing but gratitude for the one who had made their prayers come true and always looked with contempt at anyone who tried to tell them there was any other reason why the war was fought, except to set them free.

Although nearly all of them could not read a line, the Bible, with God's word in it, was in every house and from its teachings, as interpreted by their own teachers and preachers, they lived happily in the thought that in the life to come, they would nevermore be slaves.

From family Bibles in the possession of the old colored families I obtained photographs of many people who not only knew Lincoln, but also of some who served him. In many cases these are the only ones in existence.

All that the old people told me had to be authenticated by research.

I was greatly assisted by *Mr. V. Valta Parma,* for thirteen years Curator of the Rare Book Division, Library of Congress. It was due to his never-failing encouragement and critical aid that this book finally took form. He made it possible for me to meet many celebrated Lincoln scholars who approved my plan and placed their resources of Lincolnania at my disposal.

Dr. J. G. Randall, Professor of History, University of Illinois, and one of the leading authorities on Lincoln, encouraged me greatly by his letter in which he wrote:

> You have, in my opinion, a most interesting project. It is unique. I want you to develop it as a story that has risen out of your own associations and studies. Tell it in your own way and as you see it. Your first chapter is excellent, telling the story of the people of your own race who lived near Ford's Theater, of their tales, superstitions, ghosts, memories, etc. As you go on you will weave in documented material and your book will therefore have the double value of reminiscence together with historical investigation.
>
> Except for your efforts, the story of the colored people who knew Lincoln is lost. There is a remarkable story there but it is difficult to recover it. It is a disappearing story and no one can come so near recovering it as yourself. You have the power to tell it appreciatively and with the emotional eloquence which is characteristic of your people, and which you amply possess.

At Springfield, Illinois, I met *Dr. Harry A. Pratt,* Secretary of the Abraham Lincoln Association who rendered the greatest assistance with materials from that collection and his personal interest and endorsement of my undertaking.

I went to Fort Wayne, Indiana, and there met *Dr. Louis A. Warren,* Editor of Lincoln Lore and Director of the Lincoln National Life Foundation, and who gave me such aid and encouragement that I mailed him a copy of a roughly outlined plan of this book, and after examining it he wrote the following letter:

> You are to be congratulated on making ready for publication the facts you have gathered about interesting characters who were associated with Abraham Lincoln in the capacity of servants. No one else could have been quite so successful in gathering information about them as you have been.
>
> The efforts you have put forth with respect to establishing the identity of Mrs. Keckley is in itself a worthwhile contribution to Lincolniana.
>
> The many stories and bits of folklore which you have gathered about Lincoln's kindliness as revealed by his attitude toward the colored race will allow one to better understand the great heart of Abraham Lincoln.
>
> You have rightly gone on the assumption that any single incident relating to Lincoln is of importance, even as it may have to do with individuals who up until the time of your researches have been somewhat obscured.

It was my custom to pay frequent visits to the Rare Book Collection at the Library of Congress where Mr. Parma, the Curator, usually had some helpful suggestions connected with my problem. On one of these occasions I mentioned that the young colored people today were lacking in appreciation of what Lincoln had done for their race. They were listening to those who said that Lincoln was not interested in emancipation except as an aid toward preserving the Union. Mr. Parma replied that he had found an original letter of Lincoln stating his views on slavery six years before he became President and that I might reproduce it for the first time in facsimile.

In August, 1855, *Hon. George Robertson* of Kentucky gave Lincoln a copy of his book entitled *The Scrap Book* which Lincoln acknowledged in one of the most important letters inscribed by him.

It was used by Nicolay and Hay in their monumental work on Lincoln and then it seemingly vanished. A well-known Lincoln collector wrote Mr. Parma that for years he had been searching for it in vain. Mr. Parma told me that he was examining some books from Lincoln's library that Robert Lincoln had presented to the Library of Congress, when, to his surprise, he found an original letter from Lincoln inserted in the back of *The Scrap Book,* the very volume the receipt of which the letter acknowledged. How the letter found its way from Kentucky to the Library of Robert Lincoln is unknown; but the heart and mind of Lincoln which this letter reflects are worthy the consideration of all people today.

The only exact transcript of the letter ever printed follows, and a facsimile will be found in the appendix.

Springfield, Ill. Aug: 15, 1855

Hon. Geo. Robertson
    Lexington, Ky.
        My dear Sir:

The volume you left for me has been received—I am really grateful for the honor of your kind remembrance, as well as for the book— The partial reading I have already given it, has afforded me much of both pleasure and instruction—

It was new to me that the exact question which led to the Missouri Compromise, had arisen before it arose in regard to Missouri; and that you had taken so prominent, a part in it—Your short, but able and patriotic speech upon that occasion, has not been improved upon since, by those holding the same views; and, with all the light you then had, the views you took appear to me as very reasonable—

You are not a friend of slavery in the abstract— In that speech you spoke of *"the peaceful extinction of slavery"* and used other expressions indicating your belief that the thing was, at some time, to have an end. Since then we have had thirty six years of experience; and this experience has demonstrated, I think, that there is no peaceful extinction of slavery in prospect for us—

The signal failure of Henry Clay, and other good and great men, in 1849, to effect any thing in favor of gradual emancipation in Kentucky, together with a thousand other signs, extinguishes that hope utterly— On the question of liberty, as a principle, we are not what we have been—

When we were the political slaves of King George, and wanted to be free, we called the maxim that "all men are created equal" a self evident truth; but now when we have grown fat, and have lost all dread of being slaves ourselves, we have become so greedy to be *masters* that we call the same maxim "a self-evident lie" The fourth of July has not quite dwindled away; it is still a great day—*for burning fire-crackers!!!* That spirit which desired the peaceful extinction of slavery, has itself become extinct, with the *occasion,* and the *men* of the Revolution—Under the impulse of that occasion, nearly half the States adopted systems of emancipation at once; and it is a significant fact, that not a single state has done the like since—

So far as peaceful, voluntary emancipation is concerned, the condition of the negro slave in America, scarcely less terrible to the contemplation of a free mind, is now so fixed, and hopeless of change for the better, as that of the lost souls of the finally impenitent—The Autocrat of all the Russias will resign his crown, and proclaim his subjects free republicans, sooner than will our American masters voluntarily give up their slaves—

Our political problem now is "Can we, as a nation,

continue together *permanently—forever*——half slave, and half free?" The problem is too mighty for me—
May God, in his mercy, superintend the solution—

Your much obliged friend,
and humble servant
A. Lincoln

How little Lincoln thought when he penned these words that although the problem was too mighty for him then, "God, in his mercy" was to strengthen him until he, single handed, was to apply the solution.

When I arrived in Springfield the Lincoln Tomb was my first objective.

I shall never forget my impression of it as I entered the Oak Ridge Cemetery. In front of it I saw a group of colored people and as I approached I met Mr. Fay who was in charge of the monument. He was about to lead the group in singing "America." Just think of a large number of colored people, both young and old, standing about the tomb of Lincoln singing,

> "My country, 'tis of thee,
> Sweet land of liberty,
> Of thee I sing."

My mind certainly returned to the past, and I could see again all of my old folks singing this piece which Lincoln had first made a reality for them.

When the group had departed and I had examined the Fay collection of pictures, letters, photographs, I was directed how to enter the circular chamber in which the bodies of Lincoln, his wife and three sons are entombed. I went through a narrow passageway to a circular room, in the center of which was a beautiful block of stone with the name of Lincoln on it. Flags of the states in which

Lincoln lived were in holders around the room between the windows.

I was alone here—a soft light bathed the scene and a cold stillness told me that while I was in the midst of life I was with death. My earthly ambition was fulfilled! At last I stood beside the resting place of the man I loved and admired, the man who gave his life for the freedom I enjoyed. Oh, what a sensation! No words can picture it! I seemed to be petrified, and my soul was gripped with a feeling, not of fear, but with a something that told me I was in the hidden presence of one of the most beloved persons who ever trod the sod of this sinful world. He was a mortal who became really immortal because of his determination to break the chains of Slavery and make America the land of the free.

I was in the presence of Lincoln!

INTRODUCTION

By CARL SANDBURG

When reading the manuscript of this book I found myself enjoying a peculiar unity it carries throughout. It is the vivid personal narrative of a Negro boy and man who sought all that could be possibly known about Abraham Lincoln from Negroes having impressions or facts he considered worth record. "Tell it in your own way and as you see it," was the advice he received from J. G. Randall, Professor of History in the University of Illinois. "As you go on you will weave in documented material and your book will therefore have the double value of reminiscence together with historical investigation. . . . You have the power to tell it appreciatively and with the emotional eloquence which is characteristic of your people." Thus a wise teacher deepened resolves already deep, confirmed a purpose already shaped and ready to go. So we have many pages of keen writing, inevitable, spontaneous, told in its own way. There are character sketches, speech tones, wisdom of the humble set down. "I was told to see old Aunt Vina because she knew everything, and everybody, and had the memory of a mule." And why not? A more deliberate, less flowing writer would have said her memory was tenacious. The ensuing Vina is not lacking a final dignity no fate can sweep away. So we have verities, myths, ghosts, dreams, fantasies, adorations. White House servants, waiters, doorkeepers,

the barbers William Johnson and Solomon Johnson, who shaved
Lincoln in Washington, and the barber William Fleurville, who
shaved Lincoln in Springfield, they come alive and real for the
first time in any book, Solomon Johnson later becoming the first
United States government clerk of his race. We learn many gra-
cious realities about the now less shadowy Elizabeth Keckley,
dressmaker and friend of Mrs. Lincoln. We knew that only an
extraordinary ghost writer could have conceived some of the
sentences in Mrs. Keckley's book "Behind the Scenes." And
now we have no doubt but it was James Redpath who held con-
sultations with her and seemed to advise her, "Tell it in your own
way and as you see it." Included are Lincoln letters not hitherto
come to light, along with pictorial material indispensable to the
Lincoln student. Quite aside from its special interest in Lincoln
it is an important human narrative.

ACKNOWLEDGMENTS

I wish to acknowledge the generous assistance and co-operation of the many who held out a helping hand to me in my long search. I regret that lack of space prevents the recording of each. Among those who gave me major assistance are Miss Edna L. Jacobsen, Chief of the Manuscript and History Department of the New York State Library; the staff of the Public Library of the City of New York; J. E. Harper, Chief of the Appointment Division of the United States Treasury; H. E. Luhrs, Director of the Lincoln Library, Shippenburg, Pa.; M. A. Cook, Librarian Lincoln Life Foundation, Fort Wayne, Indiana; P. M. Hamer, Chief Division of Reference, National Archives, Washington, D. C.; L. Hubbard Shattuck, Director Chicago Historical Society; Donald C. Holmes, Chief Photographer Library of Congress; Mrs. Bess Furman Armstrong, formerly of the Associated Press; William C. Ashby, the Urban League, Springfield, Ill.; Paul M. Angle, Springfield, Ill.; A. H. Greenly, Lincoln Collector and Authority; Herbert Wells Fay, Custodian of the Lincoln Tomb, Springfield, Ill.; LeRoy Butler, who never failed to respond to my needs for a typist; John Linden Roll of Springfield, Illinois who gave me a copy of Aunt Ruth Stanton's story.

I am most deeply indebted to Henry P. Slaughter, Member American Negro Academy, collector of negro literature and also to William M. Brewer, Head of the Department of History, Division 10-13, Washington Public Schools, both members of the National Association for the Advancement of Colored People and the Association for the Study of Negro History.

Finally, I acknowledge my great indebtedness to my wife for the many sacrifices she has made and for the wonderful assistance she has given to make this book possible.

The discovery of de Fleurville, a native of Haiti, and the part he played in giving Lincoln a new viewpoint during the years of struggle was the most important result of my visit to Springfield, Illinois.

The full story of the Haitian, de Fleurville, could not have been told without the generous aid given me by *His Excellency Elie Lescot, President of Haiti,* while he was the Haitian Minister to the United States, and to the *Honorable Jacques C. Antoine,* Councilor and Chargé d' Affaires of the Haitian Legation.

All with whom I talked agreed that the authentication of the Keckley narrative would be welcomed by writers who had quoted from her *Behind the Scenes.* Practically all Lincoln authors have done so, as there is no other source for intimate details of the family life of the Lincolns in the White House. The genuineness of the story had always been shrouded in doubt.

PRELUDE

RECOLLECTIONS OF THE FORD
THEATER NEIGHBORHOOD

My earliest recollections are those of a little boy playing on E Street near Ford's Theater, between 9th and 10th Streets, Washington, D. C., and sitting up nights and listening to ghost stories of the neighborhood as told by the old colored people who worked and lived there, and hearing wonderful stories about Lincoln, his family, and Booth, from the mouths of some who had really seen them, and from others who claimed they had seen their ghosts.

I became interested, due to no love for these hideous apparitions, but from fear of seeing the spirits, which, I had heard, walked the streets and alleys every night, and could be seen after midnight.

Many strange stories were told by the old servants who worked on this square.

They said after Lincoln was shot it was a common thing at night to see lights in the Old Ford's Theater and to hear heavy iron chains rattling across its floors, and other strange noises. Some of the older residents said they even heard shots and people screaming in the night, and after midnight it was claimed Booth could be heard cursing his horse and tearing down the cobble-stone alley back of this haunted building.

All believed that the large dark spots on the brick

pavement in front of Ford's Theater were drops of Lincoln's blood that stained it when the dying man was carried across the street to the Petersen house. They said that every year on the anniversary of the day on which Lincoln was shot these spots would brighten into a brilliant red.

After the day's work was over, these old servants would visit one another, but they mostly met at our house. My grandmother ran a boarding house, which had a large kitchen and our sitting room in the basement, and the meals were sent to the dining room upstairs on a dumbwaiter. In these lower rooms they could talk as much as they pleased, sing, and stay out as long as they wanted, for grandmother was her own boss and really ran the house, although all of the boarders and roomers were white.

While many ghost stories were told in our house by those who could not dismiss their pet stories even long enough to think of the Lord, other topics pertaining to the life of slavery, and especially camp meetings, harvest festivals, and corn-shucking bees, were discussed by the people of the neighborhood and their relatives and friends who came from afar to visit on Sundays, holidays, Christmas, watch-meeting nights and New Year's Eve. On the latter occasion all present would devote the entire program to Almighty God and the great benefits which He had bestowed upon mankind. They would tell their experiences of the dying year and their determination to live nearer God and His teachings in the coming year if God spared them. They sang, prayed and cried the long evening through and bowed in silent prayer when old St. Patrick's bells began to toll the old year out and ring the new year in, for they just believed they would be gone to glory by next New Year's Eve.

When the last echoes of these beautiful bells died away

and the shooting of pistols and the noise of fireworks announced the arrival of the new year, they would leap to their feet in frenzy, clap their hands for joy, and begin to sing, "What a Happy New Year, What a Happy New Year."

On Christmas night, the meetings were generally more lively. I well remember Uncle George Thomas. He could "out bass" the entire gathering and how he impressed me when he struck the last note in "Old Black Joe," and everybody clapped. All kinds of songs were sung, that of the devil and the world too, songs of the old South, songs of the days to come in Glory, when everyone would be as white as snow and they could really put on their long white robes and shout all over God's heaven. They sang the songs of freedom and one about "Where their fathers died, and freedom rang." Oh! how Mr. Curtiss, who attended furnaces in the neighborhood, could pray and make everybody cry. After prayers, story telling and singing would begin all over.

Aunt Mary Dines told the story of her running away from slavery and how the hounds tracked her one night and she got away. She delighted in telling about midnight parties in barns and cabins when "Old Massa" was asleep. She said she "outdanced the living witches when the banjo played and the fiddle rang." She told about President Lincoln—how he looked, how he acted and even sang when he came to the Contraband Camp to hear the old people from the South sing and pray. She would lead the gathering in beautiful songs like "Way Down Upon the Swanee River," "Old Folks at Home," and many others of the cabin and the field and slavery. Some sang original songs pertaining to the past, the present, and the future. Finally, the earthly fervor of those present waned and they began to sing and pray about Christ, their Savior, who was born on Christmas Day.

Many churchgoers and others passed by and some clapped and others, with bowed heads, approached the old iron fence to listen to these old servants of God who claimed that religion had brought them out of the land of bondage into that happy land of freedom and they would shout, "Praise God."

God had broken their chains which had held them in slavery, then why should they not sing and be happy the night that His Son and their Savior was born? They just shouted "Glory, Glory, Glory, Lord God Almighty" for He had given to them this day a Savior who was Christ the Lord and He had brought Peace on Earth. All thought that Lincoln had been sent by God to deliver them from bondage, just as Christ was sent to deliver them from sin.

I often wondered if Lincoln, whom everybody said was in Glory, was looking down on grandmother and her friends, who were praying to join him in the land where freedom forever dwells. Or was he an unseen guest, that had left Heaven to be with these old saints below who loved him? He might! Who knows? Although they had been oppressed, they really had malice toward none and charity toward all. After singing all the hallelujahs and other songs they knew, they always closed these gatherings by singing:

"Praise God from whom all blessings flow,
Praise Him, ye creatures here below,
Praise Him above ye heavenly hosts,
Praise Father, Son and Holy Ghost."

A whispered "Amen" ended all.

One of the places that I hated to visit with my Grandmother was an old house on E Street near the old Medical School,

on the corner of 10th Street. Old "Sis" Thomas lived here
with her daughter and little son George. She came into the
neighborhood just before Lincoln was assassinated, and said
she could see ghosts all of the time, but she said she wasn't
afraid of them and knew how to talk to them. She said that
dogs howled and chickens were crowing for days before
Lincoln's death, and when a large picture of Lincoln fell off
the wall and a bird flew into the room, she just knew someone was going to die in the neighborhood.

During the Civil War, a battle was fought between the
Rebels and the Yankees on the farm where she lived and after
that, she said she could see soldiers swiftly moving across the
fields at nights. They seemed to stay on the old tobacco farm.
She gave us children some comfort, for she stated that ghosts
mind their own business and will not harm you if you don't get
in their way—just let them alone.

Nevertheless, in every home, there could be found a bottle of Holy Water, brought from St. Patrick's Church, which
was always kept near the door, and often became empty from
sprinkling the door sills and steps to keep ghosts away. "Sis"
Thomas even placed an old sieve over her front door keyhole
to keep spirits and witches out at night.

Grandmother did not believe in ghosts, and ridiculed all
stories about them, but argue as strenuously as she could, she
never gained a convert, not even from her own devoted grandson, Johnnie.

Although I had never seen a ghost, I was mortally
afraid of them, and really believed in them, for I had often
heard strange noises in Marini's dance hall, which was
next to our house, and my cousin Annie had heard the
same. A night watchman shot himself in the building one
day. I saw the police take his body away. From that time,

until I left the neighborhood, I was afraid to go out into our backyard at night.

Although nearly every colored servant was from a different part of the South, all were sisters, brothers, aunts and cousins to each other, and could tell great stories, and a few even knew how to cure sick people with herbs, and act as midwives. These were called "Grannies" by the white people. These people generally lived where they worked, not so much because the wages were low, but mainly because of great difficulties in getting to work in the mornings; for colored neighborhoods were far away and the working days were long and hard. Sleeping quarters were generally spare places in the attics, basements and above the stables and barns, so that the men could feed the horses easily in all kinds of weather. House servants always lived in the house so that they could rise early and start the fires and have the old coal stoves hot by the time the white people came down to breakfast. Some rich folks had a furnace man who attended fires. The amount he made depended on the number of furnaces he attended.

At night the children accompanied their parents, or kinfolk, as they visited from house to house. We were taught to keep our mouths shut and mind our own business. If, perchance, a child attempted to break into the conversation, the old person nearest him would shut his mouth with a slap and say "children should be seen and not heard and keep out of older folks business." Under such treatment we soon fell asleep and generally cuddled up against our parents' feet or stretched out on the floor. Sometimes, the sleepy ones had to be carried home on the shoulders, or in the arms, of the relatives.

In those days the only places colored people gathered were in the churches on Sundays, at prayer meetings once a week, and in lodge rooms, where their societies met.

The names of these lodges generally had Biblical allusions such as Moses, St. Luke, St. John, Galilean Fishermen, and so forth. Each new lodge generally was a split from an old one and received a new saint's name. Although Masons and Odd Fellows were white institutions, some colored brothers of very white skins generally got in, learned the works and left, to form a new order amongst their own people. These lodges held their meetings in secret places, alleys, backrooms of houses, cellars, etc., for fear that the white brothers would come and break them up.

There were very few prosperous religious orders except those of the Catholics, Methodists and Baptists. The Presbyterian and Episcopal churches had a few colored members, but these were as scarce as hens' teeth, and generally kept their religious customs to themselves. All believed nobody could enter the pearly gates of heaven if he had not been baptized, but some cleansed by going down under the water, and others said sprinkling would do. These partisans were in a constant warfare, which even to this day their descendants carry on.

There were no scientific discussions of the Bible at the meetings in our houses, for God's words were interpreted by the Spirit Preachers. The Bible to them was the greatest book on earth, for it contained God's word although they could not read it but desired to do so.

Every house had a Bible, if for no other reason than for those who became sick and wanted comforting. You can readily see how book agents waxed fat selling Bibles on easy weekly, or monthly payments. They were very large, to impress people, and they contained pages for family portraits, marriages, births and deaths. They rested on a separate table in the parlor, and were artistically bound in leather, and had the edges of the pages gilded.

There was no dancing that was not a sin, except "shouting"

and tapping on the floor with the feet; no swing, but the religious swaying to and fro, and no club but the church. Once in a great while, the different churches would give a big picnic to raise money, and even had excursions, but almost every week in some houses there was a parlor social gathering for the young people where they played such games as "in the well," "turning the bottle," "spinning the plate," and "swinging partners." No bridge or other card games; in fact, if a card game came into one of these old folks' home, it was instantly destroyed. Wicked people played the fiddle, for the devil was represented with a fiddle. This myth still prevails in some places.

Some really big folks lived in our neighborhood. In Washington there was nobody more important than Dr. Morgan and the Carrolls, so the old folks thought Dr. Morgan's people must be rich. The Carrolls were related to old Bishop Carroll and his brother Charles Carroll of Carrollton, who was the last person to die that signed the Declaration of Independence. Miss Minnie Morgan told us this. She was the belle of the neighborhood and to me the greatest person on earth. White persons in the neighborhood had servants and some even put their washing out. I had pennies which I earned running errands and putting coal and wood away for some of them.

Although there were only four boys on our street, we generally had a good game of ball or marbles in the alley behind Ford's Theater, because other boys from near-by streets often came there to play. Sometimes my Cousin Annie would join in. It was against the law to play ball in the streets, and we refrained from doing so because we were told that if the police arrested you, you might be sent to the Reform School and there you would stay until you became twenty-one years old and a man. We ran at the very sight of a policeman. When our games broke up, we heroes of our little games became the cowards of the evening as the rays of the setting sun beamed against the front of the old Ford's Theater and caused it to cast ghostlike shadows over our play grounds. One by one the gang stole away, and by dusk, I alone remained to beat a hasty retreat and to give up the grounds to the spirits, who I thought were getting ready to do their riding at night.

Old newspapers were kept by the old colored folk until somebody came along able to read them, so that they could know what was going on. An old one, issued the morning of Lincoln's assassination, was kept by my Grandmother until she died, and passed along to me with the other pictures which she kept. Even in her last days, she would look in it sometimes for nearly an hour and, I imagined, think of old friends who lived in the Ford's Theater neighborhood.

There were no negro Democrats, for if one had been found he would have been considered a traitor to their Savior and friend—Lincoln.

During the Civil War and for a long time after, there were a few butlers, stewards, messengers, and laborers in government departments. Very large dressmaking establishments were carried on by refined and cultured colored women, and the barbers were all colored and had large shops on F Street and Pennsylvania Avenue. Ordinary businesses were controlled by colored people, some of whom even had livery stables and packing businesses. Boot blacking furnished jobs for colored boys. The leading caterers were Wormley and Gray, who sometimes served in the White House when there were big receptions.

The elite of Washington society generally gave large social affairs, and all help and waiters were colored. Some families who entertained lavishly in large mansions had

Ford's Theatre and neighboring buildings, in old Aunt Eliza's day. Photograph taken April 14, 1865, by W. Morris Smith, shows mourning drapery festooned from the window, following the assassination of President Lincoln.

The author's grandmother lived in the house to the right of Marini's Hall, on the South side of E Street, between 9th and 10th Streets. Dr. Washington was brought up in this house. Photo courtesy of John Clagett Proctor. A drawing by Dr. Washington, showing how he painted a "voodoo" form as a child for the annihilation of Booth. His grandmother and a painter friend look on.

as many as ten servants. There were no large apartment houses, and nearly every colored man or boy was taught to start buying a home as soon as he was able. As a result, some of the most valuable parts of the nation's capital belonged to these ex-slaves.

Washington life was beautiful in the horse-and-buggy era, before the invention of a thousand mechanical devices, that do away with manual labor. It was an era when men had to earn their living by the sweat of their brow, and colored people certainly sweated. The little children ran errands for the older folk, carried wood and coal into the house from the woodshed, helped in the kitchen, washed dishes and studied their lessons. Discipline was severe on our street. Anybody could slap your jaws and say you had to get another beating, for God had said in his book, "He who spareth the rod spoileth the child," and all of our neighbors were "God-fearing people."

George Thomas' father was in Richmond when Lincoln came to see the place. He said he was close enough to touch Lincoln's hand, and he described him, and said his ghost looked just like his picture. For he had often seen it, wearing a high hat and its head hanging down, with its long arms dangling by the side of its legs. Once, when he turned into the alley to put his carriage away, after he had brought his people home from a big supper, he said that he came pretty near running into Lincoln's ghost, but the horses saw it first, shied to the opposite side, became frightened, and began to neigh. He had seen many ghosts in the neighborhood, but although they seemed to be talking to themselves, he never heard a sound coming from them, for as soon as he looked over his left shoulder and said a prayer they vanished.

The Old Folks were filled with a superstitious dread of Ford's Theater, for the original Ford's Theater had once been a church and was destroyed by fire a few months after it was converted into a theater. The present structure was erected on the ground that had been consecrated to a House of God. One old ex-slave in the neighborhood had attended Sunday school there and said the colored people left it to start the Nineteenth Street Baptist Church. She claimed the ground would always be haunted because it had become the "Devil's workshop;" and for this act alone God had put a curse on it and anything might happen there.

She knew it was doomed, and was not surprised at Lincoln's being shot there; for he should never have gone into this temple of the great Jehovah that was being desecrated by workers for the Devil.

The following quotation substantiates her belief that the theater had formerly been a church: "When the new Baptist church was built on Tenth Street, which was afterwards sold and converted into a theatre, afterwards known as Ford's Theatre, the gallery was given to the colored people."[*]

We children of the neighborhood looked upon it with awe, and I can remember the first time I became lost on my way home from St. Augustine's Catholic School. It was a cold, dreary, rainy day. I became lost from Ben Dines who took me to the school. In fact, he left me and followed the band that was passing. I began to cry from fear, and as the lights came on, I could think of but one thing, and that was of passing the old Ford's Theater where Lincoln was shot. Though weary and worn, when I turned into 10th at F Street, I began to trot and as I approached the building, I ran faster and faster, with my eyes fixed straight ahead. I imagined everything could

[*] From Special Report of the Commissioner of Education on the Condition and Improvement of Public Schools in the District of Columbia, Washington Government Printing Office 1871.

happen, and began to feel the hot and cold chills from ghosts, that were coming out of the building, for were not nearly all of the crowd who saw the murder dead? And had not my school teachers said that when you die, you don't go straight to Heaven but lingered here awhile? Didn't Grandmother say that murderers never went to Heaven and that Booth didn't have time to pray for his sins, because he was shot in a barn and burned, and his spirit could walk through any street? I was running as swiftly as my tired legs could carry me past one haunted place to another. On one side was the Theater, across the street was the house where Lincoln died, into the basement of which, in the broad daylight, I often went to carry some clothes for an old lady in the neighborhood who did laundry work, on the side, for the white folks.

I was running in the middle of the street but when I reached the corner of 10th & E Streets, I never turned my head, for on my right was the bar-room which I was told Booth had often frequented. It was here he took his last drink, Grandmother and Mrs. Thomas said. Mrs. Dines, who was the greatest ghost believer, often would tell weird stories of Booth going to this bar, for they had seen him and heard him cursing late at night in the place. She declared that the night Mrs. Lincoln died she heard crying in Ford's Theater and the place was brilliantly lighted for a few moments!

At the nightly meetings, not a child enjoyed himself, but all huddled together and with staring eyes, listened, over and over again, to the strange experiences of older folks who actually saw these ghosts and had heard them.

One night I was left to go to bed, after a great ghost-telling meeting, but I gave up and said I was scared to death. I got a slap for saying it. I had to pass through the room used as a parlor, to my little hallroom and could see on the walls the three pictures which were constantly before me day and night. Lincoln and his family, the assassin Booth, with a pistol in one hand and a dagger in the other, and the death-bed scene. I was too frightened to remember my prayers. After trying to quiet my fears, I covered my head with all the bedclothes I could find, and finally the torturesome day faded away into a land of frightful dreams. Then Booth really performed! I imagined I saw him chasing me with his dagger and pistol, over, under, and above the bed, and it was only when I escaped, by hanging from the ceiling in a spider web, and yelling, that I was suddenly awakened by my Grandmother, just as the dagger was approaching my heart. She found me nearly suffocated by a large bundle of bedding with which I had covered my head, and screaming at the top of my voice. I was so worked up, that she let me sleep with her in her bed the remaining part of the night.

This was a "ghost" neighborhood anyway, for I had been told that on the northeast corner of 10th and E Streets below the Theater, there had been a medical school, and in this place the "night doctors" would take the people's children when caught after ten o'clock, and sell them for the students to "cut up." This they would do when the weather was too cold to steal dead bodies from the graveyards and sell them to the doctors. Of course this old building was more than haunted. The block was a real rendezvous for all kinds of ghosts, besides Booth's and Lincoln's.

Up to a few years ago, my old home was still standing, and I guess I have passed it hundreds of times since the days of my childhood. When I last saw it, it stood as it did in the days of my youth, and was about the only one of a group remaining to remind me of the vanished group of yesteryears and to act as a witness and preserver of the traditions of a once great neighborhood.

The old Morgan mansion, the real manor house of the neighborhood, has lost its brown stone basement, and now is a modern store. The old medical building on 10th and E Streets has given way to a modern electric office. The old café, where Booth and other celebrities of the day quenched their thirst and exchanged bar-room gossip, is no more.

Little Italian Mary's candy store, next to the Theater, where I spent all the pennies I could make, disappeared many years ago. On the other side of 10th Street, a few old friendly buildings still keep company with the Petersen house, and I guess in their walls the departed spirits of their former owners meet nightly to converse with a few old ones who have not as yet been dispossessed of their happy hunting grounds.

But, one by one, these old places, standing like monuments of a celebrated era, are yielding to the ruthless hands of time and the crushing blows of modern improvements, and soon must pass away, like the people of my day and generation, who lived in the past.

Most of all to me, the old people of the neighborhood, both white and colored, have left no traces behind them, no one has sung their praises. History has not recorded their deeds. Grandmother seemed to have been the last one of that group to have joined the innumerable caravan that went before. She saw the World War begin. Aunt Mary Dines died shortly before in a Catholic institution. "Sis" Thomas, who cried as she laughed, lived to bury her son George and her husband many, many years ago. My own Aunt Mary and Cousin Annie recently passed away. I wonder if the souls of these good old people still hold their nightly reunions in our old home and if the spirits of Lincoln and Booth come out at twelve o'clock in the alley? They may. Who knows?

I never heard what became of Cousin Minnie and Ben Dines, who lived in Dr. Morgan's home, nor Aggie Kirk, or Tony, Italian Mary's son, who played with me in the alley. Old Dr. Morgan didn't live long after we moved away, but I understand some of his relatives became doctors and were the last to leave the place. Miss Minnie Morgan, the belle of the neighborhood, married rich, and like Miss Ada her sister, became the wife of a really big man. The old orphan asylum on 10th Street has given way to a large department store. The National Rifles, where I used to go and see the soldiers get ready to parade, is no more. Its members are nearly all dead and the place has been changed. Only St. Patrick's Church, the House of God, seems to rest securely upon its firm foundation. I know if it could speak, it would say "Amen" to all I am saying.

People and buildings come and go, but traditions of a place are handed down from one generation to another. Like Rip Van Winkle, one night when I returned to the old neighborhood, after an absence of many years, all was changed. Nobody knew me. I was the sole survivor of a once great story-telling group. I went to the old house, stood by the old railing, which, as a child, I would have been afraid to come near. I gazed longingly and listened to catch some tunes through the windows of a pitch-dark basement room.

Do they part as of old, singing "God be with us till we meet again," and with a soft "Amen" after the final prayer?

PART ONE

THOSE WHO
LOVED LINCOLN

GRANDMOTHER

Her Story of the Three C's

Grandmother was a great "race" woman, and often would walk a mile to patronize some sister or brother who was running a store or making clothes. She took no "tea for a fever," when anyone made her mad, and she surely would "bawl him out." When she started after me, I just stood up like a man and took my medicine. When the licks began to fall thick and fast, she said she was knocking the devil out of me. She died long ago, but she never struck me a lick that missed to make me a better man when I grew up, and I just had to thank her for doing so, after each punishment, although I didn't want to say so.

Everybody in the neighborhood knew me by name, if not by looks. When I began to get hardheaded and didn't hang around her skirts all day, I used to steal out to a big marble game or a game of baseball or some other, that I have forgotten now.

Then, when she would come to the door and in a voice that fairly woke up the dead, and you could hear for a mile, yelling, "Jon-nee, Jon-nee," you can bet that what I was doing, or what I was playing ended, and I flew home as fast as a hare running a race with an old hound dog.

I surely believed I took after her and was a "chip off

the old block." She often told people I did. She could read a
Bible and pronounce each hard word in it. Many times she
read the text over and over again for Uncle Ben to learn. She
got the newspaper every day for the people who lived in our
house to read, and she certainly was smart when she would tell
all of her friends the news. She had "mother wit" and "common sense" too, and could figure out of this world. When she
read the words out of the singing book for her friends to repeat
after her, she took great pains to be very proper, and when she
would say "common meter," I just chuckled, I felt so proud
of her. I knew all about our old gas meter because it leaked
and nearly killed me, but a "common" one I had never seen,
but I knew it must have been a good one, because they always
began singing when anybody called out the words.

Life was beautiful in her day. There were no large apart-
ments, but real honest-to-goodness homes, where all the family and friends met at dinner time, said the grace, and ate the
meal. No night clubs, for it was said that after 10 o'clock the air
was poisoned and everybody kept out of it who could. No meeting places but churches of God and some large rooms, where
secret societies met. No automobiles that hurried you so fast
that you couldn't see anything, but good old horses and buggies,
coachmen and footmen sitting on the front seat in grand style.
No installment buying. People just paid as they went along, and
only a few old codgers and dead-beats cheated people and didn't
pay their debts and lived above their means. The undertakers
got their money, if there were not enough pennies in the little
tin cup on the foot of the coffin to bury the dead. Many thought
the dead could not rest in peace until the undertaker got all
of his money, because he did a holy piece of work. For many
years after a funeral, the family went in mourning and stopped

buying new clothes in order to save to pay the doctor and the undertaker. You can see just why people didn't get very far in life. They all paid their honest debts and thus used up all they could earn. You can say all you please, but it certainly is a fact, that people in Lincoln's time were honest and I heard that he was so much of that, that people called him "Honest Abe Lincoln." Grandmother must have loved him because she always said she had no use for a liar. In her later days, when we would laugh over and recount the experiences of my youth, she always said the reason why Miss Minnie didn't get married early in life was that to get into the Morgan family, you had to have the three C's. I remembered this expression all my childhood life, but I never knew what it was, or had ever seen a word in my John Comely spelling book with three C's in it.

I found out that when parents were particular about persons marrying into their families, they had to have "Character, Culture and Cash," and all who married into the Clarks' and the Morgans' certainly had to have a plenty of each, especially the last.

I never grew up in Grandmother's mind and eyesight, even to the day that I bade her farewell and she too passed away. She liked to brace up her dear old frame and say, "Don't you think yourself too big for me. I'll slap your jaws if I want to, just like I use to when you lived on E Street." She was playing with me, for she lived to be older than Aunt Eliza and saw the World War begin.

THE BEGINNING OF
THE ARTIST

"Booth's Annihilation"

When I was a little boy, I had all kinds of books, and loved especially the drawing books, colored pencils and the paint box Miss Minnie gave me. I drew everything in it and everything I saw. All the neighbors smiled when Grandmother would say I was born with a pencil in my hands. In our house upstairs, in the backroom of the attic, was a funny looking old white man. I believe his name was Mr. Espberg. He surely could paint people's pictures. Many came to see him and had him make their pictures. I'd sit for hours and watch him. I went to the corner store for him for nothing. When he tried to give me anything I'd say, "Thank you, just the same." I just wanted to see him draw and paint pictures.

It wasn't long before I was drawing Lincoln, Taddie, Mrs. Lincoln, Bob Lincoln, old Jeff Davis and the apple tree, and everybody else. They may not have looked like them to anyone else, but they did to me.

Mr. Espberg always praised my work, and told my Grandmother that he thought I had talent, and to me he would say, "Keep it up, son; some day, when you grow up, you'll make pictures like I am doing and be a great artist." I never forgot the funny looking old man, with his long gray hair and big bay-window, and his mustache, which he wore like cow horns, curled up on each end. He was always broke, owed Grandmother and everybody else. She said he just kept her nose to the grindstone, feeding him for nothing and that he had to get out, before she threw him out, pictures and all. I knew she meant it, too. Once he became sick and nearly died. I surely was sorry when he had to leave. I just had to have somebody to teach me to draw all of the pictures in my drawing book, and I would have given Grandmother all the pennies I had saved in my little bank, and everything else, to let him remain in our house.

Long before he left, I was so swelled up with conceit at my drawing that I didn't want my hair cut off my head. He was my patron saint. He said I could draw and he knew it, although nobody else said so. Anyway I was satisfied. I would draw Lincoln's picture, from the one on the wall, all of the time. He would correct the work, saying it was fine. I drew Taddie and his drum and all of the other people in the picture. It was with reverent hand that I drew my Grandmother's picture—but the Lord only could tell what I did to Booth when I started on him. He had not only killed Lincoln, but one night I dreamt that he came after me and chased me all over my room. I made up my mind, if the Lord should spare me, to get even with him for everything he had done to Tad and me. Taking off my shoes and stockings like Mr. Espberg and rolling up the sleeves on my puny arms, I took a pencil in hand and began. No cartoonist who ever lived drew a more awful thing. My soul poured out its vengeance on that piece of paper.

I was truly the first great modernist and surrealist all in one. I just could not do too much to that picture. The face was long, with an awful nose like Ichabod Crane's, his eyes were jumping out of his head, his hair sticking out of his head like porcupine quills. This is what Grandmother used to say about it. His long mustache curled up like the horns of a big cow I saw in the Smithsonian grounds, and his ears looked like the devil's.

After the drawing came the assassination. I went crazy and lost my mind; I punched holes in his eyes, spat in his face, and threw dust on it; put the picture on the floor and trampled on it; then I stole Grandmother's carving knife out of the kitchen table drawer and began to carve him up. I slashed it here, and there, and everywhere—over and over again; then I took the paper again, crushed the whole thing together and threw it out of the window with an expression of hatred and revenge. I had gotten even and was satisfied.

Grandmother, who was looking through the half-open door, was just breaking her sides laughing. She took in the whole thing and when I had finished and turned to go out of the door, she patted me on the back, tenderly took me in her long arms and then led me downstairs to the kitchen. She made me go outside and gather up the pieces of the picture that were left, and even to her last day she would often take out an old scrapbook in which she pasted old pictures and clippings, and in a joking way, when pointing it out would say, "Where is the little devil who did this?"

I had always thought Booth was really crazy, because if he had good sense, as Aunt Eliza used to say, "He would never have gone across the Navy Yard Bridge where there were so many soldiers, but would have gone up in Foggy Bottom and got into that big sewer and nobody would have found him." When the big boys in my neighborhood were chased by the police, they hid in sewers until the police went by. Why was Booth so crazy? He was just dumb, that's all, for Old Aunt Eliza told me one day that the Yankees caught him hiding in an old tobacco barn and just burned him up alive. It served him right. I knew the Devil would get him and if I had had my way, that was one time I would have helped the Devil to hurl brimstone and fire upon his head, and then chained him down in Hell so that he could not come back to the little alley and ride all night scaring decent people.

Yes! The hatred for those who did anything to Lincoln was so firmly planted into my soul, that in the language of the Scriptures, as quoted by Uncle Ben, "I hated them now, and henceforth forever more."

Aunt Eliza once told me that Booth had had a good father and mother and splendid sisters and brothers, but ran in bad company, drank wine, and the little sense he had in his head burned out, and that she hoped I would never take a drop as long as I lived.

COUSIN ANNIE

Tells about the Keckley and Herndon Books

Old Uncle Ben preached about those "new time" people who studied so many books that they knew nothing, and their spirits were killed by the "letters" in them, and he said there was only one book in this world, the Bible, and in it you could find all that was necessary to carry you to glory. I thought so too, but I wanted to know something about people and things on earth and was always glad when my cousin Annie came home. She had been to college and taught school somewhere. Grandmother said Annie was unspoiled and that she "was still made out of the same old stuff as her foreparents." She delighted in telling everybody in meetings about the places she had been, the things she had seen, and the books she had read, and the people she knew.

I thought she knew more about Lincoln than anybody else did in the whole world and my eyes just twinkled when she told some one that Lincoln didn't die to save the Union, but died to save the old colored people, who lived in his day and generation.

Annie was neither too short nor too tall, too fat, nor too lean, to be a good-looking woman. Upon her face there was a constant smile and her beautiful eyes were windows of the dearest soul and she was one of the best-hearted persons I ever knew. All of Grandmother's kinfolks looked like Indians and had plaits on their heads long enough to sit on, when they had their heads bowed, when sitting on chairs. Once upon a time when I was a very little boy, I had curls down my back too. I just reasoned that I had right smart Indian blood in me, because when things didn't suit me and I became real mad, I just carried on and everybody said I acted like a "wild Indian." When Grandmother had to call me and I was outside the house, people said she gave a "war whoop" when she yelled for me.

Grandmother used to tell us all that we really had some "blue blood" in our veins, but every time I got into a fight and some old bad boys blacked my eyes and hit me in the mouth or nose, the blood that came out was red. I thought about this blood business, but decided to keep my mouth shut.

I know Annie just made the children she taught in the school stand around, because she could just drop her head, turn it on the side, push out her mouth and roll her big eyes about in her head, and begin to ask more things than a Philadelphia lawyer could do.

Annie was too nice to hold anything against anybody. She was always thinking about doing something for other people, especially little children and old people. She worked in the Church and Sunday school and enjoyed writing letters for the old folks, and reading the Bible to them. She was also on the sick committee of Grandmother's church.

Aunt Mary often said that both she and Grandmother had worked their fingers off, both day and night, raising money to give Annie an education, and the whole family was going to do the same for me.

I often looked at their hands when they told me this, and could never understand how they grew back. They said they were more than repaid for their sacrifices, as she kept a level head when she talked with the Morgans and Clarks, and used as many big words as they did.

Annie always brought many good clothes home with her, but she did not spend every penny she made upon her back, dressing up and strutting up and down the streets like a peacock. She always sent most of her money home to Aunt Mary and Grandmother. I guess to pay them back for the fingers they worked off. They said she was a chip off the old block. They knew she would never change her ways, and blood would tell, because they trained her just like they did me—on the rod and the Gospel.

Like us all she was "to the manor born." I didn't know what that meant but all of Grandmother's children were born that way, and Annie and I took after our Mother's. I heard that the other children were different and were "bred and born."

I just guessed the reason we were all so religious, and loved Lincoln so much was because we were "manor" born, and old Uncle Ben, who knew his Bible by heart preached about old-time people in the Bible with "manna."

All of the children in our neighborhood were brought up and lived on the Bible and Lincoln. White children and colored children were trained alike and would get the devil slapped out of them if anybody told their mothers and fathers about their bad actions.

Cousin Annie had even been in New York, attended all kinds of schools and read all kinds of books—and just ate up the pages like a bookworm. She was crazy about me, and I was about her, too.

Aunt Eliza said it was "because Annie knew so much, that she never forgot the place from which she sprung, nor tired of waiting on her mother and father. She sacrificed all for them. Her education hadn't made her bigger than God Almighty and man too. She had not become a doubting Thomas either, but still kept her old-time religion, and her head was not so filled with new-time trash that she couldn't listen to her folks." Annie always had many good picture books, and Grandmother had bought her a big old bookcase, from the old woman who owned our house. This was placed in the front room, and Annie was buying all kinds of books to put in it, for my Grandmother wanted me to be a reader when I grew up. There was no cheap trash in that old case, as I learned in later life.

One day there was great excitement when Annie came in with a little red book called *Behind the Scenes* by a colored woman, Elizabeth Keckley, who had been four years in the White House with "Honest Abe" and Mrs. Lincoln and her little children. It had Mrs. Keckley's picture in it.

Next door, in Marini Hall, they once had plays, and believe me all kinds of things went on *behind the scenes* but I guess the White House was better, because Lincoln lived in it, and always called on God when he needed help. I heard he surely needed Him more than once.

I just looked and looked at that book because it had everything in this world anybody could say about the Lincolns.

Uncle Ben once told me, "You know, boy, young people when they grow up soon forget the old folks; they all ain't like Annie; they just go way and go astray and forget the people who made them, but when they get sick and broke, they come back home to live off the old folks and die. You know son, 'A cow needs her tail more than once in fly time.'"

THE HERNDON STORY

Until my dying day, I shall never forget the piece Annie read us all, about a story she had read in one of the books she brought home with her. It was about a partner of Lincoln who said "Honest Abe" liked some other woman. You should have seen the faces of all of the dear old folks, whose eyes were wide as saucers, and whose ears were strained to get every word. Who ever heard of such a thing? Nobody believed it and I was just wild to draw the picture of the man who was talking about Tad's mother when his father was dead and gone to glory.

My Lord! Didn't the old folks perform? One said, "no man who puts whiskey in his head is any good, for it just moves from side to side until he loses his balance and falls down. God never did like drunken people and you might have known that they were lawyers, because Uncle Ben said they beat everybody and could get you all excited and make you lie just like they did."

The crowd was frantic and kept yelling "liar," "devil" and everything else they could think of. I guess if he had been in our square, there would have been a lynching or a race riot or something else. Annie said Mrs. Lincoln bawled Herndon out once when he stepped on her feet at a dance and he never liked her anymore.

UNCLE BEN,
THE PREACHER

Cartoon of "Riding Around the Circuit"

Annie said Lincoln never let the colored men who cut his hair, take much off because he might lose all his strength like the good old prophet of old, but a little child told him to let his whiskers and siders grow because he would need all of the hairs he could grow every place on his body if he wanted to beat the "Rebs."

Old Uncle Ben, when he preached, spoke about Lincoln's hair. He said Lincoln must have been as strong as Samson, who wore his hair long in the days of the Bible.

He said Lincoln was the only lawyer he ever heard of that was called "honest." He was poor as a church mouse and had to live in an old log cabin, sit on the rails, and shoot wild animals to get something to eat. All of the lawyers he ever saw had so much money that they kept their hands in their pockets to keep the pennies from falling out. Sis Thomas said they "just talked people deaf, dumb and blind, and if they got their hands in your pie, they would make you tell more lies than grains of corn on a cob, and would sweat you until you were as weak as a dying calf."

Uncle Ben said, that once they were looking for a great man who knew the law to be President of the United States and they could find but one in our country. He was so honest that when they put his picture in the papers and said he lived in a log cabin, and split rails, and made tables out of logs, and slept on an old dirt floor with straw on it, and had to kill bears and wild cats to eat, they just broke all of their necks running to the polls to vote, and made him the greatest President that ever lived. He was so used to saving everything of his own, and other people's, that he saved the Union and set the colored people free. The name of this great and honorable man of whom I speak was Honest Abraham Lincoln.

I nearly cracked my sides laughing at a funny old picture Annie brought me, and carried it to Uncle Ben, the preacher, to tell me about it. Gee, it looked funny! There was "Old Abe" with a tall hat on his head, and his long legs touching the ground, with a big bag of clothes on one side of the saddle and one of grub on the other. The old horse had his head and tail hanging down, and I guess he ate when Abe did—sometimes—when he made an honest dollar.

Annie said the writing said he was "riding around the circuit."

I always heard everybody say that Lincoln was a funny man, looked funny and told big jokes, like the minstrel men in the theaters, but I never heard he "rode all around the circus" instead of riding inside in a ring like the other actors.

HIS STORY OF KING
SOLOMON'S WISDOM

There was poor old Uncle Ben whom I liked best. If he was dead I just knew he never would become a ghost, because he always told everybody that when he died he was going to Glory and walk through the pearly gates and on the golden streets. He was so good that I felt sure old St. Peter locked the gates and kept him in there for keeps.

He taught me how to behave myself in his meetings and just what to say when he bore down on the Holy Ghost and began to talk about sitting down on a rock in the weary land. He was my preacher and had converted me with many little funny stories from the Bible and elsewhere. He told about little David who played on a harp, and killed a giant with a stone and some man who killed somebody with the jawbone of an ass—and Daniel who walked into a lion's den, and because he believed in God the beasts didn't tear him up. He also talked about some Hebrew children who stayed in a fiery furnace and didn't get burned. He told me about washing my face and hands and feet before I went to bed at night, for if I died before I woke, I could not strut all up and down the golden streets above. He said the good books said you "had to come before the Lord with clean hands too." When he used to tell me this story, Grandmother just chuckled because I never could keep them clean and she had the time of her life getting me to do so.

Uncle Ben often told stories to the children about bears, and foxes and every other kind of animal. Here is one I shall always remember to my dying day.

Uncle Ben once told me that when you die you can come back in some bird or other wild animal and can stay on earth till judgment day. He said King Solomon was a wise old bird and came back as a rooster, in all his glory, to rule over all of the hens and pullets, just as he had done over the old women and young gals in his days and times, and kept his crown on his head and painted it *red* so that everybody could see it and know who he was.

He then strutted his stuff and reared back and sang his songs.

When the old hens and pullets saw him coming, they were glad, and tried to get him to look at them by cackling and cackling and cackling. He did not make "fish of some" and "fowl of the other" but strutted his stuff before all.

He was so wise that he knew how to rule everyone. When he wanted to do a little flirting with some young chicken, he just made the old hens set on their eggs for twenty-one days, to keep their mouths closed and see nothing. They were afraid not to do what he told them to do, so they just fretted and fretted and became angry and disagreeable, so much so, that until this day when women keep on talking and letting their mouths run about nothing, people say "they are disagreeable as a setting hen."

When he had made all of his ladies shut up and be still, he certainly would show off. He was so jealous that he would kill any other rooster that came on his diggings, and when an old hen talked too much, he would slap her in the mouth with his wing and make her see stars, even in the day time.

He then puffed himself up like a pigeon, and carefully raised one foot after another and put it down, and made all of his beautiful feathers stick out of his body and head. He really went some. If there were some hens far away that he liked, he would call them in a very loud voice, that almost woke up the living and the dead.

Abraham Lincoln must have seen many old roosters in his day for once Uncle Ben told me that when he had to have some more men to save the Union and set the colored people free, he remembered one of these roosters who used to live in his farmyard and raise the dickens when he was young, like me. Lincoln called so loud that everyone in the world heard him and every man in the country came running to see what it was all about. The band played and they sang, "We are coming Father Abraham, 500,000 more." I don't know how many calls he made, but they say he had millions of men in the field before the war was over.

UNCLE BEN'S STORY
OF DIVINE PREPARATION

Uncle Ben told the old E Street people a story about Lincoln which I shall never forget. He said:

When the children of Israel were in bondage God raised up Moses to lead them out of it; but Moses was not to lead an ignorant horde that was uncultured and despised—a group without tradition, but was called to lead the Israelites out of bondage. He was one of them and knew his people.

In America where there was a group of God's children of a different color struggling in bondage and under the oppressor's lash, begging him not for salvation for themselves but for their children and their children's children, God needed more than a Moses of the Israelite kind, and needed one of a type unknown before. So God in answering the prayers of the oppressed deliberately created an individual to His own liking and planned his education in a manner that his language could be understood by all whom he was to lead. In short, this person had to be made to suit the purpose of Almighty God. He had to be a child of the soil, speaking the same language and experiencing the same hardships as those people who looked up to him. He had to be unlettered and uncultured in the beginning, as they were. He had come through the fiery furnace of hardships as did the Hebrew children and had to be as fearless in so doing as Daniel was in the lion's den. He had to have a heart for the most despised and rejected of people. Therefore God created Lincoln as the rough person needed for this great task. Then in His school of training He placed this child where he could know the abilities and ideas of men of a different race and color and brought him up in it.

Uncle Ben told us that he believed that Almighty God created someone to teach his chosen prophet, Lincoln, by example all that a Negro could attain with freedom and equal opportunity, and although he had never heard about anyone who had done this, he believed that some day the person would be found.

Years later I discovered that "Billy the Barber," William de Fleurville, was the answer to Uncle Ben's theory.

AUNT ELIZA

I think about old Aunt Eliza, who Grandmother said was Uncle Ben's girl in the days gone by. She was all right to me, but she smoked her pipe and even chewed snuff. When she began to let her mouth run like a train of cars you couldn't get in a word edgewise.

I never said much about Aunt Eliza's habit while she was living, and am not going to do so now, after she is dead, because nobody ever tried to change her, not even the Clarks. Everybody brought the old woman tobacco and she looked too cute as she puffed the smoke out of her little mouth, like a steam engine.

The Clarks never tried to interfere with any of old Aunt Eliza's ways and habits. They loved and idolized her and she treated them, in my day, just as she did when they were young like me.

I always thought old Dr. Morgan knew about curing people, but believe me, old Aunt Eliza had him beat to death in some things and used home medicines too. In our neighborhood there was a little boy named Ike Crooks. His legs were so crooked that he could never play hide and seek with us because when he tried to run, his bow legs would tie up one with the other, and he'd get caught before he could think how to get away. Dr. Morgan put sticks all around them and tied them up, but when he took them off, they just dropped back, more crooked than ever. Sis Eliza felt sorry for him and told his mother that she could cure him, if she put his legs in pot-likker each morning and night. The old lady did as she was told and in a few months the boy was running faster than a horse could trot, and doing the buck and wing dance like the old devil. I guess she got her potlikker knowledge from the old people who raised Tad's father.

Once every winter, my Grandmother had to buy a big goose and let it hang out of the window to freeze for so many nights and days. Then she would put it in a big pan and roast it for old Aunt Eliza, who skimmed all of the grease off the pans and stored it away in bottles. When you had a cold and your nose just wouldn't stop running, old Aunt Eliza would have your parents rub your nose, temples and hands and feet with goose grease and you would get well in a jiffy. In the spring of every year, she gave all the children in the neighborhood sassafras tea, to make our blood thin and get the old devil out. I guess there were many old lady doctors and home medicines where "Old Abe" lived, because I never saw a brass sign on any log cabin in Lincoln's neighborhood nor did I see a drugstore with large bottles in the window.

New Year's Day was a great day in the Clarks' and all of our homes. All who came just had to eat a plate of black-eyed peas and hog-jowls. Aunt Eliza said this would give us good luck for all of the new year, but if any woman came to our houses on New Year's morning, keep her out, because she would bring you bad luck for the year.

When anybody had the earache or some big pains, old Aunt Eliza would just crack one of her old dried hog-jowls and rub the marrow on them and they would get well.

AUNT ELIZA'S DEATH

Not very long after we left the neighborhood, Mr. Dines hurriedly drove up to our door in Dr. Morgan's carriage and told Grandmother that old Aunt Eliza was dying, and wanted her to come with him and go see her right away, before it was too late, for she was sinking fast.

Hasty preparations for leaving were made, all cooking stopped, house closed up, and after a few minutes spent in getting out an old tin box, containing copper coins and a little piece of smoked glass, from the bottom of a trunk, we were speedily on our way. Dr. Morgan's double team could fairly burn the wind when Mr. Dines cracked his long whip over the ears of the horses.

In a very short time, we had arrived at the end of our journey. I was going to see old Aunt Eliza for the last time as she was dying.

The Clarks, for whom Aunt Eliza worked, opened the door for us, and almost running, we rapidly ascended the long stairway to the little attic room on the third floor where the sick woman was. Rushing into the room and thence to the bedside, Grandmother found that she had arrived too late for Aunt Eliza to say anything to her, or even know her. I *had* to go in, and had crept behind the old neighbors who were standing around the bedside and drying their eyes. At intervals there would be prayers for the departing sister, then, while on their knees, Aunt

Mary Dines, who had sung so often for Lincoln, would raise a hymn with her sweet crooning voice; another prayer, then a long silent pause, interrupted only by a sob from the Clarks or from the faithful few here gathered. This went on until after midnight when old Dr. Morgan came and speedily left, as he, too, mopped his tear-filled eyes and said it would be "all over soon," for I could hear a strange noise that almost drove me crazy, coming from the bedridden patient and which Grandmother told me were "death-rattles." Even now I cannot describe the terrible sensations of those moments.

Long after midnight, the singing and praying continued, and as the rattles grew fainter, the mourners drew closer to the bed and began to look down on Sis Eliza. Suddenly she raised her head and her eyes flew open in a glassy stare. She seemed to be gazing at a large picture of Lincoln which hung on a wall at the foot of her bed. In an instant she seemed to drop her head to the pillow, all noises ceased—a whispered silence filled the room. Grandmother, who was bending over her side, put her head on her friend's breast, then took out her little piece of smoked glass from the tin box, put it in front of Aunt Eliza's mouth, and in a muffled voice said, "She's gone." An old friend of Lincoln had joined him above!

There was crying everywhere and I was crying too. I loved old Aunt Eliza, and she loved me too, and often gave me nice things to play with, but I longed to leave that room.

Uncle Ben knelt at the bedside and said a prayer for the departed soul, after which Aunt Mary Dines led the hymn, "Safe in the Arms of Jesus."

The old friends placed their hands on the yet warm head of this old saint and departed with a pitiful "Good-by," "Farewell," or "Go on, Sis Eliza, I'll meet you there soon." The last to leave was Miss Clark, whom Aunt Eliza had raised. She just couldn't stand the singing and praying and everything else. They said she had fainted and had to be carried out. Nobody would take me out, so I hid in the corner of the room, but took a peep every now and then. You know, Grandmother said that curiosity once killed a cat and that I had my share of it.

Only Aunt Mary Dines, Mrs. Thomas, and I were in that room when I was taken by the arms by my Grandmother and led to the bedside, and by force my hand was placed on Aunt Eliza's head and I was told to say "Good-by."

The reader probably can describe my feelings of that day. I never could.

In those days, friends were friends even after death, and when one departed, the dearest ones washed and dressed the body, tied up the jaws and then placed a copper coin over each eye to close it. I had often heard my Grandmother talk about people who were so dishonest that they would even "Steal pennies off a dead man's eyes"—but this was the first time I had seen them placed there. I had previously gone to see a dead woman in the neighborhood, where people put pennies in a plate on her coffin to help bury her, but I just couldn't imagine how those pennies got on the dead person's eyes. Now I could readily see for myself. I always thought about this in after life and was not quite surprised, a few years ago, when I visited Chicago, to see two large copper pennies in a museum with a label telling that they had been placed on the eyes of the martyred President Lincoln.

Grandmother told me all Aunt Eliza's friends would come to the funeral, which would be held in the Clarks' parlor. She knew the place would be filled with flowers. Grandmother said they would be beautiful and that "Aunt Eliza would make such a good-looking corpse."

Old Dr. Morgan had known Aunt Eliza the longest and

had attended her. He was going to the funeral as a mourner. I saw him wipe his eyes when he passed by the bedside to gaze into her face for the last time. He just couldn't save her. He was the dearest old gentleman I ever saw, jolly, kindly and had always a cheerful word for all. The kids adored him. He really knew Lincoln, and had been in the White House, too.

Although he was very rich he was not a "Money Doctor" but attended all, the rich, the poor, the high and the low. Those paid who could, but to his neighbors, he freely donated his services and also medicines. He would even go in the alley, at any time he was called, day or night. Once Grandmother told me he saved my life while I was very ill. He, too, has gone for many years, but today the old house stands with its brownstone front changed into a store. I pass it in silence, as a tribute to a man who was a real physician and lived for the good he could do.

While some were preparing the body for the undertaker, to come the next morning, other friends of Sis Eliza were fixing up the big front parlor of the Clark home, for those people loved the deceased as none other had done. Had she not been born in the Clark family long before the war? Was she not raised on their old plantation? Did she not nurse, at the breast, the Clark children, as she did her own? She often told me that she boxed their jaws and made them stand around, just like all the old friends of Grandmother's did me, when I went to see them.

Well, although the Clarks were devoted Catholics, they never tried to break up Aunt Eliza's faith, and even enjoyed colored folks' visits, especially when they came up to make the evening pleasant for their old friends. It was Aunt Eliza's last hour and her friends knew just what she wanted done when she died.

In the parlor, Aunt Eliza's friends were very busy getting it ready for the reception of Aunt Eliza's body. Pictures were covered with dark goods, looking glasses were turned to the walls, and every clock in the house stopped—death had been here and had taken his victim. Like the words Mr. Dines used to say, "She has gone to a better land like Old Black Joe." I was so worked up with it all! I had no hiding place, even downstairs. It was long before my Grandmother realized my condition, in the death chamber, and left the corpse, and took me by the arm and carried me downstairs to her friends. I really had been scared of living and afraid of dying, but I was worse now, for had not Grandmother's hands been all over the dead body? I just felt cold chills everywhere, when she put them on me. I certainly was happy when everything was done that could be done, and Aunt Eliza's body was on the "cooling board" and Mr. Dines drove all of the friends home in Dr. Morgan's carriage. That night, I slept with my head under all of the covers I could get, for while I loved old Aunt Eliza, I certainly did not want to see her coming into my room. I didn't care how good they said she was, or even if they did say she had gone to glory, I just wanted her to stay there, and not stop by my house to rest, on the way.

When Grandmother went back the next day, I stayed home, and stole out to play, although all of the rest of my people remained quiet and were borrowing black from everybody in the neighborhood to wear at the funeral. They even sewed a little piece of black crepe on my coat sleeve and I had to wear it. Every time I looked at my arm, I thought of Aunt Eliza with her jaws bound up and pennies on her eyes and with a big white sheet all over her. I started to tear it off many times during the thirty days we all were mourning, but I was afraid to do so, for fear that Grandmother would just kill me with that long black strap she kept in the kitchen to "make me love her more," when I did wrong and needed it. She certainly did not spare the rod when needed, and I was no spoiled child.

On the third day after death, the funeral was held. Bright and early the carriage came for Grandmother, and of course me. Nobody talked on the way. Although I had traveled the same way before, now it had no charms for me. I just wanted to stay home, but couldn't say so. When we arrived at the home we found the undertaker waiting, as were also Aunt Mary Dines and Sis Thomas. Aunt Eliza's best black silk dress was lying on a couch, with white silk stockings, and some other things given by the Clarks.

I stayed with the Clarks while all dressed the body and then I learned it had been placed in a brown, awful looking box called a coffin. When the undertaker and Grandmother had finished with it, the people present, with their heads hanging down, went into the room, to look first at the body. Then all the neighbors began to pour in and take a last look at the dead. Not a soul who had known her stayed away. I saw all of my old gang. They hung outside of the house, wanting to come in, but were scared to do so.

One by one the Clarks arrived. There were two that came from Baltimore. One was a Sister and one a young priest. Aunt Eliza had nursed them both. I saw them wipe their eyes and say some kind of prayer over her that I just could not understand. Just a little later, old Uncle Ben, her pastor, came in a big carriage. He had on real preacher's clothes, that he had had ever since he became a child of God and a leader of his flock. Mrs. Thomas told me this, and while he had no education, he knew enough to get through the world and behave himself. He just was gifted by God for preaching.

The big old room was packed. There was no religious discrimination, everybody was alike; Catholics, Methodists,

Baptists and all kinds of religious people joined in the praying and singing. Even the nice old priest from St. Patrick's Church, who used to come often to see the Morgans and Clarks, stayed to pay his respects and say something, for he, too, had often talked to her about religion and delighted to hear her tell about the time when most of the Clark children were little "shavers." She made them strong by making them suck fat meat at meals, rubbed them down with goose grease when sick with colds, and bathed their limbs with pot-liquor, just, as she said, she bet Abe Lincoln's mother did him when he was a baby. She taught them how to say the Lord's Prayer, when she put them to bed at night, just like Grandmother had done for me.

Miss Minnie Morgan came early to play the little parlor organ, and go over some hymns that Aunt Eliza's friends and Grandmother were going to sing. She was a Catholic and nearly all of the colored people were Baptists and Methodists. I kept quiet, back of everybody present, and where I could not see Aunt Eliza's coffin.

Uncle Ben certainly looked good, with his long coat hanging down below his knees. I heard afterward that he had been her pastor during the war. He met her near an old Contraband Camp where Aunt Mary Dines said she used to sing for President Lincoln, Taddy and a whole lot of real big people. Even the old watchman in Ford's Theater came to the funeral. Aunt Eliza often told me he was as poor as Job's turkey-hen and had nothing to give anybody. I felt so sorry for the Clark boy, who was studying to be a priest and also his sister, who was a "Little Sister of the Poor." After looking at the face of their old friend, they both took out little books from their pockets. One read and the other answered, then they knelt and said some beads over her, and sat down. The priest from St. Patrick's and the Clarks and Morgans also took part. Aunt Mary Dines and Uncle Ben, Thomas, and some other people could understand, but I didn't know a single word that was said. When they were through, Miss Minnie played—"Safe in the Arms of Jesus." I found myself just singing my head off with the choir. Then Uncle Ben said his prayer and began to preach the sermon. He used as his text these words, "Blessed are they who die in the Lord, for they shall rest from their labors." He just showed off before that crowd, and even the priest said "Amen" when the little band of friends and Cousin Minnie, began to yell "Amen" and "Good-by, Aunt Eliza, I'll see you soon in Glory."

I believe they forgot themselves in the big company, but they did not care. They were just plain people, who knew and worshipped God in spirit and in truth, and some said, "Lord, help us to get right all the time."

In the big sermon, Uncle Ben implored God's help upon everybody gathered therein, and even gave a long prayer for the Clarks, who took care of her, and said God would certainly bless those who looked after the poor; he then spoke of those who spread God's word on earth, and called the names of the young and old priests present who preached the Lord's word and rendered help unto the poor. (They had even given him money at times.) He just preached as long as he wanted to. Uncle Ben had never been a book preacher, just a child of God, called to spread his gospel on earth and lead a good life. His old flock had gone over Jordan. He had no church, and only Aunt Eliza was left, and he certainly kept in touch with her, for Grandmother often said he was nearly as old as she was, but was as spry as an eel. After he had prayed for all God's children and the Clarks and the great physician Dr. Morgan, he wound up on me. I can hear him now as he called out, "Johnnie, take care of your Grandmother when you grow up," and told about the little children who came unto the Lord and were members of the kingdom of Heaven. He also spoke so everybody could hear. I guess many got religion from this sermon.

When the old man finally ended his sermon and said "Farewell, Sis Eliza, I'll be with you soon in the beautiful land above, where we shall gather at the river and see God face to face, and be like Him," he suddenly stopped and just had to sit down. Dr. Morgan gave him something in a glass of water to help get himself together. I know you would have been sorry for him, just as I was, for he had lost the last member of the little flock that he had pastored for years, and only the old shepherd remained.

You never saw such a place in your life, with everybody crying, some for Sis Eliza who had gone, and Uncle Ben, who was left behind. He ended his part with the Lord's Prayer. Everybody joined in. The little choir then sang, "Go on, I'll Meet You There," then after another prayer by a tall white man, whom I had never seen before, the choir sang its farewell piece, one that Aunt Eliza liked best, "Rock of Ages, Cleft for Me, Let Me Hide Myself in Thee." The preacher gave out each verse and they sang it in "common meter," whatever that was.

After the body was put into the hearse and the mourners and friends went into their carriages, it turned up 10th St. There were no traffic officers to stop people from breaking through funerals, but no one tried to pass or drive through it, because breaking through, old Aunt Eliza said, "would give you seven years bad luck, just like breaking a looking glass."

Whether anyone knew the dead person or not, from the time that the body left the house and until it reached the graveyard, a passer-by would stop, take off his hat and bow his head when the hearse passed by. Colored and white people did the same.

I just felt that when Sis Eliza's body passed the old Ford's Theater, Lincoln's ghost must have been there to wave it farewell and was in that crowd, waving farewell with his handkerchief, while he held his big hat upon his breast and bowed when the body passed. The crowd which was standing on both sides of 10th Street between E and F Streets did this, and wouldn't he too?

Her first and last thought was of him. I shall always believe that when she was dying, and her eyes flew open, he was somewhere about. That picture of Lincoln had come to carry her home, because just before she lost her voice, Aunt Mary Dines said she was asked to sing, "Steal Away to Jesus," and then "Swing Low, Sweet Chariot, Coming for to Carry Me Home. I looked over Jordan and what did I see? Coming for to carry me home. A band of angels coming after me— Coming for to carry me home."

After a long ride we reached old Harmony Cemetery, where the body was buried, and we were driven back to our homes. After a dinner prepared by one of Grandmother's friends, who had been good enough to keep house for her while we went away, all of our friends came in, and sat around the dining-room table and listened to the virtues of the departed, as told by my Grandmother.

After the return home, I asked why I had to place my hand on Aunt Eliza. Grandmother said, it would make me not afraid of dead people. Whether she was right or not, I began slowly to lose my fear of spirits and the dead.

Nobody ever saw Uncle Ben after that funeral—poor old fellow! I just reckoned he got on the pale white horse, too, that he said was coming for us all, and rode to glory.

Perhaps Lincoln met him with the other folks at the

pearly gates and told St. Peter and all the other saints in glory about his preaching.

He was surely a nice old man and when he was not preaching and praying and singing, he could certainly make you shake all over, when he began telling some old tale of bygone days, and Grandmother would laugh until the tears ran down her cheeks, and oh! how I would grin and chuckle, when he would take me on his knee, and tell me the story of the "Grasshopper and the Ant," "Old Brother Rabbit," the "Three Bears," and many others. When he told them, they were so different from what Miss Minnie read to me from the little books she used to buy for all the children from Mr. Stuntz on New York Avenue and where President Lincoln bought his books and taffy for Taddie—or from those that came from little Addie Weedon's Aunt, Mrs. Polkaty who kept a penny book store in her basement on M Street between 12th and 13th Streets. I remember Mrs. Polkaty well, as she would seem to look clean through you, then smile. They say Tad liked her. I met Addie myself many years afterward.

Uncle Ben said at Aunt Eliza's funeral, "We brought nothing in this world and will carry nothing out of it." If this was true, I wondered where all of the rich people got their money.

People said Lincoln had nothing and was a poor man. I guess this was the reason why he was so honest—for if he had been a rich man, he would never have given a cent for good old poor people like Grandmother, Aunt Mary, old Aunt Eliza, Uncle Ben, Sis Thomas, Mr. Dines, Annie and me and would have gone on robbing the people until they became as ragged as Job's coat. I never saw Job, but I heard a great deal about the poor old man's clothes. He had some books in which he kept "texts" and from which Uncle Ben always took his. Look as I might in the Bible, I never found any books, for it contained only pages and pictures and family "likenesses." That's one time that I thought Uncle Ben didn't tell the truth, for he said he was going to *take his text from the book of Job in the Bible.* I wanted to tell him so, too, but I was afraid to do so, because when I talked back to old people I would get a sound beating, and when I began to talk my way out, Grandmother would say, "You can run your mouth, but you can't run me."

AUNT ROSETTA WELLS

Her Stories of Little Tad Lincoln and the White House

Sometimes, company came to our house. I especially remember Aunt Wells, Frank Wells' mother, who came often with her husband to see Aunt Mary Dines. They were both from the same farm and looked alike. Aunt Wells was a great talker, a dressmaker, and had been employed by Mrs. Lincoln to do plain sewing by the day. She knew the Lincolns and had worked for them and actually talked with both. Oh, me, how I would look at her while she told stories about Mrs. Lincoln and how good she was to the help! She said "she had her ways, but nobody minded her, for she would never hurt a flea, and her bark was worse than her bite."

She said little Tad Lincoln was really a little devil, and took her for a good thing. He would come into the room where she and Mrs. Brooks were sewing, thread needles for them, and sometimes hide them and make out he had lost them. Then he would tell where they were, and fly away laughing. She would threaten to kill him, if she could get him, but he knew she didn't mean it, and soon he was back again at his pranks. She thought he was so mischievous because he didn't have many children to play with.

She would often tell about President Lincoln, how he worked and acted, and said that he treated the servants like "people," and would laugh and say kind things to them, and that because he was President he wasn't "stuck up," and things had not gone to his head. Also, he was a "God-fearing man." She said that he never cursed and had his Bible and went to church on Sundays. Nobody worked in the White House on Sunday.

Mrs. Wells did the plain sewing for the family and mended clothes and bed linen, darned socks, etc:

> She wore glasses, as all her old folks did, for there were no electric lights anywhere, and gas made dim light and bad eyes. Once she said she looked all day for her glasses and that little scamp Tad kept laughing at her and running away. She had pushed them up on her head, and they were hidden in the handkerchief which covered it. At last he yelled, "Look on your forehead, Aunt Wells." She did, and there they were, and what a time he had. She said he played with everybody, even his father.

I liked to have her come to see my Grandmother. She never told ghost stories and, besides, she often brought her little son Francis to play with me. She said she didn't believe in ghosts, and had never seen one. Many people said there were ghosts in the White House. She had stayed there nights and had seen none. She always had a long argument with her friends on the subject. Although I couldn't speak in on the conversation, I certainly remembered what she said. It allayed my fears for a moment.

Mrs. Wells knew Mrs. John Brooks, who also sewed at the White House, and Mrs. Lincoln gave her two old chairs when she was leaving the White House. Tom Clark's father also helped to move Mrs. Lincoln. Mrs. Wells' husband had a team and hauled Mrs. Lincoln's baggage to the station, and also took Mrs. Lincoln, who gave something to all who helped. Mrs. Wells lived to be very old and just recently passed away.

UNCLE BUCK

I remember Uncle Buck who attended the furnaces of everybody in our street and in all kinds of weather. Everybody said he "certainly liked his tea," but I always caught him going into that saloon on the corner where Booth got his last one, and not into our kitchen, and when he was full, he certainly could toot his horn and let off steam. He said he had played in a band during the war.

People said he was a "gentleman of the old school," when he took off his hat and bowed to the ground to say "Good morning," "Good evening" and "Good-by." I never knew what kind of a place it was, or where it was, and what it had in it, or whether he attended it day or night when it was closed and all of the lights were out. If he ever went to day school, he played hookey all of the time and never saw a book. I guess he attended when it opened, by reading the Bible and saying the catechism and then he beat it for the backwoods.

I knew they never taught the A B C's in "the old school," for if they had he'd known something. If you told him the name of a letter, when he got up, he forgot it before he could eat his breakfast. He wasn't so dumb either, because if you owed him any money, he never missed the day, hour and minute in coming for it, or failed to get his "tea" before meals. He was on the dot there! It was just as easy to find any sense in his head as to find a needle in a haystack. The only thing that seemed to stay in his head was whiskey and Uncle Ben said it would remain there forever. But, thank the Lord, the prayers of the righteous got him at last and he never touched a drop after that. He also learned to read and write and helped Uncle Ben in "bassing" the choir which Aunt Mary led.

Everybody was glad when he got religion and swore off and lived like Lincoln, who never touched a drop. They say he got on the temperance band wagon. If he did, it never came down E Street with him tooting his horn.

Uncle Buck became a real religious crank, and when he went to a revival meeting with Uncle Ben, I heard that he acted as an "exhorter," and I just knew from that old foghorn voice of his that he certainly must have put "rousements" in the people, and made them go crazy with the Holy Ghost, and when he got up before the sinners and began to tell his experiences, and what a rascal he had been, and how God had saved him from the Devil and Hell, all the saints and sinners went wild. I can see him running from one side of the mourners' bench to the other making a funny noise like he was strangling, and jumping and clapping his big hands, and I can see all of the congregation shouting and clapping hands and screaming when some wayward brother had been converted by Uncle Ben and his "exhorter" Uncle Buck.

Somebody said that Uncle Buck went back down in the country, and became a local preacher himself, just as Uncle Ben was.

AUNT MARY DINES, THE CONTRABAND SINGER

Her Stories of Lincoln's Visits to the Contraband Camp—
Their Exercises for Him and
His Part in Them

You notice that I haven't said much about Aunt Mary Dines' people because she was so sweet that, like dessert, I am taking her and her family last.

Her husband and Minnie and her own Ben lived with old Dr. Morgan. Mr. Dines was the butler and drove the doctor around to see his patients. He really was so smart that when he once came to a patient's home, he kept the place in his mind, like an old fox his den, and knew just where to go to each house. Old Dr. Morgan just had to say "Take me to call on . . ." Grandmother said he would just look into his book of memory and go there. Now I call that real education. He must have gone to a different school than Uncle Buck, who was a member of "the old school" and was as dumb as an oyster and could keep his mouth shut as a clam.

I never knew what got into little Ben's head and made him so slow when anybody told him to do anything. He moved just like molasses in the winter time. He certainly did not take after anybody in his family. Aunt Mary Dines used to say he was the "old Devil himself," for he was so stubborn that if he wanted to go anywhere and thought about it, he just wouldn't go!

81

But he was "tops" when he put on his soldier's suit and acted as mascot for the National Rifles, for then he could keep step and outmarch everyone.

For many years after we moved from E Street, Grandmother always kept in touch with her old friends. Sometimes we went to see them and at other times they came to see us, until the very last of the old crowd, for one reason or another, stopped, or died.

Aunt Mary Dines was the very last one who used to come regularly as long as she could, and when she became blind, she entered a charitable institution, there to pass away the remaining days of her life.

We often went to see her, and on one occasion I determined to have her tell me the complete story of her life, all about the contraband camps where she had lived, and then to repeat the story of Lincoln's visits to the camp where she was the leader of the songs.

Although blind as a bat, her memory was as clear as crystal, and because of her active life in this camp, she had known everybody and could tell everything that had ever happened in her lifetime. I think because she had nothing to do but sit all day and hold her hands she amused herself by recalling incidents of the days gone by, but not forgotten. Aunt Mary Dines and my Grandmother were born in Prince George's County, Maryland, on a farm belonging to a wealthy bachelor. This man was so fond of his slaves that he never permitted one to be whipped, and when he died all were given their freedom by his will, and a share of his estate. His relatives who never came near him, had his will set aside easily and the slaves were ordered sold, but by court decree none could be sold outside of the State of Maryland.

My Grandmother was sold and sent to Anne Arundel County near Annapolis, and Aunt Mary was sold and carried into Charles County in southern Maryland, to a home where she was compelled to work very hard at house work and attend several children. Although she was a staunch Methodist by birth and knew all of the old hymns, her new owners, who were Catholics, sent her to their Sunday school and Church and there she learned to read the Bible and the Catechism. The little white children taught her to write.

The new owners determined to break the independent spirit of this slave girl who had enjoyed every liberty given to her by her former owner. Consequently she was whipped severely quite often, but whippings did no good, and made her more determined than ever to learn all she could, and some day, with the knowledge gained, she hoped to run away to Washington and be free.

Once, after a severe flogging, Mary came across an old newspaper describing a trip to Washington, where she had gone once with her mistress and the children on a shopping tour. She was determined, as soon as possible, to escape and obtain her freedom. By the light of the following moon she made her getaway, and traveling for many nights with the aid of friendly slaves, she arrived on the Maryland side of the Eastern Branch near the old Navy Yard Bridge. Here she met a hay-wagon going to town and she was hidden in the straw and carried to an old stable in an alley on Capitol Hill. This was one of the stations of the Underground Railroad and the hay-wagon was a "pick-up" wagon. The people who had these stations provided for the runaways until they could get to another place near free territory, although in Washington when once an ex-slave was put with a colored family he lived as a free man.

Here she remained for a few days, then went to live on the "Island" with some colored people and worked for them for a little pay and keep. When the war broke out she went to live in an old Contraband Camp off 7th

Street, near where Howard University now stands. The contrabands often lived in the old wooden barracks constructed
for the soldiers. When the soldiers would change from these
places, or the army would move away, the colored people
would move in.

Contraband camps were all around the city limits, but efforts
were made to gather them into schools by the American Tract
Society of New York as early as March, 1862. Duff Green's Row
on Capitol Hill was then crowded with this class of people, as
contraband material of war. They were taught with printed cards,
having on them verses of Scripture in large letters, and by using
the *word method* which was very successful, they were able, to
their great delight, to read whole verses in a very short time.
Mary followed this system and became a teacher for older folks.
Because of her training and her wonderful voice and knowledge
of hymns, she became the leading soprano singer of the camp,
and also the principal letter writer for the ignorant old folks.

These camps were crowded with visitors nearly every evening and especially on Sundays. Many white and colored folks
came to teach reading, the Bible, sewing, and various branches
of knowledge so necessary for them to know in order to adjust
themselves to the new methods of living. But most came to
listen to these people sing and pray and thank God for their
deliverance from bondage. Mrs. Lincoln contributed money
and sent gifts to the older people.

Not only citizens of Washington but members of the
Cabinet and their families often came to help, and according to Aunt Mary Dines, President Lincoln stopped
many times to visit and talk to them on his way to the
Soldiers' Home. He was very fond of the hymns of the
slaves and loved to hear them and even knew most of

Mrs. Elizabeth Keckley when she first went to the White House to sew for Mrs. Lincoln. Photo courtesy of Mrs. Alberta Lewis-Savoy, godchild of Mrs. Keckley.

Contrabands waiting to sing for President Lincoln. Aunt Mary Dines, who gave the photograph to the author, told how the photographer, Matthew Brady, came in a little wagon to the Contraband Camp and took the picture.

them by heart. Aunt Mary told me many stories, but the following was her prized one.

One Saturday morning, the sergeant in charge of the contrabands sounded the bugle for all to assemble. He told them that President Lincoln was coming out with some friends to visit them and wanted to hear them sing, and that everything should be in apple-pie order and gave them time to practice their pieces. Aunt Mary said the thought of singing before the President nearly killed her. All of the people dressed in their best clothes, some of which were gathered from the battlefield. Some men and boys had on soldiers' castoff blue uniforms and some had on old rebel uniforms they had picked up after the rebels had been driven away by the Yankees.

The old folks always sat together on one side of the meeting place. When all was ready, a picture man drove out with his buggy and little tent and took pictures of everybody. Presently Aunt Mary saw soldiers coming on horseback, the bugle sounded "Halt" and President Lincoln and his wife, and some more white folks, got out of their carriages, and while some sat on a little platform on the right, which the colored men had just finished decorating with flags, President Lincoln came over where the old folks were sitting and stood and watched everybody. She said Uncle Ben was a "spirit preacher," because he couldn't read a line but he just preached the gospel as God had taught him to do. He could certainly preach and pray and make everybody near him wake up when he began to moan and groan.

Uncle Ben, the oldest slave in the camp, was called on to open the meeting with prayer, and he called upon every saint in the Bible that he had heard about to bless President Lincoln and his good lady.

After he was through, all stood up and sang "My Country,

'Tis of Thee" and President Lincoln took off his hat and sang too. Aunt Mary was standing near him and heard him; she said he had a good voice. Then the commander of the camp called her aside and asked her what pieces she was going to have the people sing and to begin right away, for the President didn't intend to stay long.

Aunt Mary said she never forgot how her knees shook, as she stumbled in front of the people and opened the singing with "Nobody Knows What Trouble I See, But Jesus," always keeping one eye on the President. After the first verse, which she sang all by herself, all the colored people joined in the chorus and really sang as they never did before. To her great surprise, as she came out to call the next song, "Every Time I Feel the Spirit," she saw President Lincoln wiping the tears off his face with his bare hands. They sang for nearly an hour, and while the colored folks were singing, "I Thank God that I'm Free at Last," many of the real old folks forgot about the President being present and began to shout and yell, but he didn't laugh at them, but stood like a stone and bowed his head. She said she really believed that the Holy Ghost was working on him.

The last piece was "John Brown's Body." By this time President Lincoln must have been warmed up himself for he joined in the chorus and sang as loud as anyone there. She said he certainly had a sweet voice, and it sounded so sad, when he tried to follow her with the first tune. He really choked up once or twice.

President Lincoln returned to the camp with only a couple of orderlies on a damp, dreary evening and sent for her and said, "Well, Mary, what can the people sing for me today? I've been thinking about you all since I left here and am not feeling so well. I just want them to sing some more good old hymns for me again. Tell Uncle

Ben to pray a good old-fashioned prayer." Well, if Uncle Ben prayed the first time, he certainly did more this time, for then he was scared to death. Now he knew President Lincoln had been emotionally moved and wanted the help of God to carry on. Aunt Mary said she never heard such a prayer before. Uncle Ben just talked with God—and cried, as he begged Him to send down His loving kindness and blessings on the colored people's friend. He wanted Him to give him strength to carry the troubles of this world—and to throw around him the mantle of protection when he had finished working for the poor old folks below. He wanted the Golden Chariot, with its pale white horses, to swing low, and with companies of angels carry him to his Father above. Uncle Ben was always a praying man, but this day God must have been helping him out.

They all sang "Swing Low, Sweet Chariot," "Didn't My God Deliver Daniel?" "Go Down Moses," "I Ain't Got Weary Yet," "I've Been in the Storm So Long," "Steal Away," and they closed with "Praise God from Whom All Blessings Flow." Then Uncle Ben gave the Benediction which was as long as his sermons. Aunt Mary said that President Lincoln actually joined in singing every piece and he was so tenderhearted that he filled-up when he went over to bid the real old folks good-by.

Aunt Mary said when she gave out some words of a piece for the old folks to repeat after her, and the old people bowed in prayer, Lincoln did just like everybody else. She said he was no President when he came to camp. He just stood and sang and prayed just like all the rest of the people.

Aunt Mary said she had heard so much about President Lincoln's religion, but since she had heard him sing and pray in their camp, she just knew he was a child of God and had put his trust in Him, and that he was in Heaven if anybody else was there. A few days after the President's first visit, the old photographer, who stayed until the President left, came back and gave her the picture which she gave me shortly before she died.

I have just finished reading in a bulletin of the Abraham Lincoln Association a letter from Milton Hay to John Hay, his nephew. He had studied law in the office of Stuart and Lincoln and knew the President well. In this letter he wrote, "There were some song singers amongst us, and Lincoln was without a rival in the singing of pathetic pieces." Imagine how this quotation reminded me of the statement of Aunt Mary.

OLD AUNT PHOEBE BIAS

Her Story of the "Big Watch-Meeting" before the
Emancipation Proclamation

In recalling these old New Year's gatherings, I shall never forget the last one attended by old Aunt Phoebe Bias, before the pale horse rider carried her away to Glory.

Although she was nearly as old as old Aunt Eliza, she was nevertheless very active in spite of the fact that she was lame and bent over. The white folks for whom she worked were relatively newcomers and called themselves "F. F. V.'s." They certainly must have been the First Families of Virginia for they had nothing, and I heard lost all they had in the war.

She said that her family were slaves in Old Virginia. Once, because her husband had carelessly passed by some tobacco worms on a plant, the new master attempted to beat him. She and her son jumped into the fray and stopped him. For so doing all were severely flogged. The men were sold away down in Georgia, but she who had been severely crippled in the fight was allowed to remain on the farm since she was scarred for life and unable to do heavy work.

When General Benjamin T. Butler brought his troops into Virginia near the farm on which she lived, she just took herself up and joined his army. Soon a big boat came to his camp and carried a load of colored women to

89

Washington. She was one of them. It wasn't long before she found work with a good old Northern family and joined the Union Bethel Church on M Street.

Here is her last story told at a Watch-Meeting in our house.

During the Christmas Holidays of '62, she heard people everywhere talking about the Big Watch-Meeting to be held in her church where important white and colored men would speak about President Lincoln and the Emancipation Proclamation. She made up her mind to go.

When the last day of the old year rolled around, people from all over the city arrived early in order to get seats. She went early to get her seat on the front row, which had been reserved for the lame, aged, sick, and blind who wished to attend.

Before sundown the church was filled. To pass away the time until the services should begin at 10 o'clock, the brothers and sisters sang, prayed and spoke of their earthly experiences, just as they had done in class meetings.

Exactly at the appointed hour the pastor opened the Bible and began this memorable service with prayers, after which he preached about God, old Satan, Lincoln and the coming day of eternal freedom. After the service, a white man spoke about freedom, and the war, and then read every word in the Emancipation Proclamation from a copy which he had brought in his pocket and told them just how Lincoln had fought for it.

Now the meeting was turned over to the congregation and oh! how it sang and prayed. The very roof of the church seemed to be tumbling down.

Five minutes before 12 o'clock the minister told everybody present that he wanted no one to pray standing up with bowed head; nobody sitting down, with bended necks praying; and no brother kneeling on one knee, because his pants were too tight for him, but to get down on *both knees* to thank Almighty God for his freedom and President Lincoln too.

At first all was still as death, then as the hands on the old church clock moved toward 12, you could hear some brother or sister cry, moan or pray out loud for God to keep on guiding them when the hour of freedom came, just as He had led them out of bondage; and also they cried in loud voices for God to guide, support and strengthen the hand of the man who had brought to them their freedom.

When the city bells rang in the New Year—the year of their freedom, men and women jumped to their feet, yelled for joy, hugged and kissed each other and cried for joy. Many could not stand the excitement and fell into trances all over the house while the crowd yelled "Praise God," and kept yelling "Freed at last," "I'm so glad," "I'm freed at last," and "Before I'd be a slave I'll be carried to my grave," and many other old songs of freedom and hope. They had prayed for freedom. That night it came. One old brother who was blind as a bat yelled out aloud that he was thankful to God that he had lived to *see* the day of freedom come.

After a prolonged period of religious excitement, shouting, and singing, the pastor reminded these old people that it was really a Happy New Year. Then, suddenly, like a clap of thunder the sounds of "What a Happy New Year" rang out as it never was heard before and after singing the Doxology, the parting blessing from the pulpit was said.

Although the meeting was now over, it was such a Happy New Year for everybody, that only a few persons left this house of God until daybreak the next morning. Men and women just wept, sang and gave thanks to God Who had set them free and to old Abe Lincoln who had been the Moses who their Maker had ordered to tell the old slave owners to let his people go.

UNCLE SANDY

His Story of the Ford Theater Ghosts

I recall one of the last meetings of the old E Street people before I left the place. I had been to school for some years, could read pretty well, and was in that stage of my mental development when I took in knowledge and retained it as a sponge does water. One morning in April a newspaper carried these headlines:

LINCOLN'S ASSASSINATION RECALLED NEIGHBORS
FRIGHTENED BY HALLUCINATIONS NOISES HEARD,
LIGHTS SEEN IN FORD'S THEATER COLORED
WATCHMAN FRIGHTENED—LEAVES JOB
COLORED PEOPLE RECALL SIMILAR OCCASIONS
EACH YEAR, ETC.

Nearly every colored person on E Street bought this paper even though unable to read it. That night, all who could possibly get to our house came. Brother Thomas and Brother Dines even brought old Aunt Eliza in Dr. Morgan's carriage. Old Uncle Sandy, who cleaned up the stables in the alley, was there for the first time. He heard about the meeting and just invited himself around.

He was the funny man of the neighborhood, and came from way deep-down South. He could make you crack your sides laughing at the old tales he used to tell about the war, and how the white folks acted when they had to tell the colored people they were free. He could still do a mean buck-and-wing dance, while leaning on his cane. I don't think he had ever got religion, because Uncle Ben said "he had too much Devil in him yet to let the Savior in, and instead of getting down on his knees and praying, he would just pluck an old banjo and sing songs to the Devil all the time." When angry, Uncle Sandy certainly could deliver a sermon, in language carefully selected from the "Old Boy's" vocabulary of pet expressions.

While he had often heard and seen things, he was never so frightened as he was the night before. He asked to come around, as he was too frightened to stay home by himself. That's why this old stray black sheep was this night in the right fold.

Uncle Sandy was old too, and he didn't know exactly when he was born! All he could say was that one old Bible said he "was born in sweet potato time when old Aunt Sukey's cow Jennie had her first-born calf, which was pretty nigh the full of the moon in April" and from all that he could put together, he guessed he was round forty or fifty years old. He looked older than Uncle Ben and he just toddled along on an old hickory stick that he had brought with him from Georgia.

He was real short and inclined to be fat. I don't imagine he had had a haircut or a shave since he left the old plantation and worked his way up North with the army. He had no relatives and lived in an old deserted shack in the alley. All of the men who attended horses gave him a few pennies and tobacco, for sweeping around the stables, and kept his home in repairs for him, because from its little window he could see everything and never failed to tell them about what happened during the day.

They called him the "Watchdog of Baptist Alley," because if "cuss" words could keep a thief away, Uncle Sandy certainly had a rare collection and surely could bark them out.

After all of the old colored people, with their papers, were comfortably seated, and lemonade and some gingerbread, which we had left over from the dinner meal had been passed, Uncle Ben arose and began to read the headlines.

When Uncle Ben asked who it was who told the white newspaper men what happened last night, Uncle Sandy said he told them because it was the truth.

He said that he had lived in that alley ever since the war and had seen all kinds of things at night. Spirits had even come to his door and knocked three times, but he didn't let them in. He could guess to the minute just when Booth would be going out before daybreak—and Mrs. Lincoln, he had heard her scream often, but nothing ever happened like it did last night and he told the white men he was going to look out for another place to live.

He said, "You know how dark it was last night! Well, I heard a loud noise like thunder. I ran out into the alley and I saw lightning strike the old theater building, then it got as light as day, even the outside got light and you could see through the whole place, just as if it was made of glass. I was too scared to move and could see the people in it running about, and you could hear a woman in there screaming and crying and the crowd was raising the old dickens. Black cats filled the alley, dogs were howling and hens crowing. Then I heard men yelling, 'Get him, get him!' I couldn't move. Then I saw Booth get on a horse and come tearing at me. I really believe he hit at me with his whip, but thank God he didn't hit me. If a spirit strikes you, your face turns to the side.

"In a twinkle all was over and the place as dark as it was light before. That's all I told these men."

All looked around at each other and smiled, because they thought that Uncle Sandy was again off the water wagon and had gone on one of his sprees. He often said a little "toddy" was all that kept his soul and body together, and his pipe kept his spirits up. They told him to shut up and never tell his drunken tales to anybody.

However, their expressions soon changed when old Aunt Eliza spoke up and said what Uncle Sandy had said was the gospel truth and that she had seen it all, and more besides. She had even heard Mrs. Lincoln call for help. When she finished there was a silence and many just pressed their lips together and shook their heads from side to side. Her little attic room was very near the rear of Ford's Theater.

INTERLUDE

Slavery In The East

While talk of secession filled every home below the Mason-Dixon line, slave owners began to figure on the loyalty of their slaves to produce food and help the Confederate armies in the field, and also upon their skill in running the plantations and protecting their families.

On both sides colored servants were used by officers, and as soon as the war began slaves who ran away were welcomed into the Union army as cooks, orderlies and laborers.

There was no law to give these people their freedom or to keep them openly, but no one thought of returning them. What should be done with them? Their help was needed. General Benjamin F. Butler proposed to call them "contraband" and use them. This he did, and from time to time there was a great flocking of runaway slaves to the Union armies. The "Underground Railroad" worked more frantically than ever, and as soon as hostilities began, societies for aiding freedom were operating openly to assist the Union cause by encouraging slaves to seek freedom, and leave the fields and join the army. Bands of slaves began to follow the troops everywhere, and to care for them, and teach them how to adapt themselves to new methods of living were problems for the most learned of the Union generals.

As this account is to deal with colored people who

loved and served Lincoln, I think it necessary to review some facts concerning the Negro in the days before and during the war and the types of colored people with whom the Lincolns were surrounded in Washington and Illinois, in order that the reader may better understand what is to follow.

Slavery produced two classes of individuals, house servants and field hands. In many cases house servants were slaves in whose veins ran the blood of the owners of the plantation. Many inherited the ambition, color and particular traits of their owners. These were looked upon very kindly by the master's family. Often when the mulatto babe became large enough, the father would free it and send it North to be educated.

As a result of the above policy, even before the war was thought of, there was a class of free persons of color in the North who were educated and these formed the nucleus from which sprang the colored leaders of the Reconstruction. Most of the leading colored legislators of this period boasted of white blood in their veins. Thomas Jefferson once said, "The purest blood of Virginia runs in the veins of its slaves." The house servants being so closely connected in the family, were often loved by their white relatives, who had the women trained in first-class sewing, and the men in carpentering, blacksmithing, cooking and in nearly every trade. When freed and sent North, they became ambitious, bought homes, ran livery stables, restaurants, hotels, barber shops and some became contractors and builders.

These were the avenues generally opened to colored people before, during, and immediately after the Civil War. In Washington, many freed slaves returned from the North and with white assistance opened private schools, established churches, and formed an exclusive social set of their own.

These people were most progressive, and many bought their own freedom and that of their relatives, as well as property. They were not unmindful of the conditions of their unfortunate bondsmen in slavery.

As the war approached, more and more refugees came to Washington, and during the first years of the war, hundreds of runaway people came to Washington and remained. The older citizens organized societies to care for them and to assist them to obtain an education. Many Northern societies sent teachers to instruct and care for these "contrabands" as they were called. One of the first societies was the Contraband Relief Association organized by Mrs. Elizabeth Keckley, who was the seamstress for Mrs. Lincoln and the writer of *Behind the Scenes.* She solicited funds even from the White House, where the President's wife gave the first $200. Her organization had as its members forty of the most cultured and progressive women of her race then in Washington, who collected old garments and made them over for the poor ex-slaves. It soon became necessary to put the colored people in camps under government control. These places could be found on the outskirts of the city and free colored people visited them, to teach the contraband to read, sew and to become self-supporting. All was not work in these places, for at evening, on holidays and Sundays, scores of white people and government officials would visit them to hear their evening exercises, especially their hymns and songs. Each camp had its leader, some of whom were talented young Negroes who had escaped from slavery and could read and lead these people in singing. Some old brother generally was the leader in religious exercises. It was a common thing for a slave woman to sew until she had saved enough extra money to buy her freedom, then she would come to Washington and open an establishment. This woman would then purchase the unfortunate members of her family from their owners, give them trades, and they in turn became progressive and independent. This was done by Elizabeth Keckley who purchased the freedom of herself and son from their owner, Anne P. Garland.

In Lincoln's time, colored people were the leaders in hotel work and were trained workers, caterers, dressmakers, contractors, butlers, hackmen and mechanics. No foreign immigrants were in the field to compete with them. No doors were closed to them. All good citizens wished them luck and wanted to help them.

When Lincoln came to Washington he found that in the White House nearly every servant could trace his ancestors from slaves who had grown up as house servants. He talked freely with them and trusted them. They never betrayed his confidence in them nor did they permit themselves to be bribed to give away any secrets or information on White House affairs. "Billy the Barber" in Springfield impressed Lincoln with the possibilities of the educated colored person, and planted the seed which was to lead to the Emancipation Proclamation. In his Springfield home Lincoln had the highest respect for his servants and when he left for Washington he brought with him a young colored man, William Johnson, as valet and messenger and depended upon him for protection, more than he did on the Pinkerton Detectives, who were strangers to him.

Historians have neglected to study the lowly companions of great men, the servants, who served their masters from morn till night, who thought of their welfare every moment and who could observe them in their home, where the cares and restraints of official life are laid aside. Lincoln often sought escape by exchanging stories with his trusted messenger, William Slade of the White House, just as he did with "Billy the Barber" at

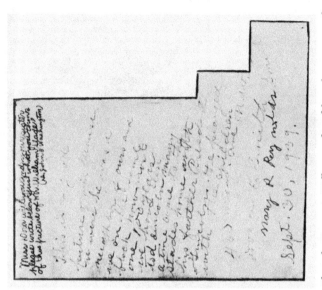

William Slade, Lincoln's confidential messenger and friend. Photo by Bruce & Hall, reproduced here by courtesy of Mrs. Mary E. Brooks, a cousin of the Slades. Testimonial regarding Slade's association with Lincoln.

Lock of Lincoln's hair, cut off after death by William Slade and given to Mrs. Mary E. Brooks. A piece of the silk dress worn by Mrs. Lincoln the night of the assassination, given to Mrs. Brooks by Mrs. Slade, and a facsimile of Robert Lincoln's signature on a verification of this. (Author's collection.) Photo of Mrs. William Slade by Bruce & Hall reproduced by courtesy of Mrs. Mary E. Brooks.

Springfield, and to some extent the valet who accompanied him from Springfield to Washington, and also with Madam Keckley the modiste, who was his wife's companion. He never treated them as servants, but always was polite and requested service, rather than demand it of them. They really knew him and loved him and protected him when necessary. Mrs. Lincoln kept no secrets from her confidential friend and dressmaker, Elizabeth Keckley. In times of stress she relied upon her more than she did on her own kinfolks.

Lincoln's views on the injustices of slavery did not all come from his visit to the slave markets in New Orleans. They were strengthened by his observation of the colored people who served him. He soon learned that these people were easily affected by environment, and with a little help would rapidly learn how to provide for themselves. They furnished an example of what freedom would accomplish and that, given the proper assistance, freedmen would become progressive, independent and self-supporting.

PART TWO

THOSE WHO SERVED LINCOLN

WILLIAM SLADE

Confidential Messenger and Friend

When I left the old E Street neighborhood and moved to the farthest part of the city, at that time North Capitol and Boundary, I attended the regular public school where all teachers were colored. Although quite small I was greatly impressed by a beautiful olive-complexioned woman who taught in the next room, but spent her lunch period in our room with my teacher. Her name was Katherine Slade, but her friends called her "Nibbie." One day while we were having Lincoln's Birthday exercises, she came into our room and gave the class a talk on her personal remembrances of Abraham Lincoln, Mrs. Lincoln, Tad and Robert Lincoln.

She said that she had even stayed many nights in the White House with her parents when storms came up and they could not get home. She and her brothers played with Tad, and he often came and played with them in their home on Massachusetts Avenue, between 4th and 6th Streets, N. W. She told many stories to our class, each one of which seemed to me more wonderful than the preceding. Now I had actually seen a person who had known Lincoln and his family and who had slept in the White House.

Miss Slade spoke about her father and mother and what they did for the Lincolns; she showed many souvenirs that Mrs. Lincoln had given her mother and then passed them around for the children actually to handle them. I well remember, even now, the fan and the handkerchief she said Mrs. Lincoln carried at a reception and later gave to her mother. When I was transferred from this school to the high school I forgot everything about Miss "Nibbie" Slade. But this break in my experiences was not destined to be forever. Many years later when I became a teacher myself, I was sent to the building where Miss Slade was teaching and my room adjoined hers.

She recalled me as "the little boy on E Street," and we soon became the best of friends. I spent most of my spare time with her, getting stories about her parents and the Lincolns. When I reminded her of the fan and handkerchief and other souvenirs of Mrs. Lincoln she said in moving around from place to place all had been lost. I wanted to know all I could about her father and Lincoln and asked questions by the score. She was always pleasant and when I told her that some day I planned to write a book on Lincoln, she talked freely, and told me many, many things, some of which I fail to recall. But the main ones I shall never forget because when I returned from school, I jotted most of them down on scraps of paper, some of which I lost, but fortunately the most important ones were preserved in an old scrapbook that my Grandmother made for me, before I went to any school and lived on E Street.

I remember especially how Miss Slade looked when she told me about Mrs. Lincoln's surprise when she first inspected the clan of White House servants. They looked so different and behaved so different from those she had been accustomed to in her little Springfield home. Many of the White House employees were held over and were experts in rendering the services that a presidential party demanded.

She said Mrs. Lincoln had no trouble in training them, for they knew better than she, what was to be done, how it should be done, and why it should be done.

Mrs. Lincoln soon found out that as a President's wife with problems of her own and her husband's on her hands, she was fortunate in having servants of the type she found when she became the mistress of the White House.

In the days of Lincoln and for many years afterward, the butler or steward was really the man who looked after everything in the servant line and the kitchen. The employer would give him instructions and often open a bank account in his name for table supplies and servant salaries and thus relieve himself of as many details as possible. In other cases, all the employer would do would be to sign the checks himself without any questions. I never heard of Lincoln doing this, however.

The colored people who worked in the White House were considered the cream of Washington's colored society and were the recognized leaders in church, fraternal and social organizations. Nearly all were members of the 15th Street Presbyterian Church, one of the leading colored churches of the day. These servants were so clannish that they even boycotted new employees; for they were jealous and fearful of their jobs when a new President took office.

The servant holding the highest rank was Miss Slade's father, William Slade—commonly called "William" by the President. He was really a confidential and constant companion and was treated by Lincoln with the greatest intimacy. Slade did not fear the President and often, according to Miss Slade's testimony, her father and President Lincoln would talk sometimes nearly all night about matters of grave concern. Lincoln just had to have somebody to loosen up on and in Slade he found the right person.

Slade was a Virginian of distinguished Southern ancestry and his wife, who was equally fair, was a Virginian also. They were old citizens of the District of Columbia but had left just before the war and went to Ohio. But as soon as the war started they came back to Washington, to their home at 464 Massachusetts Ave., N. W., where they kept a boarding-house and Slade went to the White House as steward.

He was of medium height, olive in complexion, with light eyes and straight chestnut-brown hair, and wore a little goatee. He had a wonderful disposition, never became excited, always could see the bright side of things, even when Lincoln was downcast and needed a cheering, hopeful friend. Slade was a great story teller. He was known for his collection of jokes and wisecracks, and I have often heard it said that "he had some that could make a horse laugh." Not only did Slade serve as confidential messenger for the Lincoln family, but he also acted as valet for the President, took complete charge of the colored help, made arrangements for all public and private functions (from the standpoint of food and serving), kept a set of keys of the White House and knew every diplomat, general, and statesman. He had his own private room, bought all of the food and at evenings when the Lincolns had only a few friends to dinner or a party, he would plan and assist the waiter in serving them. Being a caterer himself he often made special dishes for these occasions. Week in, week out, from morn till night, his services were in constant demand by his employer.

Many times when Slade had had the opportunity of spending his nights at home with his family, he would put his three children—Katherine (Nibbie), Andrew, and

Jessie in his carriage (which he used in traveling back and forth to the White House and also for taking him from place to place with the messages of President Lincoln) and take them to the White House where they would spend the entire day playing with Tad in the basement, in the White House grounds, or in any other part of the house that the little son of the President wanted to use.

These colored children became Tad's closest playmates and often when they had not been to the White House for some time, Tad would suddenly manifest such a strong desire to see them that he became unruly and Lincoln just had to stop what he was doing and take him to the Slade home, and leave him there to spend the entire day with the children and their playmates on Massachusetts Avenue. Two of the survivors of the Slade neighborhood, now living—Miss Dora Smith and her sister—said that Tad played with all the children and he was a real boy in the midst of real boys and girls, white and colored.

Lincoln's visits to this place were many. In front of the old Slade house, on Massachusetts Avenue, N. W., there stood an old iron figure on the side of a brownstone step. The horse was fastened to the holder and the occupant of the carriage alighted on this step. When the street was re-graded in 1873 this carriage block was covered over with dirt and is still hidden under the sidewalk.

When President Lincoln was shot April 14, 1865, Slade was at home, and because of the great crowd he was not able to get into the Petersen house to render whatever assistance he could to his dying friend. The next morning on visiting the Petersen house and being informed that the end was near and that he could do nothing, he returned to the White House knowing that much had to be done there.

Soon after Lincoln died at 7:22 in the morning, the body was taken to the White House.

Slade had everything ready, including garments for clothing the body. The suit worn by Lincoln at his last inaugural was selected. As valet and steward, it was Slade's duty and privilege to serve his employer to the last. After he had finished washing and dressing the remains and being present during the final trimming of the hair, he clipped off a lock for himself and family.

Later on it was given to his cousin John H. Brooks, steward both to Admiral Dahlgren and Admiral Farragut. Brooks also knew Lincoln and had served him many times when he visited Admiral Dahlgren at the Navy Yard. This lock of hair and a piece of Mrs. Lincoln's bloodstained dress were given to me by Brooks' daughter, Mamie, because of my long friendship with her family.

Josephine, the wife of William Slade, was a close companion of Mrs. Lincoln's and greatly loved by her. The day following the assassination, Mrs. Lincoln directed Mrs. Keckley to give to Mrs. Slade the bloodstained dress she wore on that occasion. Mrs. Keckley tells of this in her book *Behind the Scenes.*

Mrs. Slade gave pieces of the dress to various friends. In 1916, I obtained my first piece from the daughter of a friend of Lincoln's and recently, with a lock of hair, I received a second piece from the Brooks family.

Slade, who was never known to lose his temper, kept the closest mouth on all public affairs and would never discuss any of Lincoln's plans or business with anyone, although he knew much from being in contact with him day and night as his constant companion.

He never complained of long hours, even though after a strenuous day he would have to sit up all night and talk with the President, who suffered with insomnia and just had to have somebody, in whom he could confide, near him to listen to his jokes, stories and talk.

Lincoln needed not Slade's advice and I doubt whether he was swayed by it, but he did need a human comforter, a sincere friend in whose bosom he knew his secrets would rest sacred and inviolate.

To show how real was Lincoln's insomnia and desire for a comforting friend, I quote from an article in the *Washington Evening Star* in 1935.

> Lincoln's pastor in the dark days of the '60's became not merely his friend, but his confidant and his solace. Nights when the President was tortured by insomnia and these were many indeed, he sometimes sent his *servant* for Dr. Gurley and the two men would walk up and down the south portico until dawn.

Miss "Nibbie" Slade often claimed that her father sometimes knew about the President's plans before his secretaries did. Her father said that Lincoln had a peculiar manner of doing things. Often while reading or sitting alone, he would tear off a little piece of paper and write something on it and put it away in his desk, or in his vest or pants pockets, and continue his reading. Often Slade discovered these precious pieces of paper and saved them for the President.

Miss Slade asserted that Lincoln frequently would talk with her father about slavery and his emancipation plans, and that long before anyone else knew about the Emancipation Proclamation, her father had destroyed many old pieces of paper with notes upon them, and that when the final draft was written, Slade already knew every word of it. She said Lincoln would go over all of his speeches and proclamations, before he gave them out officially, and that her father had often stated how careful the President was and how much pains he took with all his papers.

Many years ago Miss Slade told the following story of the Gettysburg Address. It was the custom of the day to have the colored valet or messenger with his employer at all times to render every assistance, both in the home and on public occasions.

Whenever Lincoln went away from Washington, Slade went with him, and Mrs. Keckley often went with Mrs. Lincoln. One was to the President just what the other was to his wife—a sincere, loyal companion.

When the Presidential party arrived at Gettysburg, Pa., November 18, 1863, for the dedication services of the National Cemetery, that night Lincoln kept Slade with him at the Wills House to render any assistance he might need.

After receiving instructions as to what he was expected to say when his time came to speak at the dedication ceremony, the President locked himself in his room with only Slade present. He then began carefully to weigh every thought and carve every word in the address which has become so famous. After writing a sentence or so he would pause, and read the piece to Slade. He would then say, "William, how does that sound?" Slade, who by this time was quite a critic, would express his opinion. This went on until all was completed and the President then sent for his secretary and others to hear it. Having received the praise and criticism of his messenger Lincoln felt that even the most ordinary person would understand his speech.

Recently, I found a program of the 75th anniversary of the Battle of Gettysburg by Mr. H. E. Luhrs of the Lincoln Library, Shippenburg, Pa. In it I found a reproduction of a statement by Judge Wills on the writing of this address which, in part, bears out the statement of Miss "Nibbie" Slade.

THE GETTYSBURG ADDRESS, NOVEMBER 18–19, 1863

STATEMENT GIVEN BY JUDGE WILLS TO CHARLES M. MCCURDY, ABOUT 1890

I was President of the Soldiers' National Cemetery Association at Gettysburg, having organized the Association in July 1863, shortly after the Battle.

I had charge of all the arrangements for the dedication of the Cemetery, and it was on my official invitation that President Lincoln came to Gettysburg on that occasion. Edward Everett, who had been selected to deliver the oration, preceded the President several days, and was my guest. I also invited the President to my house and he arrived there on the evening of the 18th of November, 1863. After spending part of the evening in the parlors he retired to his room. He had his colored servant, William, with him. Between nine and ten o'clock the President sent his servant to request me to come to his room. I went and found him with paper prepared to write, and he said that he had just seated himself to put upon paper a few thoughts for the to-morrow exercises, and had sent for me to ascertain what part he was to take in them, and what was expected of him. After a full talk on the subject I left him.

Another of Miss Slade's recollections was that her father often told people that the day when the final vote on the 13th Amendment was to be taken, Lincoln, who was usually as cool as a cucumber, was excited as could be, kept in close contact with Congress every moment, and walked the floor, for he was determined that the passage should take place and the final stamp of approval upon the freedom of the colored people should become a part of the Constitution. Slade rode back and forth to Congress with all kinds of letters.

Three times the 13th Amendment had been successfully reported out of committee, but on two occasions Congress had rejected it for one reason or another. Lincoln then took the reins into his own hands, called, one by one, the politicians and leaders to his office and demanded a superhuman effort to force the passage of the bill that would give real freedom to every black man in the United States. That night, said Miss Slade, Lincoln slept as never before. He had accomplished his task.

Slade died March 16, 1868, having resided in the District of Columbia twenty-six years.

Slade was "very saving" and accumulated considerable property. He left $1481 in personal goods besides stock in the Columbia Harmony Association, Washington, D. C. His will was dated March 5, 1865, and filed March 24, 1868. A post-mortem held March 18, 1868, showed that his heart had swelled to three times its natural size, weighing 38 ounces. It was also found to have burst in three parts. His doctors gave heart disease and dropsy as the cause of his death.

His age was given as 53 years and 7 months and his birthday November 17, 1814, appeared on the transcript of death: Health Department, District of Columbia. He was considered older than this by everybody. The funeral caused quite an amount of excitement in the neighborhood because of the distinguished people who attended it.

The account of his funeral in the *Daily Morning Chronicle,* Washington, D. C., Thursday, March 19, 1868, is here given in full:

THE DAILY CHRONICLE

Thursday, March 19, 1868

Funeral of the late William Slade . . .

The funeral of the late William Slade, steward of the Executive Mansion, took place yesterday afternoon, from his late residence on Massachusetts Avenue between 4th and 5th Streets.

A very large number of persons were in attendance, among whom were President Johnson, Mayor Wallach, J. Sayles Brown, Dr. Blade, Mrs. Patterson and Mrs. Stover, the President's daughters. The corpse was encased in a yellow pine coffin, perfectly plain and covered with black cloth. Upon the coffin were laid several wreaths and crosses of beautiful flowers, some of which were brought by the President's family. The services were conducted by Rev. Byron Sunderland, assisted by Messrs. Emroy Tuston and Butler. Rev. L. Grimes of Boston and Rev. Muse of this city (colored) were also present. Messrs. Donhane, Turner (white) Louis Crust and J. T. Johnson (colored) acted as pall-bearers. The remains were conveyed to Harmonial Cemetery near Glenwood. A large number of personal friends of the deceased in addition to the family followed the remains to the grave. The old Harmonial Society of which the deceased was treasurer and of whom there are now but five (5) members were also in attendance at the funeral.

Slade had the philosophy of a Plato, coupled with the wit of an Irishman, and the love of a Negro to serve his employer, which was really a devotion. Slade did not keep all of his stories for Lincoln, but whenever he and Frederick Douglass met, he was prepared to tell a new one.

The following was told me by Mr. Haley G. Douglass,

grandson of Frederick Douglass. He said his grandfather often told it before audiences.

In Lincoln's day, colored people were not allowed to come into the White House and even Frederick Douglass who had been invited to come to a reception was refused admission until Lincoln saw him in the crowd, sent for him and welcomed him into the room.

It was the custom of Lincoln to sit at the window while reading a book or paper and occasionally gaze out of it. One evening, Lincoln called his messenger and said, "William, who is that old colored man outside with an empty basket on his arm? I have noticed him for some days, as he comes regularly, and leaves with the empty basket. Go downstairs, get him and bring him up here to see me." The command of the President was instantly obeyed and in a few minutes the old man was hobbling into the presence of his Emancipator. Embarrassed and too full of emotion to speak a single word, he endeavored to say "Good evening," but just could not get it all out.

Realizing the nervousness of the poor old man, as he was trying to get himself together, Lincoln said,

"Well Uncle, I've seen you coming here for several days with your empty basket and then in a few minutes you go away. I've waited to see if you would come again and if you did I intended to send for you to learn your story. What can I do for you?"

"Thank you, sir," he said. "You know Mr. Lincoln, I heard that you had the Constitution here and how it has *provisions* in it. Well, as we are hungry and have nothing to eat in my house, I just thought I'd come around and get mine."

After a hearty laugh Lincoln told Slade to carry him downstairs to the kitchen and fill his basket. The grateful old fellow departed bowing low with gratitude and thanking God, and Lincoln too.

No one added so much to my knowledge of Lincoln as Miss Slade. She lived the latter part of her life with relatives and friends, either in the square to the right of my home or the one to the left. During the long and intimate years, she was always ready to tell me about her parents and her own personal experiences with the Lincolns. She contributed the most to making me an ardent Lincoln enthusiast and even now when I visit the hallowed spots in the old Harmony Cemetery where forever rest the Slades, Johnsons, Brooks, Mrs. Keckley and Aunt Eliza Thomas and most of the people who knew and served Lincoln, I never fail to bow my head in remembrance of this wonderful woman who outlived all of the rest and to whom we are indebted for knowledge of the intimate life of a man so little understood—the Emancipator, Lincoln.

AUNT ROSETTA WELLS

White House Seamstress

Sis Dines and Sis Wells certainly were smart for they knew more than all the books put together about Lincoln, because both had seen and talked with him and "seeing is believing." (Uncle Ben told me this many times.)

I shall never forget that Aunt Wells often told everybody about the man who was the waiter in the White House and that he said Lincoln could eat as much ham and cabbage as any man who dug in the dirt. He ate cornbread too, and wasn't ashamed to own it, even if he was President of the whole United States. Then she spoke about the woman who cooked his victuals and the man (this was William Slade) who bossed all the help and let his children play with Taddie and stay with him sometimes, day and night.

Out in the country where Lincoln came from, she said there was a man who used to cut Lincoln's hair off, and beat him telling fish stories and knew more jokes than you could shake a stick at. He had a shop for the boys to hang around and listen to "Old Abe" tell jokes. This man was honest too, and he saved his pennies to make dollars. I always wanted to hear about him myself—but nobody knew his name.

(This was William de Fleurville, known as "Billy the Barber.")

CORNELIA MITCHELL

White House Cook

Upon the arrival of the President and Mrs. Lincoln at the White House, Mrs. Lincoln's first attention was directed to the selection of a first-class cook who could not only prepare the plain ordinary cooking demanded by the President, but also the choicest dishes, which she desired should be served her guests at receptions. She was a stickler for good food.

In Cornelia Mitchell, who was already employed in the White House as cook, she found the ideal person she sought.

Her meals were always well cooked, and good enough to be set before a king. She lived in the servant quarters with her children; and her oldest daughter was allowed to receive her company there.

This information was related to me by the daughter's beau whom I located in 1940.

Cornelia was cultured and of a splendid old Southern family background. She was well educated for a colored girl of her day, and could prepare any dish from "old corn pone and cabbage" so much liked by President Lincoln, to the finest dishes with lobster and terrapin. She was noted as one of the best cooks in the District, and the many private dishes she prepared made Mrs. Lincoln's receptions the envy of Washington's official and diplomatic entertainers. It is said that Mrs. Lincoln could put on her apron and cook as well as Cornelia herself.

In the Civil War and Reconstruction days nearly all food for receptions was prepared in the homes of the host and hostess, and each one would vie with the other in serving elaborate menus. Those were the days of big receptions and dinner parties. Elaborate homes were close together and getting from one to another was not very difficult even by horse and buggy.

Mrs. Lincoln ran the White House and was all over the kitchen. She was a wonderful hostess. The desire to excel in her entertainment was considered one of the reasons why she accumulated such a debt while in the White House.

Whenever entertainment became too strenuous for the ordinary colored servants to handle, extra waiters, cooks and help were hired from among the colored men who worked for other officials and knew just how to handle things under the direction of the White House cook, and the messenger, who acted as steward on all occasions.

Nearly every distinguished family in Washington had colored servants, butlers and cooks and entertained lavishly. White servants and cooks came later. This was probably due to the fact that Washington was considered a Southern city and held to the old ideals that good old Southern colored cooks were best. Many of them could not read or write a line, but their dishes were in demand by the most fastidious and their recipes were handed down from their mothers and fathers, who had been trained before them in the trades they were to follow. Cook-book recipes for French dishes were not so much in demand but, if necessary, they could be obtained from Jim Wormley's Hotel which was then located on the corner of 15th and H Streets, N. W., and had as its patrons the leading members of the Congressional society including Charles Sumner who considered Wormley his friend and confidant.

PETER BROWN

Butler and Waiter at the White House

Francis Wells' mother, who did plain sewing for the Lincoln family in the White House, never tired of talking about Peter Brown, the butler. She, too, had her collection of old pictures and newspaper clippings about Lincoln and her friends. I was so delighted when I found the following one clipped from the *Washington Evening Star,* February 12, 1928, that I obtained permission from that paper to reproduce it.

Peter Brown, the subject of the article, was butler and waiter in the White House during the Lincoln administration. He knew Lincoln well and waited upon the table at all meals. He was a keen observer of Lincoln's actions, and was often called upon to relate some of the little incidents that happened in private. Brown's son Robert often came to visit him and at these times played with the children of the White House, just as did the Slade children.

The article tells a story that is of great importance for it shows how closely Lincoln was observed by the servants who served him and also how familiar he was with them and their children.

(Washington Evening Star—Peter
Brown—Butler and Waiter)
(Former Slave's Testimony)

Robert S. Brown, of 1435 N Street, is a son of the late Peter Brown, who served as butler at the White House through the Buchanan administration and the first part of the incumbency of Andrew Johnson. Brown will be 78 years old April 25, having been born April 25, 1850, at Rectortown, Fauquier County, Va. He is not a talkative man and he enjoys a reputation for veracity; further, his mind is perfectly clear on the things he relates. As a Washington bootblack he won the confidence of notables in public life, particularly President Grant, whose recommendation of him was sufficient to gain him the position of coachman to President Garfield. He lived temperately, saved his money and bought a house and lot at 506 Forty-seventh Street. Yesterday he came to the business section to get his rent. Seated in the realty office of Charles S. Muir, son of the late Rev. J. J. Muir, chaplain of the United States Senate, at 1403 New York Avenue, he recalled those stirring times, in very good Washington dialect.

Now let the grizzled witness, a former slave, who had some acquaintance with President Lincoln, relate his own narrative.

Brown's Statement

My father was born a slave and became the property of Ed. Turner of Fauquier County, Va., he said. I was born at Rectortown, nearby, and was owned by Conrad B. Kincheloe, the master of the Glascock family of Virginia. Their son, Mr. James M. Kincheloe, is a loan broker in the Franklin National Bank Building in this city.

In our neighborhood there was some talk about setting the slaves free several years before the Civil War, and Mr. Priest, an Englishman engaged in conducting an "underground railroad" for smuggling slaves out of the South into the North, advised Mr. Martin and Mr. Kincheloe to let our family go, saying, "They will probably go to Washington like many of the colored people who look on that place as their heaven; when they get tired of it up there you can take them back, and they will be in the notion to stay." So they let us go, and helped us off.

Mr. Turner had been a supporter of Mr. Buchanan in his race for the presidency, and was in a position to drive a bargain or two. He kept a string tied to my father by having Mr. Buchanan appoint him butler at the White House, and, everything arranged, Mr. Buchanan agreed that my father's pay in cash should go to my former master in Virginia. I don't know the details, but they made the arrangement, and left it so my father would have upkeep for himself and family. The butler was expected to eat at the White House, and now and then some other member of the family did too. I will say that those who worked around the White House received more pay than they do now, but why that is I am unable to explain.

My parents lived first in Alexandria, where I saw coming down the road one day in a fine carriage Gen. Robert E. Lee of Arlington. He never knew I used to ride with him, because I was behind, but other people did. If I didn't ride the Lee coach it was because the driver whipped up the horses.

After five months we removed from Alexandria and went to live in a house on Twelfth Street between G and H Streets in Washington. While my father was butlering at the White House I started shining shoes around the Treasury Building, and now and then ranged elsewhere. I met lots of big men in this way—Congressmen, members of the Supreme Court, Cabinet Ministers, heads of Government Departments and natives of Washington. I used to shine around the White House, hoping Mr. Lincoln would call me, but somebody was shining his shoes and boots inside. So not long after the inauguration in March 1861, my father took me to the White House to see Abraham Lincoln. We found him in his office.

My father said, "Mr. Lincoln, I want you to see my boy."

Mr. Lincoln pulled himself to his feet, and said, "He's a handsome boy all right." Then he put his big right hand on my bare head and rubbed it over my scalp. Lord, but he made me mad; I wanted to hit him so I ducked away. I suppose I was surprised, because what the mistress did, when she wanted to punish me, was to lay a hickory across my back.

I made myself at home around the kitchen and the butler's pantry, running errands and carrying things back and forth. At this time I was eleven years old, nine years younger than

Robert T. Lincoln, and two or three years older than Tad, the youngest son, and I guess about the same age as Willie.

Robert went away to college, so I didn't see much of him except when he returned home in summer, but Tad was there all the time and kept everybody on the move, including his father. Willie was a great favorite with his family; he was quieter than the other two and died about the middle of the war. Robert was what you would call rough and ready for anything, but Tad could follow his pace.

The boys had a regular menagerie in the rear of the White House ground. Among the animals were donkeys, horses and goats, and of course bird pets came to them from everywhere. Some kind of riding tournament was always going on, and then there were sufficient animals to play circus whenever we took the notion.

The animals were supposed to be kept locked up by the hostler, but they managed to get out and roam at will about the inclosure, and they just ruined the flowers and kept the gardener distracted. They also rode the donkeys and ponies in wet weather, and just tracked up everything. Tad often drove his team of goats through the White House, and didn't care what else he did. There was no color line there; the bootblacks and other colored boys who came and peeped through the fence were invited in. Now and then we got too noisy for the cook, the hostler and the gardener, and Mr. and Mrs. Lincoln who came out to see what we were up to gave us nice presents. Tad was a liberal-hearted boy and would give away everything if he had not been stopped.

Mrs. Lincoln enjoyed fixing up for company, but the President did not like crowds so much—when he had time from official business he used to pace up and down the halls in deep thought, or he would sit for hours reading a book.

"How did Mr. Lincoln impress you personally?" he was asked. "He was a kindly tolerant man, wasn't he?"

"Yes, sir, he was kind to everybody. I never heard him speak unkindly of anyone or get out of patience. He just moved along about the same each day."

"Certain persons have circulated the report that he was careless in his personal habits. Did you ever see him walk around in his silk socks or put his feet up on the mantelpiece?"

"No-sir. I never did. When he reached the front door he took off his hat and cape and quietly handed them to my father just like any other gentleman. He was never noisy in his conversation, but he enjoyed telling jokes, and now and then he would break out into a laugh. He had a lot on him in those days."

"You heard many absurd stories, outside, about things that never happened over there, didn't you?"

"Yes, sir. People have to have something to talk about."

"Did he appear sad and downcast over the war?"

"Not that I could notice, though I suppose he had other thoughts when he was alone in his room."

"Mr. Lincoln wasn't exactly the kind of a man you best remembered from Virginia, was he?"

"No, sir. He was a poor man who learned to work hard as a boy. He knew all about life and the struggles of the unfortunate. That was why he sympathized with us colored folks, and we loved him."

"Was he a heavy eater? What dish did he like best? Did he like fancy foods?"

Brown chuckled as he ran his fingers over the iron-gray stubble on his chin:

"Fancy foods for Abraham Lincoln? No, siree. He was old fashioned about that. He liked cabbage nearly every day. He wasn't a big eater or little, just moderate. I would say he had a good appetite and digestion."

"He was the kind of a man who, if he went down South, would pass up the asparagus tips and braised beef and call for a fat 'possum?"

"That's it, you hit it right. With some yellow yams, of course. And he liked potatoes too."

"Tell about some conversation you had with him."

"Well, sir, I remembered once a meeting with him in the hall, when he called out to me, and says, 'Peter, are you hungry?' Peter was the name he gave me, after my father, though my real name was Robert. Says I, 'Always, Mr. Lincoln.'

"'Well, that's a terrible state for a growing boy to be in. We'll have to see about that!'

"He told my father to come there and said to him, 'Peter, I want you to feed this boy. He looks hungry and admits it.

Fill up his legs too, if he is like my boys, his legs are hollow.'
I didn't need a second invitation to enter the White House pantry.
Tad and I had been there before, as we said, looking for mice."

"Where were you on the night of the assassination?"

"I was home on 12th Street, between G and H about three
or four blocks from Ford's. It was about half past ten, and I was
taking off my clothes to go to bed. My father had just left the
house saying he had orders to return to the Executive Mansion
about eleven and help with a supper they intended to have, and
he would be back when he could but he didn't say what time. He
went out and I was just ready to crawl into bed when I heard a big
commotion in the street, men running this way and that, people
shouting, military giving orders, horses dashing by. When I stuck
my head out the door someone ran up saying Mr. Lincoln was
shot at the theater. My mother pulled me back in the house and
made me stay in bed. She said it was dangerous to be out and we
should stay in. We kept awake till my father returned and told
us of the excitement over at the White House. He stayed over
there trying to comfort Tad, but after putting him to bed there
wasn't anything he could do, so he locked up after awhile and
came home. Then I fell asleep."

"Who was to have made up the party over at the White
House?"

"That I couldn't say. My father just said they were to have
some kind of supper after the performance, and he was needed
there."

"How many were invited?"

"That I don't know, sir. You see, my father wasn't the steward,
otherwise he would have known how many. He only helped wait
on the table in emergencies, and I can't say whether he was to do
table duty that night."

"Were the guests coming from Ford's Theater with the
Lincolns or from elsewhere?"

"That, sir, is beyond me."

WILLIAM JOHNSON

Lincoln's First Bodyguard

In my desire to follow every avenue that might lead to information regarding those who served Lincoln I visited the Lincoln National Life Foundation at Fort Wayne, Indiana, where I met the Director, Dr. Louis A. Warren, who is also the editor of *Lincoln Lore*. The day was spent examining one of the greatest collections of Lincolniana. Among many items of interest, Dr. Warren showed me a letter from Lincoln to Secretary of the Navy, Gideon Welles, requesting him to appoint one WILLIAM JOHNSON to some position, if possible.

I had not heard of Johnson before, so, starting with this clue I was able, after much research, to uncover the story of WILLIAM JOHNSON, the first bodyguard of Lincoln.

When it was decided to have the Lincoln family make the trip through Baltimore, and Lincoln himself come directly and secretly to Washington from Harrisburg, William Johnson was the only person from his home that he selected to accompany him and be ready for any emergency. An illustration, published in the *Evening Star* of Washington, shows Lincoln arriving in Washington accompanied by a colored man and the detectives.

Lincoln decided to have Johnson continue his services at the White House, attending to his wardrobe, shaving him and acting as a handy man and private messenger for the family, but, as I have said, whenever a new President occupied the White House the old help, fearful that they would lose their jobs, instantly began to make trouble for any newcomer. Johnson was no exception. In his case there was almost an open rebellion, not only for the regular reasons, but also because of a social distinction. Johnson's color was very dark and White House servants were always light. He was mistreated in such a way that it became necessary for the President to look elsewhere for employment for him. While doing so he gave Johnson a job attending the White House furnace at a salary of $50 per month until he could find a permanent position for him. Openings were difficult to find but President Lincoln felt that since he had brought to Washington this Negro who had loyally served him and his family, it was absolutely necessary that Johnson be found work.

The President wrote several letters of recommendation. One, dated March 7, 1861, reads:

Executive Mansion, March 7, 1861

Whom It May Concern:
        William Johnson, a colored boy, and bearer of this, has been with me about twelve months; and has been, so far as I believe, honest, faithful, sober, industrious and handy as a servant.

A. Lincoln

This was followed by a letter to the Secretary of the Navy.

Executive Mansion, March 16, 1861

Hon. Gideon Welles:
Dear Sir:
        The bearer, (William) is a servant who has been with me for some time and in whom I have confidence as to

his integrity and faithfulness. He wishes to enter your service. The difference of color between him and the other servants is the cause of our separation. If you can give him employment you will confer a favour on

Yours truly,

A. Lincoln

These letters brought no results and William continued to attend the White House furnace and endure insults.

There is no record of a colored person being on the train when Lincoln left Springfield, but from the letters of Lincoln we know that William Johnson was with him, and the photograph shows him with Lincoln upon arrival. Undoubtedly he was hidden where he could be on the alert to defend the President-elect on an instant's notice, for was he not "faithful and sober?"

Having learned by chance, that President Lincoln had had one Solomon Johnson appointed to the Treasury, I wrote to Mr. J. E. Harper, Chief, Division of Appointments, for any information that could be found in the official files of the Treasury about Solomon Johnson, who was a barber. He became interested and after a thorough search of his files found that Solomon Johnson was appointed to fill a vacancy caused by the death of William Johnson, January 28, 1864.

This was a valuable discovery. William Johnson then had been appointed to a place in the Treasury. A search of the Treasury files produced the original Lincoln letter to Secretary Chase which is reproduced here for the first time, and also the appointment of William Johnson, November 30, 1861. (File:-12864, United States Treasury.)

The search was at an end. I tried to get from the District of Columbia Health Department his death certificate, hoping to secure additional information. Sorry to relate, the Health Department wrote, "All death records for the District of Columbia from 1862–64 were destroyed."

Copy of Letter in U. S.
Treasury, Appointment Division

Executive Mansion
Nov. 29, 1861

Hon. Sec. of Treasury
My dear Sir:

You remember kindly asking me some time ago whether I really desired you to find a place for William Johnson, a colored boy who came from Illinois with me. If you can find him the place, shall really be obliged.

Yours truly,
A. Lincoln

COPY
Fair Copy, "A" Vol. 2, Page 9

Treasury Department,
Office of the Secretary,
Washington, D. C.
November 30, 1861

Sir:

You are hereby appointed Laborer in the Treasury Department, at a compensation of Six hundred Dollars, per annum.

I am, very respectfully,
(Signed) Geo. Harrington,
Assistant Secretary of the Treasury.

Mr. William Johnson
File;—12864, United States Treasury
William Johnson, Laborer, $600, Six Hundred Dollars per annum. Date of appointment November 30, 1861

Lincoln was in constant touch with William Johnson even after he obtained for him a position in the Treasury and the following letters attest to his desire to assist him in earning money to add to his salary, which seemed inadequate to support himself and family. The following letter probably refers to a request for a leave of absence for him to earn extra money.

I decline to sign the within, because it does not state the thing quite to my liking. The colored man William Johnson came with me from Illinois, and I would be glad for him to be obliged, if he can be consistently with the public service; but I cannot make an order about it, nor a request which might in some sort, be construed as an order.

A. Lincoln

Dec. 17, 1862

Several years ago while visiting the State Library in Albany and consulting old newspapers in connection with my studies of Mrs. Lincoln and Mrs. Keckley, I was given every assistance by Miss Edna L. Jacobsen, Head of the Manuscript and History Sections. It is due to her kindness that permission was given to quote the following note of Lincoln and the accompanying explanatory memorandum in the New York State Library.

If entirely convenient will Mr. Atelee allow William leave of absence for today?

Jan. 22, 1863   A. Lincoln

On the reverse of this note is the following memorandum written by the historian, Benson J. Lossing:

The person named in this note is a boy brought from Illinois by President Lincoln and who attends to his wardrobe, shaving him in the morning, etc. Wishing to

have him earn more as his family are poor, he allows him to
act as messenger for Mr. Atelee (Sam'l Yorke), the Librarian
of the Treasury Department, during the remainder of the
day. This note came to Mr. A. while I was in his room, that
morning, and Mr. A. gave it to me.

B. J. L.

I think Lincoln's constant interest in William Johnson shows
us, even more than do some of his greatest public deeds and
much heralded acts, the great heart of this man. He had
induced Johnson to leave Springfield and accompany him to
Washington on a most perilous journey and thereafter never
ceased to be interested in him, but continued to assist him in
every manner possible.

Lincoln was not like many other employers who bring
servants to strange cities and then dispense with their services
and leave them stranded in a strange place without home or
employment. Although he deemed it undiplomatic to force
Johnson's presence upon the resentful servants of the White
House, Lincoln felt it a bounden duty to look out for him.

The various letters of the Emancipator showing his
great heart for those of his own race are known, but of his
acts toward this son of a slave mother nothing has been
recorded.

We have no record of the private help given this colored
man by Mr. and Mrs. Lincoln who were overgenerous to their
servants, but judging from their kindheartedness and liberality
toward others and the scant records left, it is safe to believe that
William Johnson's appeals, due to a growing family, were never
turned down. I have heard it said that the Lincolns were so freehearted that there was a fear that when their days in the White
House were over, they would leave as poor as they went in.

Old print, courtesy of the Washington *Evening Star*, showing arrival of Lincoln at Washington with his personal servant William Johnson (left-hand corner) carrying carpetbag. Photograph of a check paid by Lincoln to Johnson, the original of which is in the Illinois State Historical Library, Springfield, Illinois. There is no endorsement on the back, as it was cashed at the bank the day it was written.

BILL OF FARE

OF THE

Presidential Inauguration Ball

IN THE

CITY OF WASHINGTON, D. C.,

On the 6th of March 1865.

Oyster Stews ....

Terrapin " ....

Oysters, pickled ....

BEEF.

Roast Beef ....

Filet de Beef ....

Beef à-la-mode ....

Beef à l'anglais ....

VEAL.

Leg of Veal ....

Fricandeau ....

Veal Malakoff ....

POULTRY.

Roast Turkey ....

Boned " ....

Roast Chicken ....

Grouse, boned and roast ....

GAME.

Pheasant ....

Quail ....

Venison ....

PATETES.

Patéte of Duck en gelée ......

Patéte de foïs gras ....

SMOKED.

Ham ....

Tongue en gelee ....

do plain ....

SALADES.

Chicken ....

Lobster ....

Ornamental Pyramides.

Nougate ....

Orange ....

Caramel with Fancy Cream Candy

Cocoanut ....

Macaroon ....

Croquant ....

Chocolate ....

Tree Cakes ....

CAKES AND TARTS.

Almond Sponge ....

Belle Alliance ....

Dame Blanche ....

Macaroon Tart ....

Tart à la Nelson ....

Tarte à l'Orleans ....

do à la Portugaise ....

do à la Vienne ......

Pound Cake ....

Sponge Cake ....

Lady Cake ....

Fancy small Cakes ......

JELLIES AND CREAMS.

Calfsfoot and Wine Jelly ..

Charlotte à la Russe ......

do do Vanilla ....

Blanc Mangue .

Crème Neapolitane ......

do à la Nelson ....

do Chateaubriand .....

do à la Smyrna ....

do do Nesselrode .

Bombe à la Vanilla ....

ICE CREAM.

Vanilla ....

Lemon ....

White Coffee ....

Chocolate ....

Burnt Almonds ....

Maraschino ....

FRUIT ICES.

Strawberry ....

Orange ....

Lemon ....

DESSERT.

Grapes, Almonds, Raisins, &c.

Coffee and Chocolate.

Furnished by **G. A. BALZER,** Confectioner,

Cor. 9th & D Sts., Washington, D. C.

Menu at the Inaugural Ball of President Lincoln, found in Aunt Vina's effects by Dr. Washington. Aunt Vina's son served as a waiter at the Ball.

I knew for many years Mrs. John Brooks and Mrs. Wells who did plain sewing for the Lincoln family and both received old White House chairs from Mrs. Lincoln. They always said she was not hard to work for, was jolly and perfectly at home with them, and like President Lincoln, always treated "all of the servants like people." All of the help loved Mrs. Lincoln and said that when she was not sick with the dreadful head-aches she used to have, and was not worried about the war and things in general, she was a perfect queen to work for.

I guess it was this same kind of treatment that made William Johnson happy and contented to leave his home and old friends in Springfield and come with them to Washington where he would have no friends except his employers. If Mrs. Lincoln, who had come in contact with him daily in her home in Illinois, had been as prejudiced as historians have pictured her, he would have been only too glad to have had some excuse for getting out of the service of the Lincolns. But he was not only glad to come, but contented to be on the alert to protect his employer even if his own life was at stake on that train which brought him and the President-elect from Harrisburg to Washington.

William Makepeace Thayer knew Lincoln well and wrote many stories and books about him. From his *Character and Public Services of Abraham Lincoln,* which was published in 1864, the story below is taken:

> The Washington correspondent of the *Chicago Tribune* relates the following anecdote:
>
> I dropped in upon Mr. Lincoln on Monday last, and found him busily engaged in counting greenbacks. "This, sir," said he, "is something out of my usual line; but a President of the United States has a multiplicity of duties not specified in the Constitution, or acts of Congress: this is

one of them. This money belongs to a poor Negro, who is a porter in one of the departments (the Treasury), and who is at present very sick with the small-pox. He is now in the hospital, and could not draw his pay, because he could not sign his name.

"I have been at considerable trouble to overcome the difficulty, and to get it for him; and have at length succeeded in cutting red tape, as you newspaper men say. I am dividing the money, and putting a portion labelled in an envelope with my own hands, according to his wish;" and his Excellency proceeded to indorse the package very carefully.

No one who witnessed the transaction could fail to appreciate the goodness of heart which would prompt a man, who is borne down by the weight of cares unparalleled in the world's history, to turn aside for a time from them to succor one of the humblest of his fellow creatures in sickness and sorrow.

This statement was undoubtedly about William Johnson whose affairs Lincoln looked after from the day he brought him to Washington until he died in January, 1864, while employed as a laborer in the Treasury Department.

SOLOMON JOHNSON

Lincoln's Personal Barber

For many years I knew the members of the Solomon Johnson family and lived near them. One day while talking of my search for persons who knew Lincoln and served him, I was surprised when one of the Johnson boys told me that his father, Solomon Johnson, had been the barber for Lincoln and then proceeded to give me some facts about his services at the White House. He also told me that President Lincoln had had him appointed to a position in the Treasury and also wanted him promoted.

Carrying on the investigation about William Johnson, I accidentally discovered that Solomon Johnson received an appointment in the Treasury Department when William died.

This prompted me to call again on Mr. J. E. Harper. Soon I received from him copies of the following letters from the original files of William and Solomon Johnson. The letters show the interest that Lincoln took in these servants and how rapidly Solomon progressed in the services of the Treasury Department after he was appointed.

This boy says he knows Secretary Chase, and would like to have the place made vacant by William Johnson's

death. I believe he is a good boy and I should be glad for
him to have the place if it is still vacant.

(Signed) A. Lincoln

Jan. 28, 1864

> Treasury Department
> Office of the Secretary
> Washington, D. C.
> February 2, 1864

Sir:

You are hereby appointed a Laborer in the Treasury
Department, at a compensation of Six hundred dollars per
annum, vice Benjamin Coke, dismissed.

> I am, very respectfully,
> (Signed) M. B. Field,
> Assistant Secretary of Treasury

Mr. Solomon Johnson

I shall be glad if S. James Johnson, the bearer could
get a little promotion.

A. Lincoln

March 15, 1865

> Treasury Department,
> Office of the Secretary,
> Washington, D. C.
> February 9, 1867

Sir:

The Secretary having designated you for promotion to
a Clerkship of the First Class, I have to request that you will
present yourself to the Board established for the examination of Clerks in the Office of the Secretary of the Treasury.

Mr. West, who is the first member of the Board, will fix the time for your examination.

> I am, very respectfully,
> (Signed) Wm. E. Chandler
> Assistant Secretary

Mr. Solomon Johnson of Ohio.

> Treasury Department
> Office of the Secretary
> Washington, D. C.
> February 12, 1867

Sir:

Having been examined and found qualified to perform the duties of a Clerkship of the First Class, you are hereby appointed a Clerk of that Class in the Office of the Secretary of the Treasury, vice G. B. Ramsdell, promoted.

> I am, very respectfully,
> (Signed) H. McCulloch,
> Secretary of the Treasury.

Mr. Solomon Johnson.

Desiring to carry further the studies of the lives of these two men, I again had a conference with Mr. Harper, who in spite of the great amount of labor necessary in finding data pertaining to appointments in the Lincoln administration, found a second file for Solomon Johnson.

Not content to be a laborer, which was at the time of his appointment a "big" job for a colored man, and in spite of the demands of a fast-growing family, Solomon Johnson devoted himself to study, and in a short time became the first colored United States Government clerk. This took place about three years after his original appointment. A few years later due to Government reorganization plans, he was appointed to a second-class clerkship and later reappointed to the first-class clerkship position.

His record as stated in the letter of R. Burr and his own letter to Secretary William Windom and the other letters herein reproduced, shows that he knew Lincoln and served him.

James M. Comly, Postmaster
R. Burr, Assistant

POSTOFFICE, COLUMBUS, OHIO.
April 5th, 1877

Hon. John Sherman,
    Secretary Treasury U. S.
Sir

Permit me to commend to your favorable notice Mr. Solomon Johnson, a colored man, a clerk in the Office of the Third Auditor of the Treasury.

During the first year of the War, Mr. Johnson was employed in my office (Quarter Master's) Went from there to Washington, with a Military Company, organized as a body guard to President Lincoln. Was employed for some-time at the White House, and was the first colored man ever appointed to a clerkship in any of the Government Departments. Has had now long experience in that capacity, has always I believe proven faithful, is a very worthy man. He very naturally desires promotion. I take pleasure in earnestly commending him to your kind consideration.

Very truly yours,
(Signed) R. Burr

Washington, D. C.

May 26th, 1881

To the Honorable,

William Windom

Secretary of the Treasury.

Dear Sir:

I respectfully take this method to place before you my case for your favorable attention at such convenient time as without prejudice to calls of your office, you may be pleased to give it.

I am a colored man and a voter. Have a family.

I was first appointed in the Treasury Department by the late Chief Justice S. P. Chase then Secretary of the Treasury, in 1864, upon the request of the lamented Abraham Lincoln, whose trusted attendant I was at that time.

Shortly after my appointment I received several promotions until the one distinguishing me as the first colored man appointed to a Clerkship under the Government of the U. S. I was assigned to duty in the Internal Revenue Division of the Secretary's Office, and also assisted in the Mail Division of that Office. I remained thus employed until the year 1870, when at my own request I was detailed with expert Clerks on Accounts in the Office of Commissioner of Customs, for several months. Also served in the Warrant Division till 1876, when I was assigned to duty in the Third Auditor's Office which place I have filled until temporarily called to duty in the Loan Division, recently, as a Second Class Clerk.

It will be seen, Mr. Secretary, that I have been on duty in various positions in the Treasury for more than seventeen years, and as intended, have become informed as to the workings of the Department, generally, and so far as I am aware or have reasons to believe, given approving satisfaction to my Official superiors.

During this time of service, I have been able to give

myself a fair knowledge of law which I read at the Howard University, and have endeavored to improve myself in such liberal culture as becomes a good citizen.

In view of my long and faithful service I trust that I may receive such recognition as in your judgment you may find proper to give me; and that my unfortunate race relations may not be a bar to such recognition.

I take this method, because I do not wish to trouble my friends to intercede in my behalf; and being a stranger to you I did not wish to personally intrude, perhaps at a time when you would be occupied on important Official duties. If I have erred in so doing, please pardon me.

I have papers to substantiate what I write if granted at any time an interview.

> I am very respectfully
> Your Obedient Servant
> Solomon Johnson
> Third Auditor's Office.

Solomon Johnson was born in Petersburg, Va., and in 1875 stated that he was thirty-three years old. He was recruited by the 54th and 55th Massachusetts Volunteer Regiments (colored) but rejected on account of physical disability. However, he served in the Presidents guard and in other ways continued his services to the cause of the Union. Being a fine barber, Solomon Johnson continued to make extra money in shaving his patrons after his official hours were over. Until recently colored men who controlled the barber trade in Washington sent special barbers to wealthy white men's homes to shave and cut their hair.

Most of the colored men then in Government services as laborers and messengers depended on outside work to help them in supporting their families. Nearly everyone not only did the work required by the Government, but also served as house servants and valets for their chief without extra compensation. They served him faithfully at his home, before Government time, and often into the night at dinners and receptions.

Many Government messengers in Washington even to this day, especially those assigned to important officials, keep up this custom.

Solomon Johnson died in Washington, November 24, 1885.

PART THREE

THOSE WHO REMEMBERED LINCOLN

AUNT VINA

Her Home and Souvenirs of Lincoln

My fondest hope, when a child on E Street, was realized when we moved to the other side of the city away from the place of spooks, haunted houses and dreaded tales. I felt then that I would hear no more ghost stories about Lincoln, Booth and Mrs. Lincoln. I had always wished for the time to come when I could run away, like many of the larger boys in the neighborhood. Then all that would be left for me to see would be pictures and I could shut my eyes and swiftly pass by them. When we arrived at our new home, I thought the place very beautiful, and the surrounding scenery filled me with the greatest ecstasy. There were no brick sidewalks and cobblestone alleys to make blisters on my feet when I went barefooted. "Cops" seldom stopped, as they hurriedly rode on their spirited horses up the dusty roads.

No big houses. Just a row of two-story frame houses with large rooms. As I gazed in front, I saw for the first time in my life a large green field that lay for miles in every direction, with here and there a mighty oak, or a mammoth spreading elm beneath which boys were playing. Some cows were also grazing in the field. In the distance, against the blue sky running from east to west, was a large stretch of woods.

To the west, on what is now First Street, another grove of woods extended to R Street. To the east, on Lincoln

Road, a large orchard covered a great distance. It contained real apples and peaches and other fruit. Up First Street I saw a real running stream of water and a meadow, and on the corner nearest us, in an old lady's barn, there was a large well with an old oaken bucket hanging by its side. We brought our water from it.

A few days after we began to live in our new house, a neighbor who was called "Sister" Payne, and who lived next door, came in to make herself acquainted with my Grandmother. Both were glad to meet each other and from the very first, they became the greatest of friends. I liked "Sister" Payne too and began to work for her, driving her old horse and caring for the cows. My courage fell one evening when I heard her tell my Grandmother that she came from St. Mary's County, and began to tell her about the ghosts of her neighborhood. She could see spirits even in the house where she lived and I was working. When Grandmother would tell her about Ford's Theater, and the reputed haunted spots of our neighborhood, she would reply with her remembrances of Booth, Mrs. Surratt, Dr. Mudd, Tom Gardiner and the places their ghosts visited. She said one night after twelve o'clock, she heard and saw Booth kicking and cursing his horse as he raced across the old Navy Yard Bridge and up Good Hope Hill. Once she had even seen him in a field with a crutch in his hand, limping and trying to make his getaway. Her people, the Hawkins, were still living on the old farm where they were born. Her family could see, but were not afraid of spirits.

When I was informed that in the different woods that I saw, there were graveyards, I wanted to return to my old home. In the front of the distant woods was Glenwood Cemetery, on one side St. Mary's Cemetery, and on the other Prospect Cemetery. On First and R Streets was old St. Patrick's graveyard which had been abandoned for many years and now resembled the forest primeval, with here and there a weather-beaten stone slab to remind you of its former use. Beyond the orchard, on the right, was the most flourishing of colored cemeteries—Harmony. There were only two approaches to all of these burial grounds, R Street and Lincoln Road. These crossed each other a short block from where I lived and I could see every funeral that passed. This place with its dark nights I considered worse than my old E Street neighborhood. What I had thought was such a paradise of freedom for my poor ghost-scared soul was really a gathering place for spooks, who could leave their graves and indulge in their nightly revels on the field in front of the house, and wage great ghostly battles when one graveyard gang crossed the other a little distance away.

It was not a very long time after we moved to our new home and surroundings that I was sent to a public school which was quite a distance away. I traveled through different neighborhoods, white and colored, and had to fight my way through them many a time.

At school I met new friends, whose mothers and grandmothers had ideas similar to mine, and in whose homes could be seen the very same type of pictures—"Lincoln and His Family," "Deathbed Scene," "The Assassination of President Lincoln," and the circular colored lithograph of the bust of Lincoln.

I found in my friends' homes many scrapbooks containing pictures and stories about Lincoln, some of which I had never heard of before. They contained nearly everything that could be pasted in them—pictures of Mrs. Lincoln and Tad; Booth, the assassin; copies of the 13th Amendment to the Constitution; addresses to colored people about freedom; the part colored soldiers played in the Civil War; Lincoln's addresses to the contrabands

and colored citizens; and even one offering reward for the capture of Booth and his associates.

I remember my greatest sensation was when one old man,
who kept an upholstery shop, let me put my hands on an old
black necktie that he said Lincoln once wore. It looked just like
any other tie, but I just felt funny when I put my hand on it.

Our teacher often took the class to visit the Capitol and the
other public buildings. In the former I saw for the first time the
"Signing of the Emancipation Proclamation" by Carpenter. In
the parlor of the Kirks, an old Yankee family on E Street, there
was a large copy over the dining-room mantel, but it was not a
painting. When I first saw it I just couldn't help dropping my
jaws, and gazed with fixed eyes on the men who were sitting
beside the President. I knew somebody just had to help him, but
this was the first time I ever saw a picture of them. Most of them
were really strong-looking men, because they wore their hair
long, and must have had strong voices, because they had plenty
of hair on their chins. When I was large enough I often went to
see this picture, for I was born and bred on the Emancipation.

We also went to the old Smithsonian Building where we saw
many interesting things. There was a large hat and a long black
coat, beneath which had been placed a card, which the teacher
read, and told us they had been worn by President Lincoln.
In this case were many other things he wore, including an old
Scotch plaid shawl, just like the one Grandmother wore.

I also saw a plaster head of Lincoln with the eyes closed as
if he were dead. The teacher said it was "his death mask and
was made after he died." I didn't see any bullet holes in it however, and I knew Booth had a pistol and shot him.

In another case we saw a little statue of Mrs. Lincoln

ORDER OF THE PROCESSION.

FUNERAL ESCORT IN COLUMN OF MARCH.
One regiment of Cavalry.
Two batteries of Artillery.
Battalion of Marines.
Two regiments of Infantry.
Commander of Escort and Staff.
Dismounted officers of Marine Corps, Navy, and Army in the order named.
Mounted officers of Marine Corps, Navy, and Army in the order named.
All Military officers to be in uniform, with side arms.

CIVIC PROCESSION.

MARSHAL.
CLERGY IN ATTENDANCE.
The Surgeon General of the United States and Physicians to the Deceased.

| PALL BEARERS. | **{ HEARSE. }** | PALL BEARERS. |

On the part of the Senate.

Mr. FOSTER, Connecticut,
Mr. MORGAN, New York,
Mr. JOHNSON, Maryland,
Mr. YATES, Illinois,
Mr. WADE, Ohio,
Mr. CONNESS, California,

On the part of the House.

Mr. DAWES, Massachusetts,
Mr. COFFROTH, Pennsylvania,
Mr. SMITH, Kentucky,
Mr. COLFAX, Indiana,
Mr. WORTHINGTON, Nevada,
Mr. WASHBURNE, Illinois.

Army.

Lieut. General U. S. GRANT,
Major General H. W. HALLECK,
Brevet Brig. Gen. W. A. NICHOLS.

Navy.

Vice Admiral D. G. FARRAGUT,
Rear Admiral W. B. SHUBRICK,
Colonel JACOB ZEILIN, Marine Corps.

Civilians.

O. H. BROWNING,
GEORGE ASHMUN.

Civilians.

THOMAS CORWIN,
SIMON CAMERON.

THE FAMILY.
RELATIVES.
The Delegations of the State of Illinois and Kentucky as mourners.

THE PRESIDENT.
THE CABINET MINISTERS.
THE DIPLOMATIC CORPS.
EX-PRESIDENTS.

The Chief Justice and Associate Justices of the Supreme Court.
The Senate of the United States, preceded by its officers.
The House of Representatives of the United States, preceded by its officers.
Governors of the several States and Territories.
Legislatures of the several States and Territories.
The Federal Judiciary, and the Judiciary of the several States and Territories.
The Assistant Secretaries of State, Treasury, War, Navy, and Interior; and the Assistants Postmaster
General, and the Assistant Attorney General.
Officers of the Smithsonian Institution.
The members and officers of the Sanitary and Christian Commissions.
Corporate Authorities of Washington and Georgetown, and other cities.
Delegations of the several States.
The Reverend Clergy of the various denominations.
The Clerks and employees of the several Departments and Bureaus, preceded by the Heads of such
Bureaus and their respective Chief Clerks.
Such Societies as may wish to join the procession.
Citizens and Strangers.

The troops designated to form the escort will assemble in the avenue, north of the President's
House, and form line precisely at 11 o'clock A. M., on Wednesday, the 19th instant, with the left resting
on Fifteenth street. The procession will move precisely at 2 o'clock P. M., on the conclusion of the
religious services at the Executive Mansion, (appointed to commence at 12 o'clock meridian,) when
minute guns will be fired by detachments of artillery stationed near St. John's church, the City Hall,
and at the Capitol. At the same hour the bells of the several churches in Washington, Georgetown,
and Alexandria, will be tolled.
At sunrise on Wednesday, the 19th instant, a Federal salute will be fired from the military
stations in the vicinity of Washington, minute guns between the hours of twelve and three o'clock,
and a national salute at the setting of the sun.
The usual badge of mourning will be worn on the left arm and on the hilt of the sword.

Portrait of Aunt Elizabeth Thomas, heroine of the Battle of Fort Stevens. From the original now in the possession of her grandson, William A. Grant, of Washington, who loaned the picture to the author for this purpose. Old Stone Spring House at Fort Stevens, near which Lincoln was standing when Aunt Thomas warned him of danger.

dressed up in a beautiful dress that she once wore, and I thought then that it was the one that her colored dressmaker, Mrs. Keckley, made.

On another journey we saw in front of the old courthouse building a statue of Lincoln on a very high marble column, and we were told it was the first one ever made of Lincoln after he died, and that many colored men, women and children gave pennies to build it.

Once, I remember, just as clear as if it were yesterday, all the children put in for street-car fare and we went on a long trip to see a statue of Lincoln freeing a colored man. Gee, this man was looking so happy, as his chains had been broken, and he was on one knee trying to get up! It was called the Emancipation Statue. We also had Emancipation Day exercises in all the colored schools and a grand parade down Pennsylvania Avenue.

I could never forget my early training about Lincoln, because Grandmother and Mrs. Payne constantly told the same old stories over and over again.

Into whatever house I went with a new companion, I found that everybody held Lincoln in the same high esteem. In most of the front rooms there were many old pictures of Lincoln pasted on the walls of the sitting room over the mantelpiece. This was the uniform custom of old colored people everywhere—in the cabins, huts, old barns and even sleeping rooms. They just had to have Lincoln near them, they loved him so.

I never lost my love for the old people of my race and their stories and began to take a greater interest in them as I progressed in school. I always was a great reader, and read every book about Lincoln I could get. I had visited every place that I could, to add to my special storehouse of knowledge concerning my people's Emancipator, and had mapped out a well-planned procedure for collecting materials to write a book.

I wanted to become a teacher like Annie and finally succeeded in becoming one, and earning a large enough salary to allow me to lay aside a few dollars monthly for books and excursions into the surrounding country where I could obtain first-hand knowledge about Lincoln, from the very mouths of people who knew him and loved him.

From old family records, lectures and addresses of prominent colored and white speakers, I found out that even in these days there were quite a large number of old people living in the backwoods of Maryland and Virginia who were still illiterate and living under the same conditions that had prevailed in Lincoln's time. They were so far off the main highway that they had never seen an automobile, nor an electric light and didn't care to do so. They were just living in hope of dying and joining their friends above. These dear old folks had a large amount of valuable material that had been forgotten in these days and times, and much that had never been published on the Emancipator of my race. If this could be collected, it would serve to do much in establishing another viewpoint of the man a whole race loved and honored so much, but how, when, and where could I find these cherished spots? I asked Mrs. Payne these questions. She said she knew some in the country, where she used to live and would carry me to see them, but I'd have to be just like them and not put on airs while I talked to them.

I was told to see old Aunt Vina because she knew everything, and everybody, and had the memory of a mule. Mrs. Payne said she lived way down in Charles County, and was in her prime when Lincoln was shot. She could plow, hoe a garden and shuck corn equal to any man. She never could be taught to read anything, even the Bible, and got no further in her schooling than to learn the first letter of the alphabet.

If you told her to say her "letters" instead of saying, "Aunt Vina, say your ABC's" she did not know what you meant. Her great old head was too full of common sense, and religion, and mother wit, to let anything else enter her brain; yet, if she once heard anything, she had it, and never forgot it, and really carried things straight in her mind. She was one of those poor old souls who wanted to know about the Lord, and the Devil and everything in the world, and hence let no opportunity pass to obtain this end. She lost her old man Ned, soon after the war, and never wanted another, for she did not think any man good enough to take his place.

One bright morning I left with Mrs. Payne to go down in the country to see old Aunt Vina. No one in town knew her. I took an old team and with Mrs. Payne traveled for hours and she pointed out the same spots as before. When we came to an old grove of gigantic oaks, we entered a rough single-track dirt road and were told that about a mile down this road old Aunt Vina used to live. Was she dead? That was the question that worried my mind. If alive, would she be too old to remember the things I wanted to find out? As we journeyed along we passed, here and there, a deserted barn, cabin or "big house." We saw no signs of life anywhere, not even a chicken. It was the most deserted and forlorn place I had ever seen.

Suddenly, as we came out of these woods, we saw a beautiful opening with a prosperous-looking garden and many little flowering bushes surrounding an old log cabin that had been whitewashed and looked whiter than snow.

Mrs. Payne said this was where Aunt Vina lived and somebody must be living in the place. Before we stopped at the door, a quaint old lady, bent with age, leaning heavily on a hickory stick, with piercing eyes, a feeble voice and a head of hair as soft and white as cotton came out of the door to see who it was that was coming from the great world beyond those trees, to see who was living with herself and God.

We were invited in, and after some statements by Mrs. Payne about who she was and to what people she belonged, Aunt Vina remembered her, and was so glad to see her that her mouth ran a mile telling about the changes that had taken place since she was a child and born in the very same old cabin. She didn't know who I was and asked about my people, where they came from, to whom they belonged, and finally just why I came with Mrs. Payne to see her.

Aunt Vina may have been living down in the sticks down behind the sun, and lost everything, but her memory was still alive, and her tongue rolled about in her little mouth so fast that when I had finished answering one question after another, I felt as if I had been through a third degree by young Abe Lincoln when he was riding the circuit.

One of the hardest things to do is get some important information out of these kind old folks. They must be certain that your motives are pure, and that you are not there to trick them into saying anything that would harm them, or to hurt the reputation of an old friend.

Unscrupulous relic hunters had beaten them out of some of their most cherished objects, given them by their slave owners, and shrewd land dealers had caused many to sign away their little shanties and cabins. Aunt Vina was over-cautious with me until I told her what I was trying to do and that I wanted the whole world to know how dear Lincoln had been to the colored people of his day and that I felt if anybody in this great world could help me out it was she. Yes! it was she. While I was talking she kept nodding assent, and after Mrs. Payne said

I was all right and that she had known me from childhood when I came to see her with the Hawkins many years ago; that I had been raised by a God-fearing Grandmother, and been taught to love and respect the aged, and had been taught to love Lincoln all of my life, Aunt Vina just couldn't be too free with her knowledge.

I asked Aunt Vina if she had seen Lincoln, and she said:

"Yes, I saw President Lincoln during the war." Then she told me how some colored people on the farm just made up their minds to go to Washington to see Lincoln inaugurated, and she herself was one of them. The Yankee soldiers had told them they were free, and they intended to see the man who had given freedom to them. Nobody dared to stop them either. They traveled all night in an old ox-cart with straw all over the floor, had bags of food and arrived in Washington the next day in time to see the parade go up the Avenue.

It was grand, and there were even some colored soldiers marching in it and riding behind the generals on horseback. Lincoln rode with his wife on the back seat of his carriage and just as he passed the place where she and a large crowd of colored people were standing, he took his hat off, smiled and bowed to them. Mrs. Lincoln bowed too, and waved a white handkerchief. Aunt Vina said she could see it as clearly in her mind now as she did with her eyes that day.

Her little old cabin room was covered with pictures, from the floor to the ceiling, and she passed her time looking over piles of pictures and old papers she had brought from Washington and other parts of the country. She, too, had had many children but they were now all dead, and she hoped, "gone to Glory." Her children had hoped some day to return to the place of their birth and spend the rest of their days on the farm with her, but something must have gotten into them, for they never were willing to stay in the old cabin after they had been up North and in Washington. These members of her family used to send her pictures, papers, and books on the war from the North where they lived. Hence all of this material, which she had collected for years, while waiting for them to return and read and tell her all about the contents of the books and pamphlets.

She was so glad to have me read some of the old papers and tell her about the pictures most of which I had never seen anywhere before. I was almost overpowered to know, that in this out-of-the-way deserted spot, I had found one of the most valuable collections of Lincoln material I had ever seen. Over the fireplace hung a picture of soldiers reading to a family of slaves, by the light of a fire, the Emancipation Proclamation. It was old and almost covered with smoke and dirt, but it told a story of the greatest event in the world to me. It was the message of God to man through Lincoln, notifying the colored people that they were free. Next to it was a copy of the Emancipation Proclamation itself, which her boy Henry sent to her during the war. That was the first thing he sent back from the army. He was killed in that war. On the other side of the picture was a poorly framed copy of an appeal to the colored people to help in capturing Booth, etc. As I had never seen or heard of this broadside before, I longed to have it, but hesitated to ask her for it.

Her children who went away to work during the war sent back to the old home anything of interest they hoped to keep, because they only stayed in rented rooms and in some of these, several persons slept. Her other son, Charles, had been a headwaiter in a large hotel in Washington and waited on Lincoln at the supper after his inaugural ball. She showed me a menu card that Charles sent her. Strange, that this old soul who could neither read nor write could tell you the name of each paper she had, also the subject of the old pictures. If you told her anything about a picture or paper, she would squint her little eyes and tilt her head, while you were talking and suddenly she would give a sharp jerk to her head and smile. I guess it meant, "I have it, go on." In a black frame she had a program of the funeral exercises with a little piece of black crepe hanging above it. She said Charles sent it to her. On one side wall she had pasted with flour paste, many years ago, several pages of *Leslie's Weekly* of April, 1865. It was full of pictures of the assassination.

She entertained me for hours while I smiled and nodded. She only took time out when her little old corncob pipe would go out and need relighting. She just knew everybody, and I believe she hadn't had an opportunity to talk her tales for months, and was using me to let her information out.

She said she was so glad I came, for she had always been worried about her things being thrown out and destroyed after she died, for, said she, the white folks around where she lived had Rebel parents and they were Rebels even to this day. I took only a few things that I didn't have in my collection, but prized an old copy of a report of the House of Representatives offering a reward for the capture of Booth. There were blue lead pencil marks around the first and second pages. Her son Henry had told her to keep this, because it told how two colored women helped to capture Booth.

I also took a Memorial Poem on the death of Lincoln by H. H. Duganne, a photograph of the Capitol Prison where the conspirators were jailed while waiting trial, and also an engraving of the conspirators. There was a photograph of the first Cabinet of Lincoln in 1861. As I had never seen one like it, I brought it away. As I took these precious things she seemed to be so happy and would say, "God bless you, son! You can have everything you want, for I know I'll be gone too, soon, and someday you may find use for them."

She would not take a single penny from me for these things. She just wanted to know that someone of her race, who loved Lincoln, would have them when she was gone.

Did she know the Surratts, the Mudds and the Gardiners? Sure she did, and could tell you their entire history, who they were and what people in the county said they did. She told me that young Tom Gardiner was living in Washington and if ever I got a chance to see him, he could tell me about Booth and what he did in the county.

Old Aunt Vina knew Susie Jackson and everybody in the county could never understand why Susie let Lincoln be killed when she knew that in Mrs. Surratt's home, where she worked, all the plans had been made. When this news got out every colored person for miles around felt it a disgrace to their race that she didn't tell about what was going on, because the war was over and nobody was going to hurt her. Aunt Vina said she would have crawled to Washington on her knees to save Lincoln if she had been in Susie's place. You can't imagine the feeling of these old Lincoln lovers against one of their race, who could have prevented the tragedy that brought sorrow and broke every old slave's heart.

I asked her if there were any other old people living in the neighborhood like herself who knew anything. She said, no— they were either all dead or gone away, and she guessed she would be gone, too, if she could, but she just liked the place where she was born and she guessed she would die there and be buried in Mt. Hope graveyard with all of the other people who were carried there after the war. The Government gave her a pension and she was still living on it and the good neighborhood storekeeper saw that she didn't want for anything, and never had any change coming back after her insurance was paid. Aunt Vina said it was in his name, and he was going to see to it that she was buried where she wanted to be by her old man, Ned.

HER DESCRIPTION
OF LINCOLN'S FUNERAL

When the word came down in the country that Lincoln had been shot, and soldiers could be seen riding everywhere and even across the very farm on which Aunt Vina was then living, she said there was but one thought in every colored person's mind in southern Maryland, "Try to help the soldiers capture Booth, and then go to Washington to the funeral."

While the body was lying in state in the Capitol, Aunt Vina said a large number of colored people stood in line all night to get a "peep" at the dead President's face. Although she was tired, sleepy and hungry she stood in line, too, and when the time came to pass by the dead body, she just had to take out her handkerchief and cry like a newborn baby. She was not the only one to do so, for there was weeping and wailing and praying all the night long in the line that was waiting to pass.

She said the corpse looked so peaceful and she believed it had a smile on the face. At last she had really been close enough to look into the face of her Emancipator, even though he was dead.

Before and after the ceremonies in the Capitol, the procession moved on its way through lines of mourning people. Aunt Vina said it appeared as if every colored person in the world was there, praying and crying and weeping, falling down on their knees, and bending over until their heads nearly touched the ground, in reverence and grief, as the body passed by. In the procession there were many colored soldiers too, and they certainly looked as good as the white men when they marched by, with tears just pouring down their cheeks. Some of them were so sad that they just couldn't help getting out of step with the band, which was playing the saddest music she ever heard. "Many even broke out of line and had to sit down on the side of the street. They just could not stand that music and march a single step farther." The old lady was now wiping her eyes with her hands. She said she had seen Lincoln in life, and death, and hoped to meet him again face to face in Glory, very soon, and if any man ever had prayers enough to carry him to Glory, Lincoln surely had them that night and day, because even the little colored children, who had never seen him, added theirs to those of the older people.

"Now, sonny," said she, "you can read for yourself and see that colored soldiers were the first in line in front of the corpse when it was carried to the Capitol from the White House, and the last to bid it good-by in Washington, and the colored Methodists in Baltimore sent the first message of sympathy after Lincoln died."

Aunt Vina said, "The day that Lincoln was shot, my husband Ned, was in Baltimore attending the African Methodist Episcopal Conference and before the conference was over, Bishop Payne told all the preachers Lincoln had died. The preachers then got themselves together and passed a motion of sympathy and sent it to Washington." She said that she always heard that this motion, by colored people, was the first one passed by anybody after the news was given out that the President was dead.

Then she told me to open the larger of the two books she had given me, and read where her husband had made pencil marks in it and I would learn something more about our race.

On opening the book, *Lincoln Memorial* by William T. Coggeshall, she asked me to read the pages that were turned down for her. On page 132 I read the following:

> First in the order of procession was a detachment of colored troops, then followed white regiments of infantry and bodies of artillery and cavalry, navy, marine and army officers on foot; the pall-bearers in carriage; next the hearse, drawn by six white horses—the coffin prominent to every beholder. The floor on which it rested was strewn with evergreens, and the coffin covered with white flowers. Then followed physicians of the late President, then the grand hearse and the guard of honor and the pall-bearers, Capt. ROBERT LINCOLN and little TAD, the President's favorite son, in a carriage, and TOMMY behind.

Then she turned over the pages and said to me, "Read the other pages, 137–138."

> The coffin was carried into the depot, followed by the distinguished gentlemen, civil and military, before mentioned, and deposited in the car which had been prepared for its reception. At the door of this car the Rev. Dr. Gurley again briefly addressed the God of the living and the dead in a solemn and appropriate prayer. Ten minutes before eight o'clock a pilot engine was started to ascertain that the track was clear, and at precisely eight o'clock the funeral train was put in motion.
>
> The military escort remained in line in front of the depot until the train started, and as it commenced to move, presented arms, as a last token of respect. As the train moved off by the Soldiers' Rest, which is rear of

the depot, the Eighth Regiment United States colored artillery, were drawn up in line and presented arms until it passed.

When Willie Lincoln died, the remains were taken from the White House and kept in a vault in a Washington Cemetery until the Lincolns should return to Springfield and bury them in their family site. This fact was forgotten by many. When Lincoln's body was carried back to Springfield, the remains of Willie were taken back also, but in a way to attract no attention whatever from the ceremonies over his father's.

The remains of little Willie Lincoln, who died in the White House, December 21, 1862, at the age of twelve years, was placed in the interior of the hearse car, immediately in front of those of his father. Mrs. Lincoln requested that no display be made of her son's remains, but that they might be privately removed to Springfield.

Just a few weeks after I saw old Aunt Vina, one morning she was found dead in her bed and was given a Christian burial by the storekeeper who looked after her affairs, and his own also. This was one occasion on which I didn't arrive too late for an interview. Death robbed me of many other opportunities.

AUNT ELIZABETH THOMAS

Heroine of Fort Stevens

Washington lies in a low area on the Potomac River, but is surrounded on the northern side by high elevations. From one side to the other of the District of Columbia, in Civil War days, there were forts that controlled the incoming roads. Later, these old abandoned barracks were changed into schools for colored children. General Early after getting into Maryland attempted to capture Washington by coming from the North. He had to pass this Fort Stevens to succeed. As Grant's troops were in Virginia, much excitement was caused in Washington when it was found out that Early was about to attack from the North in an area protected by this Fort.

Every effort was made to strengthen the place. Loyal citizens as well as available military men endeavored to help while awaiting assistance from across the Potomac. Even Lincoln and the Cabinet were excited and rushed to the spot.

Not far from the Fort Stevens area was a locality known as Vinegar Hill where many colored people of German and Indian mixtures had built their homes. It was with sadness that they witnessed the destruction of their homes and barns to make room for breastworks.

Below this vicinity between 16th Street and what is now Georgia Avenue, in Brightwood, was a large tract of eighty-eight acres belonging to a colored woman, Elizabeth Thomas. It was a most beautiful spot and practically controlled the entrance to the city and was the most important location of all. A large part of this was taken to build Fort Stevens. It was needed and needed badly. The cattle, pigs and chickens were needed to feed the soldiers and the buildings were in the way and must go. While patriotic to the cause, this old colored woman did not like giving up her all, especially when there was no hope of ever getting the property restored. She resisted the army's action and finally was forcibly removed from her home by having it torn down over her head, and they piled her furniture around her under an old sycamore tree. She had a six months' old baby named Maria in her arms. Fight as she might for her home, she found that she could do nothing, and exhausted, with her child in her arms, sat down to rest under the sycamore tree, which is still standing. Here she saw all of her life's savings destroyed. The officers who had handled the situation with as much diplomacy as possible, finally called in the assistance of President Lincoln, who had visited the spot several times before and on each occasion had been quite friendly with the old colored woman.

Arriving just as the home was being torn to pieces to make a magazine, and seeing the livestock being driven away, Lincoln hastily moved toward the spot where the unfortunate woman, with her babe in her arms, was crying as if her heart was breaking. She had cried until she was exhausted, and felt that all was lost forever.

Bending affectionately over her, Lincoln listened to her pleas for her home. Then he said, "It is hard, but you shall reap a great reward." When Lincoln told her that when the battle was over, he would see that she was paid for all her stock that was taken away and that her home would be restored, she readily consented to go with him to her barn, which the soldiers had turned into a house, and put her furniture in it.

She loved Lincoln, and believed so much in his word that when the "Rebs" came she cooked for the Union troops, and between times helped with the ammunition which was stored in the stone basement of her old home. During the battle she even had her old shotgun by her side, to kill any "Rebs" who tried to hurt Lincoln. You know in those days the gun was a handy instrument in the hands of every colored man or woman. Now she forgot self and home and was fighting for Lincoln, for she had contributed her all to prevent the capture of Washington.

During my boyhood days we often went out to Mrs. Thomas' in Brightwood to have school picnics and some teachers boarded all of the summer with her. She certainly liked to tell her story about Lincoln.

Regularly as clockwork each year, the members of the Grand Army of the Republic, who had taken part in the battle, held their reunions on Mrs. Thomas' porch and about the house, which had been restored, and here they all told stories of the fight.

One old barracks had been changed into the Military Road School for colored children. I knew nearly every teacher, and with these Mrs. Thomas, the patriot of Brightwood, was always most friendly. They kept her supplied with the latest news, and newspapers and gossip. Mrs. Thomas often told the following story at G.A.R. reunions, and the old soldiers who were at her side during the battle, confirmed it.

While the battle was raging and bullets were whizzing everywhere, Mrs. Thomas was busy as a bee doing her duties in helping the defenders of the fort. Suddenly she looked out of the basement window and saw Lincoln standing upon the bank of the newly constructed trenches.

Forgetting everything, she excitedly yelled to those near him, "My God, make that fool get down off that hill and come in here." Just then a bullet felled an officer near the President, and he left the dangerous spot.

She said Lincoln just had to smile when she yelled at him. She was so afraid he might get hurt. The President kept his word and came back to see her often and laughed over the battle, but he was assassinated before he could see that she was paid the $6,000 damages.

Historians of the Civil War, who knew the story of Fort Stevens, have not mentioned this heroine, who gave all she could to Lincoln and country and relied on the promise of the Emancipator of her race for reward for damages. But the newspapers of the day in which she lived, annually wrote of Aunt Betty and even took her picture at the regular Grand Army of the Republic reunions which were held on the old battlefield.

When the boulder was dedicated on the spot on her farm where Lincoln stood in the battle, Mrs. Thomas was the main guest of honor and the accompanying picture by a newspaper photographer shows her in the stand with the speakers.

Miss Eva Chase and Miss Rachel Bell were two teachers who spent twelve summers regularly with her as boarders. They were great Republican women and G.A.R. workers and attempted to write the story of her life. I felt real lucky, some time ago, when the surviving one, Miss Bell, who had known me for years, stated that they had collected much valuable material on Mrs. Thomas, and were going to write an article on her, but now that I was writing on the people who loved Lincoln, and Aunt Betty certainly was one, she was going to give me everything on Mrs. Thomas that she had. She kept her promise and from these clippings, notes and photographs,

I have written the following account after conferring with her grandson "Billy" Grant.

While the nation seemed to have forgotten Aunt Betty after Lincoln died, the National Federation of Colored Women's Clubs—a nation-wide organization, on September 22, 1924, heard this program at Fort Stevens with the leading men and women of her race in attendance. Miss Bell, who knew Mrs. Thomas better than anyone else, was President of the Elizabeth Thomas Citizens' Association, and gave me the program showing Mrs. Thomas as she looked fifty years after she had taken part in the battle; she was seated in the grandstand while the orators of the day praised her for her part in saving the city.

From an old faded family portrait, I was able to restore the features of Mrs. Thomas as she looked about the time of the Civil War.

A life-long fight was made by Mrs. Chase and Miss Bell to get Mrs. Thomas the money Lincoln had promised her, but who died before he could see it fulfilled.

The *Washington Evening Star*, Wed. Oct. 17, 1917, carried the following article which gives the story of Mrs. Thomas almost like the story told to her friends and relatives and which formed the basis of my story:

MRS. ELIZABETH THOMAS
DIED AT BRIGHTWOOD

❧ ❧ ❧

Her History Was Connected With
Fort Stevens Where Lincoln
Was Once Under Fire.

Mrs. Elizabeth Thomas, whose life history was closely connected with the history of Fort Stevens, where President

Lincoln was under fire when Early made his attempt to capture Washington, died Saturday at her home on the site of the old fort in Brightwood, D. C.

Mrs. Thomas died from blood poisoning, resulting from a three-year-old wound sustained while working in her garden. Funeral services were held this afternoon at 1 o'clock at the Trinity A.M.E. Church, 781 Morton Street northwest. Interment was in Harmony Cemetery.

Mrs. Thomas was the former owner of the site of Fort Stevens. Her great grandmother was Nora Butler, a famous belle of colonial days, who created a sensation by eloping with Morning Glory Proctor, an Indian council man.

Mrs. Thomas was ninety-six years old. She was born in Charles County, Md., moving in her early childhood to the home on the site of Fort Stevens. The family bought a farm of eighty-eight acres.

During the Civil War, when the division of the Confederate army under Gen. Early made its attempt to capture Washington, the home of Mrs. Thomas was taken by the defenders of the National Capital.

William V. Cox, who now owns a portion of the land where the fort stood, tells of the meeting of President Lincoln and Elizabeth Thomas in his "The Defenses of Washington." He says:

Her Meeting With Lincoln

"The Fort (Stevens) had two magazines, one where Emory Chapel now stands, and the other to the west, where the depression is still visible. The house of Elizabeth Thomas, who is still alive (and known to most of us), was torn down and the cellar enlarged for this magazine."

Aunt Betty says: "The soldiers camped here at this time were mostly German. I could not understand them, not even the officers, but when they began taking out my furniture and tearing down our house, I understood. In the evening I was sitting under that sycamore tree—my only house—with what furniture I had left around me. I was crying, as was my six-months' old child, which I had in my arms, when a tall, slender man, dressed in black, came up and said to me: 'It is hard, but you shall reap a great reward.' It was President Lincoln, and had he lived I know the claim for my losses would have been paid."

After the war Mrs. Thomas for many years prior to her death lived on the Fort site, where she was always working, tending her garden and raising poultry.

Great interest attaches to old Fort Stevens through the fact that there, for the only time in the history of the United States a President was actually under fire. No other President was under fire while an incumbent of the office.

Association Named for Her.

Mrs. Thomas, during the later years of her life, was active in civic work and was president of the Elizabeth Thomas Citizens' Association, which was named in her honor.

Two daughters, Mrs. Martha Grant and Mrs. Eliza Johnson, seventeen grandchildren and eighteen great-grandchildren survive her.

JOHN HENRY COGHILL

Living Witness of Booth's Capture and Death

In after years during one of my travels I found still living John H. Coghill who in spite of his advanced age was as strong a lover of Lincoln as he was during the war.

John Henry Coghill is the son of the late Buck Coghill who died at eighty years of age and Mary Coghill who lived to see her seventy-fifth birthday. Both were slaves of the Gravatts in Caroline County, Virginia.

To this couple there were born thirteen children, five boys and eight girls, five of whom are still living: John, eighty-eight; Thomas, seventy-five; Henster Golden, eighty; Sallie Pratt, fifty-five; and Lena Coghill, forty years old.

John, the last known survivor who was present when the barn on Garrett's farm was fired and John Wilkes Booth was killed, was married twice and now has two living children by his first wife who died twenty-two years ago. His son John is sixty-five years old and his daughter Anna forty-five years old. There is one grandchild living.

While his first wife was from Virginia, his present wife Ella was born in Maryland. She is seventy years old. All of these people are hale and hearty at this time, and John who uses tobacco moderately, only uses glasses occasionally when reading. He has always been and still is a great walker, and although retired as janitor of the St. Thomas Episcopal Church, he still can be seen at his old job when the present janitor needs assistance or is away from his duties.

John Coghill is of medium build and quite erect and walks with a fast, brisk gait. He is quite light in color with very fine hair and his head is getting quite bald. He has small piercing eyes and a drooping mustache. His mind is still very clear and he recalls almost to the very day the most minute details about the Booth killing on the Garrett farm.

He is very reticent but when once he knows and likes you, he becomes a very delightful conversationalist. This is true of nearly all old colored ex-slaves whom I have interrogated even to this day. Coghill recalls many famous members of St. Thomas Episcopal Church, including President Franklin Delano Roosevelt.

Coghill tells this story from what he actually saw, and what took place on the Garrett farm—however, it is of value to note the part that loyal colored people played in the actual capture of Booth, the assassin, although Susie Jackson, a colored woman in Mrs. Surratt's employ, failed to prevent it by telling about the meetings of the assassin in Mrs. Surratt's home. Coghill had heard of the Emancipation Proclamation and had just found out that freedom had been given to all colored people who could get out of Virginia into the Yankee lines.

Coghill was a slave on the Gravatt farm, across from the Garrett farm, and was probably the first person to see Booth coming to it, riding back of Mr. Jett on his horse. When he saw this strange man with a crutch in his hand, he thought that he must be the man who had shot Lincoln. He was in the road driving the cows to the barn for evening milking when he stepped aside to let the man pass. That night he overheard the white people in the house say that this strange man was Booth, the man who shot Lincoln. He also saw the Garrett boys leaving on horseback, and felt that something was going to happen. Early on the second morning while getting the cows up, he saw about two dozen Yankee soldiers on horseback rapidly riding up and surrounding the old barn near the Garretts' house. A few other slaves had come to see what was going to take place. The soldiers drove them out of harm's way. He witnessed the firing of the barn, saw soldiers bring Booth out of the burning place and lay the body on the Garretts' porch, and after a while, saw it placed in a colored man's wagon and surrounded by soldiers and driven away. He was so glad that the man who had murdered the one he loved had met his doom and that he had witnessed the end.

To substantiate this fact, I quote from *Lincoln Memorial* by Wm. T. Coggeshall (p. 105):

> Meanwhile the pursuing forces on the Virginia side of the Potomac were watchful. They consisted of a detachment of twenty-six men of Company D, 16th New York Cavalry, commanded by Lieut. Doughtery, accompanied by two of Colonel Baker's experienced detectives. The cavalry landed at Belle Plain in the night and immediately started out in pursuit of Booth and his associate, having previously ascertained from a colored man that they had crossed the river into Virginia at Swan Point. The cavalry crossed the Rappahannock at Fredericksburg, and moved down the Bowling Green Road, and then over to Port Royal. There they obtained news of Booth from an old colored man, who said that four men, in company with a Rebel Captain, had crossed the Rappahannock a short time previous, going in the direction of Bowling Green, and added that the Captain would probably be found at that place, as he was courting

a young lady there. The Captain was found at the hotel in Bowling Green and taken in custody. From him it was ascertained that Booth and Harrold were at the house of John and William Garrett, three miles back toward Port Royal, and about a quarter of a mile from the road passed by the cavalry. Returning, they arrived at Garrett's home about three o'clock on the morning of the 26th. The Cavalrymen were posted around it by Lieut. Baker, a brother of Colonel L. C. Baker, and Lieut. Conger of Colonel Baker's force.

HIS PERSONAL STATEMENT

I was born on Ellis Gravatt's [sic] farm in Caroline County, Virginia March 11, 1852. Our farm was on the opposite side of the road from Garrett's farm. Both farms had a meadow in a valley between which ran the main road.

One evening just at dusk while my uncle and I were driving the cows home, we saw Jett with a man holding a crutch sitting behind him on his horse. They went into the Garrett farm and up to the house. Jett and the two Garrett boys were friends so I guess that is why Jett carried Booth to their farm and leaving him there went to Bowling Green to notify the soldiers that he had captured Booth and had him in the Garrett's house.

Ned Freeman a free colored man had a little farm just inside of the Garrett farm. It faced the road and his house was probably about a half city block from Garrett's house.

The next evening I saw some soldiers riding rapidly by and going to Bowling Green. Soon after this Ned Freeman told my father that the Garretts put Booth in the tobacco barn which was quite near their house. They feared that the soldiers would set fire to their house in order to make Booth come out. I never heard anybody say who the lame man in the house with Jett was until the troops returned early the next morning, just before day as we were getting ready to milk and take the cows down into the meadow. The white people never would talk about this affair. There were only a few colored people on these farms because most of them had gone away because they were free.

It was only when a few colored people saw the soldiers ride up into the Garrett's yard that they went into the Garrett's yard to see what was going to happen. After a little while I saw the soldiers putting fire to the tobacco barn. We were as near to it as the soldiers would let us come. There were no white people around except the soldiers. I didn't hear the shot, and in the smoke and fire the soldiers rushed into the barn and brought out the body before the fire could burn it. When Booth died his body was put into Ned Freeman's wagon with another white man and surrounded by soldiers. Ned Freeman drove his team away to Barge Hole. I later learned that the man who was put into the wagon with Booth was Harrold. There was only one man on the horse with Jett. Where Harrold came from or how he got into Garrett's house I never heard.

I heard that Jett and the Garrett boys got plenty of money and that Jett bought a large farm on the Rappahannock River with his share. They said Jett went to Washington and got the money.

Ned Freeman told us that Bill Rawlins who ran the ferry piloted the troops to Jett's house in Bowling Green. He said Jett got Booth in King George County but brought him to Garrett's house because it was a safe place to keep him until the troops came. Bowling Green is about 16 miles from the Garrett's house and Barge Hole is about 20 miles from the Garrett's farm. Port Royal is 2½ miles away on the Bowling Green Road.

The old tobacco barn in which Booth was shot was made of logs and not very high. Where the dirt fell out between the logs the soldiers could look through the holes and see everything in the barn. I saw it hundreds of times. Inside beams ran across it from side to side to hang tobacco on. You could easily touch these beams with an ordinary step-ladder. Beneath the tobacco the Garrett's kept old tools.

All the facts are as clear in my mind now as they were when I stood watching the barn burning and saw the soldiers put Booth in the wagon and Ned Freeman drive it away.

All who saw the body and Ned Freeman said the soldiers shot Booth in the back of his neck. You are the first person I have ever given my complete story to, but have talked it over with my people hundreds of times.

Yours truly,

(Signed) John Henry Coghill

TOM GARDINER

How He Knew the Conspirators and Booth's Plans

Some of the old people told me that the Gardiners at Silver Hill, Maryland knew all about Booth and what he did just before and after the assassination. They were white folks and I did not feel that I could go to them. Aunt Vina said that Tom Gardiner, the son of old Squire Gardiner, knew things that had not been told; that Booth had visited him the week before Lincoln was shot. So I planned to get him talking if I ever had the chance.

The opportunity came unexpectedly when in the spring of 1912 Tom Gardiner came to me for some dental work. He had been sent to me by an old-time school friend who had married Gardiner's daughter.

When I began to talk about Booth's escape through Maryland and his death in the tobacco barn, Gardiner said that he was a young man at the time and was so connected with the events that he had told no one, because if he had, he guessed the Union soldiers would have hanged him too.

I wanted his story for my Lincoln collection and asked him to write it out for me. This he did and I record it here for the first time just as Gardiner wrote it, his queer spelling and all.

PERSONAL STATEMENT BY HIM

(Received Fri. May 10, 1912)

Six weeks before the Assassination of President Lincoln, John Wilkes Booth, the Assassin was in Charles County Maryland pretending to want to buy a farm. He stopped with Doctor William Queen about one week. During that time I was invited to the Doctor's to see Mr. Booth, had considerable talk with him upon general topics, found him very pleasant and agreeable. I invited him to my father's, Thomas Gardiner, thinking I would be able to sell the place. He stayed with me three days, then by his request, I drove him to Doctor Samuel Mudds house. There he stayed a week. During the time there, Booth, hired a saddle horse from Squire George Gardiner. When he left Mudds house, he left this horse in the care of Chanler Thompson, the Stage driver at T. B. Prince Georges' County, Maryland, then took the stage to Washington. On Tuesday, then it was known that his intention was to capture Lincoln alive, but, finding that he could not catch him without his Cabinet with him. On Friday he decided to take his life; Booth being familiar with all theaters. He took Herrold to the theater, showed him the crank to use to turn all lights at once, telling him when he heard the Pistol shot, turn out the gas, then he could walk out among the audience and it would not be known who committed the deed. But Herrold's heart failed him. Therefore it was that he (Booth) leaped from the box to the stage, turning to the audience saying, six semper Tyranus [*sic semper tyrannis*]. In the jump he broke his leg. He hobbled from the stage in the rear of the theater where the horse he hired from Allison Naylor, awaited him. Then he struck out for T. B. Prince Georges' County, Maryland. Arriving there he put out for Dr. Samuel Mudds where he received surgical attention. Dr. Mudd set his leg, then went to his fathers, secured two black saddle

horses, returned, took Booth and struck out for Aquire Creek
where he hired a boat and was put across into Virginia. Before
Dr. Mudd could get back home the soldiers and detectives were
at his house. Mr. Williams, head detective, went in the house and
had a talk with Mrs. Mudd. She told him that her husband set
his leg, but she did not know the mans name, but he had left his
boot behind. Brought in the boot, Mr. William turned down the
top, and in the lining was written John Wilkes Booth. During the
time Dr. Mudd got to his fathers, turned the horses out in the
field and walked over to the house. Mrs. Mudd told Williams,
there comes my husband. So Williams met him and had a talk.
He denied he set anyone's leg, not knowing that his wife had
told anything. So Williams placed him under arrest and all left
for Bryantown. Just before getting to Bryantown they met a
man by the name of Daniel Thomas, my wifes Uncle, asked him
some questions, found out that he knew Dr. Mudd and had met
him that morning and another man on two black horses going
through Bryantown. So they took his name and address for witness. Stopped in Bryantown a short time and brought Dr. Mudd
to Washington. The next day Soldiers were sent to search the
swamps from Bryantown to Newport. They were three days upon
reaching Newport. They were told that a man of the discription
had been put across the Creek into Virginia. About one weeks
time he was found in a barn in Virginia. He refused to surrender,
the barn was fired, Booth's body was brought to Washington.
The Government had a trial. Mrs. Surratt was hung, Dr. Mudd
sent to prison for life. Shortly after imprisonment, Dr. Mudd
tried to make his escape, crawled through the toilet hole to
swim away, but was captured and placed in close confinement.
The second year Yellow fever broke out. Dr. Mudd offered
his services to cure it. He was successful. Therefore President
Johnson pardoned him for services rendered after nearly

four years. Mr. Williams, dective, I knew personally. Dr. Samuel
Mudd married a Miss Dyer who was my Second Cousin. Since
Dr. Mudd's return from prison, we talked the matter over sev-
eral times. John Suratt, Mrs. Suratts son was known to be with
Booth several times in the County and city.

(Signed) Thos. E. Gardiner

Silver Hill, Md.

WILLIAM J. FERGUSON

*The Only Witness of All the Phases of
the Lincoln Assassination*

When Lincoln was shot the shock and confusion of the moment was so great that few of those present in the theater could give a clear account of what occurred. As the years passed, survivors of the audience told conflicting tales of how they saw Lincoln shot. The stories of these "eyewitnesses" did not impress me as worthy of credence and I was always on the lookout for someone able to prove that he actually saw Lincoln at the instant the shot was fired.

In my search for Lincolniana, it was my custom to pay weekly visits to the old book stores and curio shops where I purchased old photographs, autographs and Lincoln items.

One of my favorite places was on the north side of E Street, just around the corner from Ford's Theater. To this shop came distinguished people, actors, Lincoln collectors, and visitors interested in antiques.

One evening I was called on the 'phone by a man who introduced himself as William J. Ferguson, an actor in the cast of "Treasure Island," playing at a local theater. He had visited the curio shop hoping to find a picture of the interior of Ford's Theater and was informed that I had a number of such photographs some of which might interest him.

When I told him I had a photograph of the entire stage of Ford's Theater taken the day of the assassination with the scenery set for the "American Cousin" and also a diagram of the theater showing the box in which Lincoln sat, he wanted to purchase both of them, but I told him neither was for sale. He then asked for a copy of the stage picture explaining that he was on the stage facing Lincoln at the time of the shooting and that he had been searching for a picture to prove that he was the only person in a position to see the actual shooting. No one else, he assured me, witnessed the entire drama from the moment Booth fired the shot until he leaped to his horse in the alley behind the theater.

My excitement in at last locating a real eyewitness can be imagined. I promised that he should have a copy of the picture as soon as it could be made. A few days later the photograph was mailed to Mr. Ferguson at the Lambs Club in New York.

Weeks passed without an acknowledgment, but on the 1st of March, 1916, I received a letter returning the photograph on which Mr. Ferguson had indicated his position and that of Laura Keene and Harry Hawk. Miss Keene was coaching Mr. Ferguson on the lines he was about to speak. Harry Hawk had turned toward the rear to make his exit leaving only Ferguson in a position to see the puff of smoke and Lincoln's head sag forward.

This picture with Mr. Ferguson's annotations is here reproduced for the first time. Four years later the Ferguson story was published in the *American Magazine* of August, 1920 but without this vividly descriptive illustration.

The stage at Ford's Theatre as it looked on Friday, April 14, 1865, and as William J. Ferguson marked off on it the exact positions of Hawk, Laura Keene and himself on the night Lincoln was shot.

Confirmation of his story appears in this letter on Mr. Ferguson to Dr. Washington. Plan of the interior of Ford's Theatre, showing the location of boxes #7 and #8 where Lincoln and his party were seated. From the scrapbook of Joseph S. Sessford, theatrical manager and ticket-seller at Ford's Theatre, and now in the author's collection.

PART FOUR

THE SPRINGFIELD REVELATION

William de Fleurville,

Also Known as

William Florville

and

"Billy the Barber"

WILLIAM DE FLEURVILLE

or William Florville ("Billy the Barber")

Of all Lincoln friendships, that with William Fleurville is perhaps the most interesting from many angles. First, it was the oldest in Springfield, and second, it was the oddest, being with a colored man.

It has always been a question in my mind why Lincoln had such confidence that the Negro, if freed, would become a good citizen. So far as the world in general knew he was surrounded only by colored people who had been slaves and others recently freed; a group of unschooled people, humble, with knowledge of nothing else than that of the hoe and plow; a people with no known history but that similar to the most ignorant of primitive groups; physical beings uncultured, unlettered and unsung.

These poor children of nature knew but one thing—that Almighty God rules the world, and from tradition they had heard that some day their bonds would be broken by death and then they would be free. In this extremity their hopes and songs were all of the hereafter. Earth had no claims for them, but Heaven was a land of freedom and pleasure where all their sorrows would be healed. I knew that these American representatives of an African people, snatched from freedom and transplanted into slavery by a people foreign to them in every way, had traditions unwritten, a spirit to fight on equal terms with others, a desire to die rather than to be slaves—a spirit of honesty and devotion to duty, and a spirit of gratitude for favors rendered, even by those who opposed them. I had been told, that God only knew why he allowed this group of His devoted children to suffer. Only God saw in them material for a new race, although the schooling and labor must of necessity be severe to bring these rough seeds to bear fruit in a barren land. He knew that with proper leadership and in the proper time, these poor children would at His appointed time become the most loyal and obedient class of citizens that was needed in what America was destined to be—a land where freedom really dwelt—a land where race and color are not barriers—a land where East is really East, West is West, and men are men.

I wanted to go everywhere that Lincoln and his family went. I felt that in Springfield, where Lincoln lived and was buried, there were also some old people left, or if there were not, then some descendants certainly were in this place and these could tell me stories they had remembered.

I had a friend named Charles Pickett who had come to Washington from Springfield with Speaker Cannon and had also served Senator Cullum. He lived with my mother-in-law for many years and he related many Lincoln stories and Springfield stories as told to him by his people.

Charlie said the old people of Springfield told how nearly every colored person in town lined the streets, stood on boxes, waved and yelled as Lincoln passed by on his way to the station to entrain for Washington. While many were glad that he was to be made President of the United States, nevertheless many colored people were so sad to see him go that it was with tears in their eyes that they said "Good-by" and others waved a sad "Farewell."

While many rich white folks could go to Washington to see their friend inaugurated, all the colored could do would be to ask God in their prayers to keep him safe from harm and bring him back to them so that they could again be free to tell him their troubles. He had been the lawyer to whom all the colored folks in Springfield went in time of need, which was often, and now he was going away. While all the white people were happy, the colored felt that he would never return to plead for them and their rights anymore. Charlie said he heard that the day when Lincoln's body was brought back, every colored person in town who could get a few pennies, bought and wore a little black crepe on his arm and stood in line to see the funeral procession pass by. Some of these old people even went to Chicago to attend the ceremonies and they said that the hearse was drawn by two black horses, each attended by a colored groom dressed in black with a crepe hatband and crepe badge. In Springfield I later learned that the old horse Lincoln used to "ride the circuit" was led behind the coffin by an old colored man who had known Lincoln for many years.

My friends, the Picketts, had arranged for me to stay at the home of Dr. and Mrs. S. A. Ware, and when I had been comfortably provided for, I was invited to eat breakfast with her and her husband, who was a physician. When I told Mrs. Ware the object of my visit to Springfield was gathering material for a book on Lincoln and the colored people who knew him and facts I could weave together to prove the theory I had always entertained, etc., she smiled and said to me:

"You can study Lincoln in the large mirror before you on the dining-room wall." Then she began a story that answered the question as to the source of Lincoln's belief that the Negro would respond to education.

She said that her great-grandfather was a barber named William de Fleurville but went by the name of Florville, and was born in Haiti and that the mirror originally hung in front of the barber chair in which Lincoln sat while being shaved and having his hair trimmed. She stated that her brother, who had recently died, made a study of everything pertaining to Fleurville and that the main facts about him were as follows:

> William de Fleurville was born in Cap Haitien, Haiti, West Indies, about 1806. In this island at this period there were constant revolutions, one faction in power today, and another tomorrow. In 1821–22 the great revolution took place and it became necessary for de Fleurville's godmother, his only relative, to flee the country and go to Baltimore, a city where Catholics found a haven. She immediately put the boy in St. Mary's Convent. After a little while she died and the Orphan's Court bound him out as an apprentice in a barber shop. He soon learned the trade. While learning the barber trade he secured employment as a general all-around man in the home of Dr. Elias H. Merriman who later moved to Springfield to continue his practice of medicine there.
>
> The old French town of New Orleans, Louisiana, had always been a mecca for the various wealthy Haitians, not only because the French language was spoken there, but because of its French atmosphere and localities similar to those of the various French settlements in the West Indies.
>
> De Fleurville didn't like Baltimore, its people, its language and the climate, and resolved to go West to New Orleans and St. Louis where his relatives stated he followed the Father Marquette trail that every Haitian child knows in detail. Here he could again live in an environment

similar to that of his childhood days, and hear and speak his native language.

It didn't take long for de Fleurville to see the conditions of the blacks in these towns where they were held as slaves. He saw them bought, whipped and sold. He even heard of many free Negroes who were captured and sold at auction in these cities. These towns were celebrated for their large slave markets. Spurred on by the high price paid for Negro flesh, traders would seize any Negro who could not prove his ownership, place him on the block and demand a price for him. Once incarcerated, there was no appeal either to the Louisiana or Missouri law which a colored person could make to prove he was not a runaway slave. While most free Negroes had their "free papers," many were lost by carelessness, some were stolen, and in some cases slave traders, upon seizing and searching a victim, would destroy the "free papers" and hold the possessor as a runaway Negro.

De Fleurville having been born a freeman in a free country feared that he too, a stranger, might suffer the loss of his liberty, and decided to leave these dangerous places for one where he could be free to do as he pleased and not live in dread of being captured and sold.

In J. C. Powers' *Early Settlers of Sangamon County* we find the following:

> On a hunting excursion from St. Louis, he (de Fleurville) sailed up the Mississippi, into the Illinois, and thence the Sangamon River. It was in the fall of 1831. It was late evening. As he approached the village (New Salem), he fell in with a man wearing a red flannel shirt and carrying an axe on his shoulder, just returning from a day's labor in the woods. They fell into an easy conversation, and walked to a little grocery store together. The tall man was Abraham Lincoln who soon learned the stranger was a barber, nearly out of money and aiming to reach Springfield.

This was enough to enlist the good will of Mr. Lincoln who took him to his boarding house (Rutledge Tavern), told the people of his business and situation. That opened the way for an evening's work among the boarders, and the next morning, he started on his way rejoicing, and reached Springfield the second day.

This was in the fall of 1831. Powers knew both Lincoln and de Fleurville, hence in all probability while he was gathering material for his book he consulted de Fleurville, as he did others whose names and family records are in his book. Herndon knew all about the friendship between Lincoln and Fleurville, but made no reference to him in his books.

We see how easily Lincoln and de Fleurville became acquainted and how Lincoln desired to help him by getting him work enough from this boarding house to make expenses for the balance of the trip.

The first person de Fleurville met in Springfield was Dr. Elias H. Merriman whom he had known in Baltimore and worked for when a boy. Dr. Merriman immediately assisted him. He soon secured employment in the home of General James D. Henry, a noted fighter in the Black Hawk War.

As soon as he could procure the necessary equipment for his office, he opened the first and only barber shop in Springfield in 1832. From that time until his death he became famous as "Billy the Barber." In 1831 he married a fair-complexioned woman whose name was Phoebe Rountree. She was born in Glasgow, Kentucky, February 4, 1811. Five children were born to them, Samuel, Alseen, Sineet, Varneel, and William.

He had the best citizens as his customers, and by thrift became one of the wealthiest men in the community in spite of the demands of a family of five children.

De Fleurville possessed commendable musical talent, playing well on several instruments, including the flute and violin. The latter is said to be still in existence and in an excellent state of preservation. It was well known that he was in demand at the town socials among the best people and that he often was accompanist for Lincoln when the latter was spending an evening at an important social function. An interesting comment on his musical abilities is found in the following quotation from the *Sangamon Journal*,* Aug. 22, 1835:

> The Springfield Artillery made their first appearance in full uniform yesterday . . . .
>
> Attached to the company is a military band, who have new instruments, and promise to make adepts in their profession.
>
> "Jack" Hough was leader of the band, and John Ives, Amos Camp, and "Billy" Fleurville were among the musicians, the latter playing the clarinet. The company was uniformed in blue with red cuffs, and a wide red collar extending down the front of the coat, and tall red plumes waving from their helmets.

The article states that each member of these organizations bought his own uniform.

As a business man, de Fleurville advertised his shop. Almost constantly he kept a witty advertisement in the *Illinois State Journal* and as it became necessary from time to time to move his shop he sought to make it more attractive with a large collection of paintings and engravings to amuse and entertain the "troubled minds, so their gloomy despair would vanish."

De Fleurville from time to time ran a special feature in the *Springfield State Journal.* It was in the form of comic prose and poetry about his services and place of business and was designed to attract new business.

* Illinois State Historical Society, Vol. 3, Jan. 1911, No. 4, p. 26.

His barber shop was the "club house" of Springfield to which nearly every man in Springfield would come to give and hear the latest news. It was packed nearly every evening. This place was Lincoln's second home, and if he could not be found elsewhere, he was sure to be in de Fleurville's shop swapping tales with the owner and other patrons, making new business contacts and discussing the leading topics of the day. If there was one spot in Springfield where he could be *free* to stand before the tall stove and swap yarns with the "boys," it was in this place of merriment and business.

Lincoln gained many a customer here, often left his law books here for days. This shop was his free breathing place and he came to it daily to give, and to take in the little debates that were in the constant making. So close were the relations between Lincoln and de Fleurville that an editorial in the *Illinois State Journal* was published with the following information:

"Only two men in Springfield understood Lincoln, his law partner, William H. Herndon, and his barber, William de Fleurville." The latter knew from the beginning that Lincoln's great purpose, after becoming head of the nation, was the preservation of the Union; that Lincoln was not politically an abolitionist, and that he thought that emancipation, if it came, would be incidental to the defeat of the Rebellion. De Fleurville liked Mrs. Lincoln and she was fond of him, but he had no use for, nor would he tolerate the drinking Herndon in his place.

De Fleurville was very thrifty. Almost from the beginning of his business career he began to acquire property. At one time he owned practically a whole city block, 8th Street to 9th Street on Washington Street, Springfield. His first property was purchased April 1, 1836. Between 1836 and 1864 he acquired twelve distinct pieces of property and in 1848 he purchased four lots for $100 each. They

were situated halfway between the Public Square and Illinois
Wesleyan University, whose trustees bought his property, paying
him $1,200. Lincoln was his adviser and attorney in every legal
matter. Another de Fleurville enterprise was the first clothes-
cleaning establishment in Springfield. One of his advertisements
mentions it.

His donations to the Catholic Church were large for his
time, some running as high as $700 at a time. He also gave
liberally to other churches and charities.

I was told that the lifelong friendship between Lincoln and de
Fleurville certainly manifested itself in business, because from the
very beginning to the end, Lincoln was his attorney in nearly every
transaction and was his confidential adviser in all legal matters.

While Lincoln himself had very little to invest in real estate,
the fact that he was able to advise de Fleurville in his dealings
shows plainly the Emancipator's ability in handling civil as well
as criminal matters. Lincoln knew real estate. He was a surveyor
and knew the country and could tell "Billy" just when property
was to be bought at a bargain. Undoubtedly this knowledge was
correct for his client certainly made a success as a real-estate
dealer. The two letters of Lincoln here reproduced are proofs
of Lincoln's relations to de Fleurville's real-estate affairs.

Bloomington
Sept. 27, 1852

C. R. Welles, Esq.
Dear Sir:

I am in a little trouble— I am trying to get a decree
for our "Billy the Barber" for the conveyance of certain town lots sold to him by Allin, Gridly and Prickett—
I made you a party, as administrator of Prickett, but the
Clerk omitted to put your name in the writ, and so you
are not served— Billy will blame me, if I do not get the

thing fixed up this time— If, therefore, you will be so kind, as
to sign the authority below, and send it to me by return mail,
I shall be greatly obliged; and will be careful that you shall not
be involved, or your rights invaded by it.

Yours as ever

A. Lincoln

Attached to this letter is the following explanatory note by
the son of Prickett:

The Billy the barber—alluded to in this letter, was an old
colored man who lived here, a barber by profession. He also
played the flute at the Evening Entertainments. In those
days our Music on such occasion was the flute Piano Violin
or harp and Billy often played or Served on the Table at My
Mothers home Entertainments. My Father in connection
with Allen & Gridley laid off an addition to Bloomington. He
gave Billy two lots, in Consideration that he shave him during
his lifetime, which Billy did, and he also shaved him at the
time of his death. Billy failed to have his deed recorded &
lost it—a fact he did not discover until after the death of My
Father. He then got Mr. Lincoln to get another— Wells was
the Administrator of My Father's Estate— The Widow of old
Billy Sold the lots Some years after his death for $2500—
Some of his children are Still living here.

Thos. C. Prickett

Springfield,
Feb. 10, 1860

Mr. W. Packard, Esq.
Dear Sir:

William Fleurville, a colored barber here, owns
four lots in Bloomington, on which I have been paying the
taxes for him several years, but which I forgot to, though
under promise, when I was at Bloomington last—will

you please collect the ten dollars fee we spoke of, add enough of your own money, pay all the taxes due, and send me the receipt or receipts? If you will I shall be greatly obliged; and besides, will return you the money you advanced by the first mail. William Thomas, Larrimore and others there know about these lots.

Yours truly,
A. Lincoln

Mrs. Ware related how wide-awake her great-grandfather was when it came to the making of a dollar, and he was always trying to do something to advertise his business. She spoke particularly about his poetry and his newspaper advertisements, but had none to show me. Imagine my delight when a Lincoln collector and scholar in Springfield gave me the following clippings from Springfield papers:

Illinois State Journal, March 23, 1833
William Fleurville, the barber king of the village, announced that he had erected a new barber pole, against which the storms of factions, the hurricanes of the prairies, a common size earthquake or a runaway team will dash in vain.

July 20, 1833, the *Journal* carried another article:

William Fleurville announced that he had removed his barber shop west of the Court on the Public square.

NOTICE EXTRAORDINAIRE

The subscriber feels himself called upon to apologize to his trusty subjects, for closing the Palace door against them during the audience hours on Friday last. It cannot be supposed that my high station precludes me from the attacks of sickness. Therefore be it known, that on the day above written, the stomach of his majesty manifested utter rebellion to the lawful deposits made by order of the Princess Royal; I regret to state, that they were removed notwithstanding the remonstrances of *my* Secretary, and, in short, of *my* whole Cabinet, including the Knight of Industry; consequently I was completely prostrated; I could not have taken a friend by the nasal organ and flourished my razor without serious hazard to the jugular. In addition to these facts noted, it may be properly stated, that my eldest son (heir apparent) is cutting his teeth—a crisis that needs all the care and kindness of a devoted parent. Times are pregnant with important events. Among them, and not the least, is the approaching election. I am personally friendly to all the candidates. No one of them has any reason to fear my opposition. I shall exert myself to secure the election of them all. To effect this object I would say to them that nothing is so necessary as to have "a smooth face." I am adept in making smooth faces. My terms are very moderate. I shall rise in price on some after the election.

June 14,   Wm. Fleurville

In an article to the same paper in 1835, he writes:

My government is in a prosperous condition. New subjects daily present themselves, and if my kingdom continues to increase I shall appoint a register, whose duty it shall be to attend on application for office.

While I take pleasure in acknowledging the loyalty of my subjects, I rejoice that I can communicate to you in a formal way that the Heir Apparent has finished cutting his teeth, and is progressing to manhood as fast as times will admit.

For the past season I have attended to my subjects daily, with the exception of two or three days during which, owing to the treatment of my mineral physician, my bursers stuck out in bold relief and were so swollen that it was impossible for me to articulate. Nevertheless, Secretary Marberry his barber assistant attended regularly.

In conclusion, his majesty would suggest the propriety of his subjects (particularly those whose names are registered) to pay into the treasury all demands that may be found against them, as the pecuniary affairs of the government at this time is not in a very flourishing condition.

William Ashby of Springfield who has contributed so much to this account of Fleurville thinks the facts were that in his "register" were plenty of overdue accounts for shaves, hair cuts, beard trimmings. What he wanted his subjects (customers) to do was to pay their assessments.

Sangamon Journal
March 4, 1837

WILLIAM FLEURVILLE

Hair Dresser & Barber Shop & etc.

They who could get the public favor
Must learn to utter some palaver;
Sound their own fame—or at least show
They'll hold the trump while *others* blow.

Know fashions votaries of either sex,
I am "Habile" in this art complex
For such as wish (if such there be so silly)
Mere red or white (but why 'paint the lilly')

Powders and Puffs, cosmetics too I'll find—
All things, indeed, not needed to adorn the mind.

To such as care for curls, for top knots seek—
Heads I can dress as a la Kemble or as a la Grecque.

I've skill for those, whose hair to curl or cut,
Even those who dash with a bald occiput—
And I never force one unnatural grin
On those who yield to *me* their chin;

While waiting too for the art tonsorial
You may see my specimens of the art pictorial
Perhaps too it is well to hint, that
I'm at last becoming a democrat.

Peoria Register and Northwestern Gazetteer, Feb. 24, 1838:

William Fleurville, lately from Springfield, and more
recently from Bloomington, located permanently in Peoria,
a few doors above Brooks and Cogswell's. Advertisement
started Jan. 6, 1838.

The following advertisement in the *Sangamon Journal,*
Springfield, April 2, 1841, is most interesting as it shows his
religious desire to remember the Sabbath day and keep it holy.

> *Sangamon Journal*
> Springfield
> April 2, 1841

Barber Shop Removed.

The subscriber has removed the shop once occupied by
him a few doors east of Johnson's City Hotel where he will be
glad to wait upon those who will favor him with their custom.

He would also inform his friends that he will not hereafter, open his shop on Sundays, but that he may serve
all he will keep his shop open late on Saturday nights.

> Feb 25th 1870
> John Henry Coghill Born Meh 11th 1852
> Payton Sale " Aug 10th 1852
>
> I do here by certify that the above
> are Correct. Ellis Gravatt
>
> Test
> Hcol E. Gravatt
> tal J. Gravatt

John Henry Coghill, a former slave, at the foot of Emancipation Monument, and the record of Coghill's birth and date of sale, given to him by his master, Ellis Gravatt. Coghill is apparently the only living witness of Booth's capture and death.

William de Fleurville, also known as "Billy the Barber." Reproduced by the author from a photograph owned by Mrs. S.A. Ware of Springfield, Illinois, great-grand-daughter of de Fleurville, and used with her permission.

Anxious at all times to give his whole attention to business on week days, he hopes to be indulged on the Sabbath in devoting his time to those duties which properly belong to that day.

March 19, 1841
Wm. Fleurville

Illinois State Register
Sept. 3, 1841
Wm. Fleurville, Barber & Hair Dresser

Billy will always be found on the spot,
With razor keen and water smoking hot;
He'll clip and dress your hair, and shave with ease
And leave no effort slack his friends to please.
His shop is north-west of the public square,
Just below the office of the mayor;
Strangers or friends may always find him there,
Ready to shave them well or cut their hair.

On Sunday until 9 o'clock he'll shave,
And then to church he'll go, his soul to save.
To his old customers, for favors past,
His gratitude, indeed, will ever last;
He hopes by attention and efforts rare,
A part of public patronage to share.

Illinois State Register
Nov. 12, 1841

Billy Fleurville
    "Billy the Barber"

    Has removed his shop to a new building opposite the north front of the State House (on Washington Street).

The pressure of the times have so embarrassed the people and affected the minds of many, that the *Razor* is not to be trusted in the hands of any but the skilled barber. The papers tell of men, most every day who are in the habit of shaving themselves, or committing suicide with this dangerous instrument. To prevent such a fate let every man who is hard run (and who is not) call on Billy and he will take off the beard with such ease, and cut the hair with such skill, that his patron will forget that he ever had the *blues*. And then Billy has a large collection of paintings and engravings to amuse and entertain the troubled mind, which will so enliven their spirits that the gloom of dispair will vanish like the dark before the glory of the sun. To the young men, who would like the girls to be pleased with them, Billy would say, "come and I'll fix you off to take their eye." Old bachelors, under the operation of Billy's skill can be made to look ten or twenty years younger than they really are; thus they may at the eleventh hour, secure for themselves a wife and a dozen of little ones. Farmers and strangers are particularly and respectfully solicited to give Billy a call.

His charges were reasonable. For shaving one year $15 (75¢ a month). For cutting men's and boys' hair, 15¢; and 20¢ for cutting girls' hair.

While spending the night at the Rutledge Tavern with Lincoln, Fleurville conversed freely with the boarders and answered many questions about himself and his native land, Haiti. One of Fleurville's relatives in Chicago said that from that night Lincoln always seemed interested in the land and people from which Fleurville came. Hence when he became President, it was not surprising that he had a bill passed recognizing the independence of Haiti, and also had placed in it an offer of steamship passage to any person who wanted to go and live there. At first there was no colored Minister wanted from Haiti by the State Department, but Lincoln said he would receive one, and a colored man from this island home of William de Fleurville was received by the great Emancipator with all of the honors given to any other diplomat. Undoubtedly Fleurville's influence upon Lincoln during their long acquaintance had much to do with bringing this event to pass.

Mrs. Ware seemed to be delighted when she was telling me about Fleurville's devotion to the Catholic Church, about his generosity to the poor and about his giving to all kinds of churches that needed assistance.

I was not surprised, therefore, when I read in the One Hundredth Anniversary Edition of the *Illinois State Journal,* November, 1931 an article by Bernard J. Walsh on the History of the Catholic Church in Springfield, under the title "Growth of Catholicism in Community during 97 years," that the first Mass in Springfield was celebrated "At the home of William de Fleurville, a West Indian known as 'Billy the Barber.'"

Although he was Catholic, he helped with his contributions the establishment of the First Christian Church, now the largest Protestant church in Springfield, Illinois. The Christian Church was built in Springfield with money donated by its members and anyone else in the community who would give to it. It was to be used by all sects alike. Then the Mormons came to town to gain converts and the idea of their using the Church did not appeal to the members so they went to the contributors and got the following release, dated Springfield, May 27, 1839:

The undersigned subscribers to the building of the church on lots one and two in Edwards' addition to the town of Springfield, understanding that difficulties have arisen in relation to the use of said Church or meeting house, do appoint and direct that said meeting house or church, be held and used exclusively by and for the use of the church established in Springfield, calling themselves the Christian Church, the said meeting house being the same used by that church since the year 1834.

Stephen T. Logan	[Lincoln's second law partner]
Elijah Iles	[Lincoln's captain in Black Hawk War]
John T. Stuart	[Lincoln's first law partner]
John F. Rague	[Architect of the Illinois State Capitol and the Iowa Territorial Capitol Bldgs.]
John Todd (Dr.)	[Brother of Mrs. Lincoln's father]
William Fleurville	

(and 35 other leaders of the town of Springfield)
Recorded in the Recorder's Office in Springfield.

It was said in Springfield and Chicago where I met some of Fleurville's descendants, that the saddest moment of his life was when he bade Lincoln good-by, after cutting his hair and trimming his beard for the last time. Both reviewed the principal events of their friendship of many years. Both had met as poor strangers, both came to the same town to establish themselves in vocations that would provide for their future. Lincoln went into law, Fleurville into business. From lowly beginnings one became the greatest of American citizens—the other, the highest that he could attain to because of the color of his skin, a successful business man and a Christian.

Fleurville often said to members of his family that when Lincoln left he felt he would never see him again, and when they shook hands and said "Good-by," there was a momentary pause while one gazed into the eyes of the other. Then the President-elect turned and slowly left the old shop where he had spent so many delightful hours.

Mrs. Ware said from the time the news of Lincoln's assassination reached Springfield, April 15, 1865, until Fleurville died, he was never the same. His high spirits went when his old friend was shot and although invited to join the funeral party with Lincoln's best and oldest friends, preferred to go in the funeral procession with the colored citizens of Springfield because he was one of them and felt as they did, that his place was with the colored group who felt Lincoln's passing the most.

On April 3, 1868, Fleurville made his last will and died ten days later. He was buried by Thomas C. Smith and by the same undertakers that buried Tad and Mrs. Abraham Lincoln. His illness, which was very severe, was short and Dr. George D. Allen who attended him made thirty visits from April 1st to April 13th, and charged the estate $56 for services rendered.

Fleurville left all his personal property and income from his property to his widow, Phoebe Fleurville, and made her executrix. After her death the real estate was divided equally among his children and his adopted son, Samuel Henry Fleurville.

With Fleurville's passing, the city of Springfield lost one of its most colorful characters. He had seen it grow from a mere hamlet into the capital of the state. He had known and served not only its leading citizens, but the state's most celebrated politicians, who came to the meetings of the Legislature and also to attend sessions of the Circuit Court.

As a musician he had played at many of its most important gatherings. As a Christian he had helped establish a house of worship as a tribute to the religion of his Haitian forefathers and had assisted other religious denominations in doing likewise. As a father he had successfully raised and educated a large family and amply provided for them. As an uncommissioned ambassador of a little faraway island, he had so conducted himself that the name Haitian came to be respected by all and stood for liberty of smaller groups; and as tradesman his business methods were above reproach.

His early education and his associations never went to his head so that he forgot the people of his native land and those of his own color in America. Throughout a long life he constantly strove to carry out the principles of friendship and love for all. His funeral was one of the largest ever held in Springfield and was attended by the most distinguished people of the city which he had helped to develop and which he loved so much.

PART FIVE

ELIZABETH KECKLEY

*Companion and Confidante
of Mrs. Lincoln*

ELIZABETH KECKLEY

Companion and Confidante of Mrs. Lincoln

Madam Elizabeth Keckley was the most celebrated colored person ever connected with the White House. She not only had the perfect confidence of Mrs. Lincoln, but also that of President Lincoln.

As author of *Behind the Scenes,* Elizabeth Keckley is known to every thorough student of Lincolniana. The book has long been considered the greatest of all source books on the life of Mary Todd Lincoln during the four years she spent in the White House and for several years after.

Mrs. Elizabeth Keckley was born in Dinwiddie Court House, Virginia, about 1818. Her mother was light complexioned and intelligent, with aristocratic slave-owner blood coursing through her veins. Her mother's name was Agnes, and Elizabeth was her only child. Mrs. Keckley stated that she knew very little about the man she thought was her father, George Pleasants, who was slave to a man named Hobbs and was allowed to visit her mother only twice a year. He was sold, sent from the neighborhood and never returned.

To Mrs. Linnie Moore, wife of the late Professor Moore of Howard University, Mrs. Keckley stated just before her last illness that one day her mother told her that her real father was her master. Her *reputed* slave father was very dark, her mother fair, and Mrs. Keckley was fair with magnificent features and a wonderful personality.

When about eighteen years of age, Elizabeth Keckley was given by her owner to a friend, Alexander Kirkland, and after four years she bore him a child named George.

In St. Louis where she was taken with her child, she became an excellent seamstress and was able to take care of seventeen members of her owner's family by working hard, early and late, at her trade.

Here she met James Keckley, a yellow man whom she had known years before in Virginia, and was permitted to marry him. He became dissipated and proved a burden instead of a help-mate, and was a slave, instead of a free man as he represented himself to be. They lived together eight years when he died from his own abuses. She never married again, neither have I ever heard of her being especially fond of any particular man.

Determined to purchase the freedom of her son George and also of herself, she saved whatever she could lay aside and finally received the following promise from Anne P. Garland, her owner:

"I promise to give Lizzie and her son George their freedom, on the payment of $1200. Anne P. Garland June 27, 1855."

When Mrs. Le Bourgois, one of her patrons, heard of the above promise, she solicited from her friends money enough to lend Mrs. Keckley to make up the $1200 needed to secure her free papers. Mrs. Keckley promised to pay back every cent and did so.

In St. Louis, August 13, 1855, her "free papers" were drawn up and the transaction closed.

Know all men that I, Anne P. Garland of the County and City of St. Louis, State of Missouri, for and in consid-eration of the sum of $1200, to me in hand paid this day in cash, hereby emancipate my Negro woman Lizzie, and her son George.

The said Lizzie is known in St. Louis as the wife of James, who is called James Keckley, is of a light complexion, about 37 years of age, by trade a dress-maker and called by those who know her Garland's Lizzie. The said boy, George is the only child of Lizzie, is almost white and called by those who know him Garland's George.

Witness my hand and seal, this 15th day of November, 1855

Anne P. Garland

Witness: John Wickham
            Willis L. Williams

Mrs. Keckley left St. Louis in the spring of 1860 for Baltimore where she remained six weeks before leaving for Washington. At this time it was necessary for free people to be vouched for by someone who had the power to do so. A patron of hers, a Miss Ringold, a member of General Mason's family from Virginia, volunteered to render the assistance needed. Mrs. Keckley soon was sewing for the best people in Washington, chief of which was the family of Jefferson Davis, Senator from Mississippi. She was constantly employed here until the South seceded. Here she heard all of the plans of the South, but was true to the trust placed in her and never revealed them to anyone.

When Mrs. Lincoln came to Washington, Mrs. McClean, a daughter of General Sumner, introduced Mrs. Keckley to her and she commenced to sew for her. In a very short space of time, Mrs. Keckley had sewed in the families of the President of the Union and also that of Jefferson Davis who later became the President of the Confederacy. She was known to all as Washington's most famous seamstress and employed twenty girls in her establishment.

Not long after coming to Washington, her son, George Kirkland, who was then a student at Wilberforce University, enlisted in the Union Army as "White," and was killed in the Battle of Lexington, Missouri (Wilson Creek).

When Mrs. Lincoln heard this news, she wrote to her cousin, Mrs. Elizabeth Todd Grimsley, the following letter:

Sept. 29, 1861
Executive Mansion

My dear Lizzie,

I know you will be sorry to hear that our colored man-tuamaker Elizabeth, lost her only son and child in the battle of Lex. M. She is heart-broken.

She is a very remarkable woman herself.

Your attached cousin,
Mary Lincoln

Mrs. Lincoln had lost her son Edward in 1850, so this loss of Mrs. Keckley made them both mothers of sorrow, and it was possible the comfort that each gave the other cemented a friendship between them unknown before in American history, a President's wife and a colored woman.

Mrs. Keckley had no one to look out for her, so Mrs. Lincoln suggested that she apply for a pension, and after some coaxing, succeeded in having her do so. Owen Lovejoy of Illinois was one of the Lincolns' best friends. He was a minister, and it was probably Mrs. Lincoln's idea that he take up Mrs. Keckley's case. At first there was some difficulty in getting it through, but he stated he would see it was accomplished, even if he had to take it to Congress. Finally, this trouble was surmounted after he left for Illinois, and his brother completed the work. In the beginning, George had been known as just "Garland's George," which meant that he was a slave belonging to Mrs. Garland, but when he grew up he learned more about his real parentage, and at college in Wilberforce, went by his real father's name, Kirkland. He had enlisted not as George Keckley or George, Garland's Negro, but as George Kirkland.

For many years, I searched the records of troops in the Civil War for 1861 looking in vain for George Keckley. I looked under Ohio, Missouri, and in the death lists for the early settlers in the West. I knew that Mrs. Keckley received a pension, and if I could find her application for it, I could then know about the boy's parentage and other information required to be filed when such an application was made, which might lead me to find out about George's enlistment papers.

One day I went to the Veterans' Bureau, and was told by Colonel Hatch, the officer in charge of the Civil War Claims, that all old Civil War Pension records had been sent to the National Archives, and that I might find what I wanted there under Mrs. Keckley's name as mother of George. There I discovered that Mrs. Keckley's son George had served in the Civil War and that she did receive a pension. Photostats were ordered and are reproduced for the first time. Here are the full records of Mrs. Keckley's life and that of George.

STATEMENTS OF
MRS. ELIZABETH KECKLEY

Washington, D. C.—1863

I, Elizabeth Keckley, being duly sworn, do testify and say, that, about twenty-three years ago, I being then, the Slave of Hugh Garland, of Virginia; I was by him married to Alexander Kirkland (a white man) by whom

I have one Son, "George W. D. Kirkland," whose father died when said "George" was eighteen months old. In Eighteen hundred and fifty-five, I purchased myself of Mrs. Garland, paying *Twelve hundred Dollars* for myself and son. For three years after that, my Son paid me out of his wages, over one hundred Dollars per annum. He then went to School until the time of enlistment; I still owe more than *"One hundred Dollars"* for his schooling, and was depending on *him* to pay this, and give me other Support as I might need. About eleven years since, I was married to "James Keckley," a colored man, but have never received any Support from Him: and for more than three years, He has lived in Missouri, and I in this—Washington City.

I still owe *One hundred Dollars* of the money advanced to me, by friends in St. Louis for the purchase of the Freedom of myself and Son. Having borne this, as a mother, purchased him with definite toil and labor, once willingly laid his life upon the altar of his country; I ask the usual pension to a Mother, who has given her only Son, to whom I looked, and on whom alone, next to God—I depended.

Elizabeth Keckley

District of Columbia

SS

County of Washington

On this 18th day of April A. D. 1863 personally appeared before me Justice of the Peace, of the District of Columbia Elizabeth Keckley, a resident of Washington City in the county of Washington and District of Columbia, aged thirty-nine (39) years, who being first duly sworn according to law, doth on her oath make the following declaration, in order to obtain the benefits of the provisions made by the act of Congress approved July 14, 1862: That she was the widow of Alexander Kirkland, and mother of George W. D. Kirkland, who was a private in Company D, commanded by Captain *Richardson,* in the first Regiment of Missouri, in the war of 1861, who was killed in the battle of Wilson Creek on the 10th day of August A. D. 1861.

She further declares that her said son, upon whom she was in part dependent for support, having left no widow or minor child under sixteen (16) years of age surviving, declarant makes this application for a pension under the above mentioned act, and refers to the evidence filed herewith, and that in the proper Department, to establish her claim.

She also declares that she has not, in any way, been engaged in, or aided or abetted, the rebellion in the United States, that she is not in the receipt of a pension under the 2d section of the Act above mentioned, or under any other Act, nor has she again married since the death of her son, the said George W. D. Kirkland.

Elizabeth Keckley

Washington, D. C.

Personally before me, William S. Clary, Justice of the Peace in and for the County of Washington the above mentioned named "Elizabeth Keckley" who being duly sworn doth dispose and say that the two foregoing statements are true and correct, to the best of her knowledge and belief.

Wm. S. Clary, J. P.

Mrs. Keckley was granted a pension of $8 per month commencing August 10, 1863. The pension was later increased to $12. It was stopped upon Mrs. Keckley's death which is recorded as of May 20, 1907. (See Pension record of Elizabeth Keckley M.C. 6135 in files of the United States Archives Building, Washington, D. C.)

This little pension which when granted was a mere pittance, became Mrs. Keckley's sole income in her last days, and having been saving, when she was too feeble to work, she was able to support herself as she had always done.

While sewing for Mrs. Lincoln, she had her dressmaking establishment at 1017—12th Street where she lived in the home of Mr. Walker Lewis. He was one of the leading caterers of the city and kept a boarding house, which was patronized by the most distinguished leaders of colored people then in Washington.

Mrs. Keckley was one of the most liberal contributors to the 15th Street Presbyterian Church, where the Pastor, the Rev. Henry Highland Garnet, ministered to a most select group of members. Mr. Lewis and Mr. William Slade were Trustees. The church furnished Mrs. Keckley's only outlet for relaxation and as long as she could possibly go she attended regularly every Sunday.

So devoted was she to her church, that when she was old and had stopped sewing, many supposed her destitute, not knowing about her pension, and thought she lived on alms given her by the church. It was even said that the church buried her when she died and also donated the tombstone, which now stands at the head of her grave.

Having heard this, I thought so too, but one day while walking down the street in front of my house, I met an elderly man whom I had known for many years. Seeking information from every source, I inquired of him if he knew Mrs. Keckley, and was surprised to learn that he had known her intimately for many years, so that when she made up her mind to have her will made out, she called upon him to do it. He told me that I could go to the Probate Court and not only get a copy of the will he had written for her, but also a statement of the final settlement of her affairs. The next morning, I went to the court and obtained copies as shown in appendix. Mrs. Keckley had money enough left at her death to pay all

Mrs. Elizabeth Keckley, while a teacher at Wilberforce University. The picture was given by Mrs. Keckley to Dr. William Board while he was a student at Wilberforce now in the author's possession.

Copy of Lincoln's funeral expenses from the records in the National Archives, showing $360 paid to Mrs. Keckley (recorded Kickly) for services to Mrs. Lincoln. Courtesy of Archivist Hamer.

of her bills, buy a grave and tombstone and then leave to the Home of Destitute Women and Children a neat sum of $179.11. Mrs. Keckley had never told a single person that she received a pension.

To her most intimate friends, she would at times speak about her son who was killed in the first battle of the war at Wilson Creek, but her constant talk was about Mrs. Lincoln and Tad, and very seldom about her own son George.

After giving up sewing, Mrs. Keckley left Washington to become a teacher of Domestic Art at Wilberforce University. Here she prepared the exhibit of that school for the World's Columbian Exposition, in 1893. She taught here for two years, 1892 and 1893. While here, she also assisted the matron in the management of the girls and was adored by all students.

At Wilberforce, she had a large trunk in which she had kept pieces of goods that she had saved from the various dresses that she made for Mrs. Lincoln, and gave pieces to her favorite pupils to make pin cushions out of them.

I also learned that when she became an inmate of the Home for Destitute Women and Children, which she helped to found, she paid for her room and board, and also upon the insistence of her physician went out for a carriage ride once a week. Yet those in this institution never heard about the pension she received, nor money she had in the bank, and even her closest friends never knew that she received a cent. She always held her head high and never discussed her private affairs.

ELIZABETH KECKLEY
THE WILL

I, Elizabeth Keckley, declare and publish this to be my last will and testament.

I give, bequeath and devise to the *National Association for the relief of Destitute Colored Women and Children* all the property of which I am possessed.

I appoint *Rebecca J. Cole* to be executrix of this my last will and testament, and request that she be not required to give bond for the performance of this duty.

ELIZABETH KECKLEY

ATTESTED AND SUBSCRIBED in the presence of the testatrix and of each other in the city of Washington, District of Columbia this 14th day of November 1905.

WITNESS:

Sara F. Bullard

Lo. Layette M. Hershaw

ELIZABETH KECKLEY
FINAL SETTLEMENT STATEMENT

Died May 24, 1907

The Will—No. 14586

District of Columbia Probate Court Book No. 66 Page 428

First and *Final* Account

Cash on hand	$ 12.04
Death Benefit	50.00
Gift	4.00
In S. Fund	428.25
	$ 494.29

National Bank of Washington, June 1, 1907

Cash on deposit—$428.25

Cash in possession of decedent—$12.04

There were no debts due on estate of decedent.

Copy of final Account of Rebecca J. Cole, Executrix
October 28, 1908.

Court expenses		$ 10.00
Fountain Peyton, Atty.		10.00
Law Reporter		5.00
Washington Bee		5.00
Mrs. Frazier, Nurse		7.50
T. H. Hillyard, Mending clock		1.25
James H. Winslow, funeral expenses		104.00
Columbian Harmony Society, vault, etc.		10.00
L. H. Hershaw, Atty for drawing up will		10.00
Thom. Heany, monument		100.00
Insurance household goods		1.00
Car fare		2.00
Commission on $494.29 at 10%		49.43
	Total	315.18
	Balance	179.11
	Total	$ 494.29

Distributed in accordance with the provisions of the last will and testament of said deceased as follows to wit:—

To the National Association for the Relief of Destitute Colored Women and Children $179.11

Mrs. Alberta Elizabeth Lewis-Savoy was her godchild. Mrs. Keckley having been present when she was born, and when her mother Mrs. Walker Lewis died, she acted as mother for Alberta and her sister. The training Mrs. Keckley gave these girls still shows itself in the carriage, refinement and culture of this lady, who still lives.

From a statement given me by Mrs. Lewis-Savoy I quote as follows these extracts:

She carried on an extensive dressmaking business and taught young colored girls how to sew, fit and design pretty dresses. She had a figure on which she draped the dresses. I forget the name she called the figure; but she taught the S. T. Taylor system of cutting and she sent out from her dress-making establishment finished dressmakers. Many seam-stresses owe their success in life to the thorough, painstaking instruction given by Mrs. Keckley.

While living with us on P Street, Mrs. Keckley gave me a piece of black thread and told me that it came off a dress of Mrs. Abraham Lincoln; and she also gave me a little piece of Valenciennes lace that came off a white linen cambric dress worn by Mrs. Lincoln.

Mrs. Keckley was a woman of refinement and culture, always careful of her associates— She carried herself gracefully and well poised and had a striking and pleasing personality.

She was very particular and exacting and insisted that the young girls whom she was teaching to sew in her establish-ment sit erect at all times; and never allowed them to pin their sewing on their knees. This of course, was to prevent them getting a stooping posture.

I think the best of all descriptions of Mrs. Keckley was writ-ten for me by Mrs. Eva N. Wright, who knew her very well and was almost a constant companion of hers while she was a teacher at Wilberforce University. She wrote:

Mrs. Keckley was light mulatto, tall and graceful in bear-ing. In profile she suggested the Grecian type, thin lips, and an aquiline nose, high cheeks, twinkling eyes and a keen sense of humor. Always entertaining and never without dignity.

The following passages are from letters given me by persons who knew Mrs. Keckley at different periods of her long life. Mrs. Keckley lived for some time during her last years with the family of John Gray, who had been one of Washington's leading caterers during Lincoln's times. His daughter LeBerta sent me a letter from which I have copied the following:

> She was a woman of high ideals, character and dignity. As I remember her, she was very reserved, refined, intelligent and unobtrusive. Her voice was soft, pleasing and convincing. She did not often speak of her past life but would tell those about her that she had put an account of it in a book which they could read. "I do not like to burden others with the sorrows of my past," she would sometimes say.
>
> In her declining years she was unusually straight for one of her age, walked with a graceful movement and a steady pace. Her manner was most dignified at all times. She usually wore a long black dress with a white fichu at the neck when dressed for the street. At home she wore either a white or a black and white wrapper. She was always neat and kept a very tidy room.
>
> There were certain rules of decorum she always observed. She never left a company of people or an individual with her back turned toward them or him. She did not linger after telling her friend "Good-bye." She would say "Good-bye means I am leaving so why continue to remain?" She considered it inelegant to cross the street except at the intersection. She was courteous to the "Nth" degree and to every favor requested she never failed to say, "I thank you."
>
> Women in high official capacity were her customers. Adjoining her establishment was that of Madam Estern, colored, a fashionable hairdresser. Both of these colored establishments served the very best people of the city and vicinity.

Tom Clark, who served some time as a Deputy Recorder of Deeds for the District of Columbia, wrote of his recollections of Mrs. Keckley:

I frequently heard my parents speak of her. She was a magnificent-looking woman, tall, stately and with an imperious-looking face and features of such distinction, that she would have been an outstanding personality at a social gathering of Louis the Fourteenth, when the Bourbons were at the peak of their power and still had an abundance of brains.

I often talked with Mrs. Laura Fisher who was one of the post-graduates of Howard University, and a retired Washington public school teacher, and had known Mrs. Keckley from the time she joined the 15th Street Presbyterian Church until she died. In fact, Mrs. Keckley was a constant visitor to her home and was very friendly with the whole family and even gave her oldest sister a copy *of Behind the Scenes.* Mrs. Fisher said:

> Mrs. Keckley was one of the most picturesque women that walked the streets of Washington, and wherever she went, people would turn to admire her carriage. She was so much out of the ordinary in looks and dress, that people would turn and wonder what nationality she belonged to.
>
> Members of the Presbyterian Church would often come on Sundays to see Mrs. Keckley walk down the aisle to her pew, and every eye would turn to see her because of her queenly walk, and to admire the beautiful and fitting way that she was gowned; refined and rich, but not gaudy.
>
> From her contact with the best that the white society could produce she had absorbed culture and had a conversational ability that would have done credit to a Mrs. Lincoln or some of the best-educated persons who patronized her. She was a leader in nearly all of the church activities, and always gave most freely of her means for its support. She was very fond of children and young people, and delighted to be with them. Being a witty and wonderful

conversationalist, full of life, her company was courted by all. She could charm you when she gazed into your eyes and gave you a smile. The church was her life and she always attended its meetings as long as she could do so, which was nearly fifty years.

When she was spending her last days in the Home for Destitute Colored Women and Children, there were two teachers of this school who saw and conversed with her daily, one of them Loretta Simms, now connected with this Institution, wrote:

> I recall very clearly Mrs. Elizabeth Keckley while she was with us during the last days of her life.
>
> Although here for a short time, I saw her daily. She kept to herself all the time and only went out for a ride once a week when Dr. Cole, the Superintendent, made her do so.
>
> She seemed sad and despondent all the time, talked to the inmates here very little, wrote very little if any, and read her Bible the greater part of the time. She seemed to have lost interest in everything, appeared worried and really pined away.
>
> She often talked about Mrs. Lincoln and Robert and sewing in the White House for Mrs. Lincoln. She told Dr. Cole, the Superintendent, about her book and to Mrs. Anna Eliza Williams, the kindergarten and first grade teacher, she told many things about her affairs. Mrs. Keckley and Mrs. Williams talked together very often, and came in contact almost daily.
>
> She always kept herself very neat, fixed her hair upon the top of her head, and generally wore an old black silk dress with a little train. She carried herself erect and walked sprightly up to the time she was taken ill and died. She left nothing except a few old clothes.
>
> She was sick only a very short time and died quietly in her little room which was on the first floor of our old

building across the street where the Banneker Center is now.

She was an excellent talker, had a wonderful memory, quiet and polished voice, and her language was refined and correct.

(Signed)

Loretta Simms

Loretta Simms also told me that "Miss Eliza Williams was at this Institution when Mrs. Keckley was there. Mrs. Keckley would talk with her very freely. I think she can give you some valuable information about Mrs. Keckley. I heard that Mrs. Keckley wrote a book that hurt her. I never saw a copy. Mrs. Keckley told Dr. Cole and Mrs. Williams about the book."

Mrs. Anna Eliza Williams wrote me as follows:

In reply to yours of June 11, '38 I am compelled to return to early childhood, when I lived on New York Avenue between 12th and 13th Streets, N. W., in a little brick house with queer attic windows, in order to show you the connection.

It has been torn down to make way for the stately Temple at the corner. On the north side of the street near the end of 12th was a little candy and notion store kept by a Mrs. Stuntz. All the children in the neighborhood came to this store to buy a penny's worth of taffy. Very often we would stand on the curb to see General Grant's children pass by in their little pony cart. Sometimes they would go into the store—to buy taffy too, we supposed.

It was at this store that I first saw Madame Keckley. She was tall with long black or dark hair. As a child when I saw her I thought she was an Indian. Later on I found that she was a dressmaker and sewed for Presidents' wives and Big Folks.

The children had a fad of collecting "Memory Buttons." Knowing her relation with the "High Ups" and finding that she lived on 12th Street between H and New York Avenue with a Mr. and Mrs. Walker Lewis, I went to her home with others, to beg for buttons; she gladly gave us a button. I had no contact with her for years afterwards; because of loss of my parents, I was placed with guardians.

Years later I was employed at the Home for Destitute Women and Children. I had been there for several years when Madame Keckley was admitted as an inmate. Her position in the home was a very trying one. Here I learned to know her. I found her polished and intelligent above the women of her time and while painfully reserved she was as truly cultured as the women with whom she had had years of contact—the wives of Presidents and women of higher life. Her language was always well spoken. I would often go to her for a story about the White House children, in order to inspire the tots I taught. The stories were very interesting.

I asked her about the book she had written on Mrs. Lincoln and if she would let me see a copy if she had one. She sighed and became depressed—saying her copy has been misplaced, that the book had been suppressed. She said her object in attempting to write the "Life of Mrs. Lincoln" was because Mrs. Lincoln had been a true friend to her and by selling the book she would be able to help her, as Mrs. Lincoln was in poor circumstances. She also said the book caused her much sorrow and loss of friends. She never thought of injuring such a loyal friend.

Madame Keckley said she was in New York City when she started the book, and from what she said, she must have seen Mrs. Lincoln very often. Madame Keckley must have had abiding confidence in someone who helped her with the book. She said, "He pretended he

was my friend and wanted to help me make the book a success." He persuaded her to turn over to him the letters she
had from Mrs. Lincoln so he could get certain extracts; that
he could understand better by seeing some of the letters. He
was not to print anything very private or personal. Only facts
that would make the book a success.

She saw Robert Lincoln before she entered the
"Home." He was so hostile to her that he could not be
made to understand her true motive for writing the book.
Mrs. John Brooks, her two daughters and sons often visited Madame Keckley. An artist by the name of Mrs. Wilson
painted a large picture of "Madame K" which stayed in the
"Home" for a long time on exhibition.

There were two white relic hunters who came to see if
Madame "K" had any White House relics. She had none to
my knowledge. I have been unable to find a report of when
Madame "K" was admitted to the "Home." I have given you
in a rough way what I know of Madame Keckley.

(Signed) Mrs. Anna E. Williams

Mrs. Keckley's presence at the Home was known only to
a very few old acquaintances of the church and her pastor. It
was as she wanted it to be. The room was a little dingy one in
the basement with one window facing the setting sun. Over
the dresser was a picture of Mrs. Lincoln. On the dresser were
a comb and brush and her Bible. A little table with a pitcher
and bowl in one corner, a straight chair in another, and a rocking chair constituted all that was in this room, except an old
trunk containing the few clothes she owned. She passed away
in peaceful sleep, from a paralytic stroke, on May 26, 1907,
after an illness of only a few days.

Thus passed from this world one of the most persecuted of women. One who, through love, carried throughout life a condemnation undeserved, just because she loved her friend, Mrs. Lincoln, with a love that never died.

In the old Harmony Cemetery in Washington, D. C., is to be found all that remains of most of the illustrious colored people who loved and served Lincoln while he was in Washington. On a beautiful knoll, facing the east beneath a mammoth spreading elm tree rests forever all that remains of Elizabeth Keckley.

These ashes are entombed far beneath the surface, while the greenest sod drapes a mantle over the little mound leveled by time and nature's elements.

Far from the maddening cries of those who would destroy her, and surrounded by the last earthly homes of her dearest friends she lies while waiting for the last trumpet to sound.

I shall never forget my first visit to this sacred plot. A peculiar deathlike stillness spread throughout the cemetery, not a human sound could be heard to disturb the chorus of the birds who seemed to have gathered in the leafy boughs of this magnificent old tree to add their music to that of the organ of the winds, and to sing their daily requiem for this departed soul who loved nature and its God so well, and who sacrificed all for a friend whom she could never cease to remember, and with whom I feel she now associates again in that happy land above where the wicked cease from troubling and the weary are at rest.

Mrs. Keckley's name and date of death are carved on the face of her tomb, and she selected these words from Psalm 127, second verse, to be inscribed beneath them:

FOR SO HE GIVETH
HIS BELOVED SLEEP

All admit that in Elizabeth Keckley, Mrs. Lincoln had a true and devoted friend. For some unaccountable reason Mrs. Lincoln would yield to Mrs. Keckley when her husband could not get her to budge. When she was sick from her dreadful headaches, she wanted to see no one, nor have near her any one but "Lizabeth" and even when she spent that horrible night in the Petersen house waiting for the end to come to her loving husband, she kept up a constant cry for Mrs. Keckley.

It has been written that Mrs. Keckley's power over Mrs. Lincoln was uncanny, and just a kind word, or a pleasant smile from her would bring the desired result. Is this strange when she complained of the treatment of her closest acquaintance, for if ever a poor soul needed sympathy Mrs. Lincoln did. Mrs. Lincoln's niece wrote that even as a child, Mary Todd would always run to her old Mammy for comfort and protection, and when she found Mrs. Keckley, she naturally did the same with her.

In every emergency, she had a true friend and comforter in her colored modiste, who stood by her when all others had fled. So close to the family was this mulatto woman that she even washed and dressed the body of little Willie when he died. Mrs. Lincoln clung to her colored friend when her husband was snatched from her side by the assassin. During the six weeks that she remained alone in the White House in a nervous collapse, resulting from the experiences of that dreadful night of April 14, 1864, she would not let Mrs. Keckley leave for a moment.

Interesting verification of Mrs. Keckley's services to Mrs. Lincoln at this time of stress is to be found in the copy of a bill given here and a photostat of which appears in the Appendix:

BILLS FOR PRESIDENT LINCOLN'S FUNERAL
Paid by the Commissioner of Public Buildings

To Elizabeth Kickey [Keckley]

To Services as first Class Nurse & attendant on Mrs.
  Lincoln from April 14th to May 26th, 1865. 6
  weeks at $35.00 per week $210.00

Traveling & incidental expenses in attending Mrs.
  Lincoln to her home in Chicago, Ill. & return trip
  to Washington. 100.00

Amount expended in requisite mourning apparel . . .   50.00

$360.00

Finally, when Mrs. Lincoln was able to travel, Mrs. Keckley did not leave her at the old railroad station, but at Mrs. Lincoln's insistence accompanied her to Chicago.

Aunt Rosetta Wells knew Mrs. Keckley very well and said she was as tall and straight as an arrow, and didn't take "tea for the fever" from anybody and was the only person in Washington who could get along with Mrs. Lincoln, when she became mad with anybody for talking about her and criticizing her husband. Annie also found articles in old newspapers giving Mrs. Keckley the very devil for writing *Behind the Scenes.* The old folks said it was a great book and told the truth and it was just because Mrs. Lincoln liked this colored woman that some of the newcomers had tried to harm Mrs. Keckley; but Uncle Ben, who said he never told a lie in his life, prophesied that some day she would be a saint in glory and her manners would be handed down by generations unborn, because she told the truth, as God had given her the light to see it, even if she was "Behind the Scenes."

"BEHIND THE SCENES"

Story of Mrs. Keckley's Book

I believe I would have remained merely a collector of Lincolniana and this book would never have been written but for a bombshell, in the form of an article sent to the newspapers by a National Press Service, stating that Mrs. Keckley was not the author of *Behind the Scenes.*

I felt that the duty of protecting the name and work of Elizabeth Keckley rested upon me and that I should set at rest forever all doubts as to Mrs. Keckley's relations with the Lincolns and her book *Behind the Scenes.*

In Grandmother's day, the old folks said "Lizzie" Keckley had her sewing establishment first on Pennsylvania Avenue, then on 12th Street. They all either knew her or had heard a great deal about her. Aunt Rosetta Wells knew her well, for while she and Mrs. Brooks were doing the plain sewing for the White House, Mrs. Keckley would come into Mrs. Lincoln's room at any time and stay for hours. They said she fairly lived in the White House.

While I had heard of Mrs. Keckley as far back as I can remember, and knew scores of people who knew her, I never saw her. I believed that Mrs. Lincoln had a hand in writing the book *Behind the Scenes,* because Mrs. Keckley, proud, reserved and tight-lipped would not have published it without Mrs. Lincoln's knowledge and consent. I could not understand why

Mrs. Keckley would never defend herself or tell who helped her to write the book.

She would only say "It is all a sad memory," and refuse to discuss the book at all. Was she shielding someone? Was there anything more to be said about a woman that had not been said about Mrs. Lincoln by those who hated her?

I have told of Mrs. Lincoln's love for colored people, and how she relied upon them more than upon her relatives, when she was in need, and how she was a great admirer of Frederick Douglass and Rev. Henry Highland Garnet.

The first step toward proving that Mrs. Keckley wrote *Behind the Scenes* was to establish beyond question Mrs. Lincoln's close personal interest in Mrs. Keckley and that Mrs. Keckley was actually employed in the White House. This was accomplished when, on a visit to Springfield, I found in the Illinois State Historical Society Library an undated letter from Mrs. Lincoln to George Harrington, Assistant Secretary of the Treasury, of which the following is a copy:

Executive Mansion

Hon. Sec. Harrington
     Dear Sir:
     I am under many obligations to you, for your frequent kindnesses to me, and will only request you to add another name, in the place of Ellen Shehan & will promise not to trouble you again. The woman, who is most estimable, is named Elizabeth Keckley, although colored, is very industrious, and will perform her duties faithfully. I do not believe, I am making a vain request of you—and I will not trouble you again.
     Please insert her name in place of the other, I presume you will not object to her not entering upon her duties, until the middle of April, you see Mr. Harrington,

I am calculating on your kindly agreeing to my proposal.

Very respectfully,

(Signed) Mrs. Lincoln

My belief that Mrs. Lincoln knew of the book *Behind the Scenes* and had a hand in writing it was substantiated when I found in the *Argus* of Albany, New York, under the date of April 15, 1868, the astonishing caption, "Mrs. Lincoln's book," and the article which follows:

MRS. LINCOLN'S BOOK

It is announced that Mrs. Lincoln has written a book. The volume will contain much that is interesting, as it will give an inside view of the White House during her four years residence there. It is probable that she was impelled to this from the fact that her old admirers and flatterers snubbed her so rashly when she proposed to sell her cast-off clothes, and the fine presents which she found were worth nothing to her.

When plain "Mrs. Clarke" exposed these articles for sale, the relic hunters and gossips came to stare at them, but none to buy. The office holders and the contractors came not at all. Mrs. Lincoln was justly indignant. And to give vent to her indignation, and to show up the base ingratitude of the men upon whom she had conferred benefits that had led them on to fortune, she determined to write a book.

We are now told that the book, in spite of all sorts of efforts to keep it back, is nearly or quite ready for the press, and will soon make its appearance in print. An Illinois editor has been permitted to look through some of its pages, teeming with all that is rich and rare in Radical rule and rascality. Hundreds of prominent members of the Radical party are painted in colors that will make them still more prominent, but, if possible, far

Mrs. John H. Brooks (Hannah F.) in whose aunt's house in Broome Street, New York, the book "Behind the Scenes" was written by Mrs. Elizabeth Keckley. Photo used here by courtesy of her daughter, Mrs. Mary E. Brooks, who owns the original.

Mrs. Elizabeth Keckley in later life and her grave at Harmony Cemetery. Mrs. Keckley's photo, courtesy of Mrs. Alberta Lewis-Savoy, daughter of Walker Lewis, in whose house Mrs. Keckley lived.

less respectable. The Illinois editor gives me an inkling of what is to come. He refers especially to the case of John A. Logan. In connection with this fresh-blown statesman, Mrs. Lincoln records the history of a diamond ring—a splendid solitaire.

When Logan presented it to her he gave her to understand that it cost him several hundred dollars. Remembering how few there were of Logan's friends with whom his word was as good as his well-endorsed bond, she sent the ring to a New York jeweller with a request that he would tell her the value of it. As she anticipated the ring turned out to be worthless—or very nearly so, the jeweller placing its value at eighteen dollars—and it was returned to Logan with a message which he probably remembers.

From this little incident we may form some idea of the quality of Mrs. Lincoln's book. It is to be hoped that she will not suffer herself to be deterred from publishing it. The public will readily take a hundred thousand copies, and from its sale she will realize quite as much as her cast-off finery would have brought her.

I think the first ground for questioning the authorship of the book was based on the mistake of the Carlton Company in *printing* the copyright notice as filed in Pennsylvania instead of New York. It appeared on the back of the title page as follows:

Entered according to Act of Congress in the year 1868, by

ELIZABETH KECKLEY,

In the Office of the Clerk of the District Court of the United States for the Southern District of Pennsylvania.

This mistake was brought to my attention by Mr. V. Valta Parma, Curator of the Rare Book Collection of the Library of Congress. He realized that the weakest link in the work of writers on Lincoln was the uncertainty as to whether *Behind the Scenes* could be accepted as an authentic source and he had been searching the Copyright Archives for evidence regarding the actual authorship.

Mr. Parma told me that he had found the original copyright entry and showed me the huge record book of 1868 in which applications for copyrights were entered by Mr. George F. Betts, clerk of the United States Court for the Southern District of New York. Turning to the entry for the Tenth of June he pointed out that here was proof that the author resided in New York and that Elizabeth Keckley not only claimed that she was the author but that she was the proprietor, that is, owner of all the rights connected with the copyright.

A transcript of this copyright entry follows:

Southern District of New York ss

Be it remembered, That on the *Tenth* day of *March* Anno Domini 1868

(*Elizabeth Keckley*)   of the said

District   has   deposited in this

Office the title of a *Book*

the title of which is in the words following, to wit:

Behind

the

Scenes

or

Thirty years a slave and Four years in

the White House

by

Elizabeth Keckley

formerly a slave but more recently Modiste &

Friend to Mrs. Abraham Lincoln

the right whereof—*she* claims as *Proprietor & Author* In conformity with an Act of Congress entitled "An Act to Amend the several Acts respecting Copyrights."

George F. Betts
Clerk of the Southern District of New York.

The American Literary Gazette & Publisher's Circular of April 1, 1868, published by George. W. Childs, 600 Chestnut Street contained this notice on page 304:

G. W. Carlton and Co.
Will publish early in April A Remarkable Book entitled
Behind the Scenes

By Mrs. Elizabeth Keckley 30 years a slave in the best Southern families and since she purchased her freedom, and during the plotting of the Rebellion a confidential servant of Mrs. Jefferson Davis where "Behind the Scenes" she heard the first breathings of that Monster's Secession. Since the commencement of the rebellion and up to date, she has been Mrs. Abraham Lincoln's Modiste (dressmaker) confidante and business woman generally. A great portion of her time having been spent in the White House in the President's own family. Being thus intimate with Mrs. Lincoln and her whole family as well as with many of the distinguished members of Washington society, she has much to say of an interesting nature in regard to men and things in the White House, Congress, Washington and New York. She discloses the whole history of Mrs. Lincoln's unfortunate attempts to dispose of her wardrobe, etc, which when read will remove many erroneous impressions in the public mind, and place Mrs. Lincoln in a more favorable light.

The book is crowded with incidents of a most romantic as well as tragic interest, covering a period of forty years. It is powerfully and truthfully written and cannot fail to create a wide world interest not alone in the book, but in its gifted and conscientious author. It is perfectly authentic. One Vol. 12 mo. 400 pp. cloth. Illustrated with portrait of the author. Price $2.00

Having satisfied myself as to Mrs. Lincoln's knowledge of the book previous to its publication, there was only one thing more that I needed to find out—*who helped Mrs. Keckley write the book.* No trace could be found of the records of the Carlton Company. Only their advertisements remained. In the *New York Commercial Advertiser,* was found the following announcement which gives Mrs. Keckley credit as author of *Behind the Scenes* and gives the approximate date of publication:

SATURDAY APRIL 4, 1868
NEW PUBLICATIONS

———

A LITERARY THUNDERBOLT
will be launched from the press of

G. W. CARLTON & CO.
in a few days, entitled

BEHIND THE SCENES
by Mrs. Elizabeth Keckley

For 30 years household slave in the best Southern families, since she purchased her freedom, and during the plotting of the Rebellion Mrs. Jefferson Davis's confidential servant, where "Behind the Scenes," she heard the first breathings of Secession. Since the commencement of the rebellion, and up to date, she has been Mrs. Abraham

Lincoln's *modiste* (dress maker), confidential friend, and business woman generally; a great portion of her time having been spent in the White House in the President's own family. She has much to say of an interesting, not to say startling nature, in regard to men and things in the White House, Washington, and New York. She discloses the whole history of Mrs. Lincoln's attempt to dispose of her wardrobe, &c.

The work is thoroughly authentic and truthful, 1 vol., cloth, illustrated with portrait of the author. Price $2.00

The book was reviewed under "Just Published" in the *New York Commercial Advertiser,* April 16, 1868.

Mrs. Keckley has told her story plainly and clearly and with sufficient piquancy. Mrs. Lincoln speaks her mind freely in the book, and occasionally criticizes very sharply some persons in whom she evidently lost confidence.

On Saturday, April 18, 1868, the following notice appeared in the advertising columns:

"Notice" A Literary Thunderbolt launched this day from the press of G. W. Carlton & Co. entitled "Behind the Scenes."

On Wednesday, May 13, 1868, an additional notice appeared in a New York paper with the words:

White House Revelations
or
Behind the Scenes

On Saturday, May 30, 1868 in the regular advertising notices of
the G. W. Carlton Company in *The New York Library*, I found
this advertisement:

> Behind the Scenes The Great Sensational
> Disclosure by Mrs. Keckley $2.00

If Mrs. Keckley did not write *Behind the Scenes,* she would
have complained about the use of her name in a way that
might ruin her business. I have not discovered a single book
reviewer, journalist or politician who, at the time the book
was published, claimed that Elizabeth Keckley was either a
"pseudonym" or was assumed to hide the real author.

Fortunately there were living in Washington, scores of
people who knew Mrs. Keckley intimately. Some had lived
with her, and others were her last attendants in the old home
in which she died. Even her old pastor was alive and was called
upon for corroboration.

I interviewed old friends and acquaintances of Mrs. Keckley.
One told me that he had made signs for her and that Mrs. John
H. Brooks knew her so well that if I went to see her, I might get
some real facts. I had known Mrs. Brooks ever since I was a boy
and played with her boys, Dan and Reggie, and later on taught
school in the same building with her daughters. I felt sure that
if Mrs. Brooks knew anything, she certainly would tell me.

Mrs. Brooks was one of the leading colored citizens of
Washington. She was related to the Slades and her husband
was steward for Admirals Dahlgren and Farragut.

When I saw Mrs. Brooks she instantly recalled the
days long passed and told me that she had known Mrs.
Keckley ever since she was a little girl and had lived with
her aunt on Broome Street, New York. Then she began to

tell me about the writing of *Behind the Scenes*—and without any questioning, told me how James Redpath used to come to see Mrs. Keckley, and spend the afternoon writing what she told him. The next day he would return, read what he had written, and then write down more for the next day. She said she was in and out of the room all the time waiting on both grownups.

Mrs. Brooks was blind at the time I called, and her daughter Mamie who was present at each interview, wrote the following statement of what her mother told me:

> Mr. William Slade, who was President Lincoln's messenger and much beloved by him, was my mother's and aunt's (Mrs. Bell's) first cousin, and to us he gave a lock of President Lincoln's hair, and Mrs. Slade, his wife, gave us a piece of the dress that Mrs. Lincoln wore the night of the assassination. We still have both.
>
> When Mrs. Keckley was employed by Mrs. Lincoln as seamstress, she became very intimate in my family and that of my cousin, William Slade. She was sent to New York on business and stayed with Mrs. Bell, 543 Broom Street from time to time.
>
> Our house on Broom Street was a very large one with two immense parlors and was used by my aunt for rooming and boarding. One parlor was for the family and the other was used for private business by our guests. The most celebrated colored men and women of that day boarded with us. A few of whom I recall were: Frederick Douglass, Representative Rainey, Senator Revels, General Smalls, Martin Delaney, members of the Liberian Society, Rec. Stella Martin, Congressmen and their families from Washington. All of these men knew and consulted Mrs. Keckley on important matters because she could get the attention of the President and Mrs. Lincoln.

Many abolitionists visited her because she was so close to Mr. and Mrs. Lincoln and could probably influence them.

Mr. Walker Lewis' boarding house on 12th Street in Washington, D. C., catered to the same type of boarders. Mrs. Keckley lived with them in Washington and with us in New York.

During the fall and early winter of 1867, while Mrs. Keckley was trying to sell Mrs. Lincoln's clothes, she stayed at my aunts boarding house and as my aunt's helper, I was constantly in her room and the parlor, doing small things for her and observed what was going on. She wrote greatly at night and every morning many white men would come to see her in the private parlors about the writings. No white women ever came to see her at our house. One man by the name of Redpath would spend several hours every evening with her. Everybody in the house knew that Mrs. Keckley was writing a book on Mrs. Lincoln and that Mr. Redpath was helping her compile it. He was a medium built, red-faced man, and generally wore a reddish brown suit. He was quite pleasant to all of us. He would take down her story each evening, read what he had compiled, and the next evening return for more facts to be arranged. I was constantly in and out of the room, taking ice water, etc., and doing little errands for her.

[The name is "Redpath"—not Ridpath, the historian.]

The book was published after she left us to live with Mrs. Amelia Lancaster, another friend of hers living at No. 14 Carroll Place, New York City. Mrs. Lancaster was a very fine hairdresser and worked for the leading society people of New York. She taught many young ladies the trade of hair dressing. To help herself out financially, Mrs. Keckley took in some sewing at Mrs. Lancaster's but did nothing but attend to business and write her book while with us.

Everybody in New York and Washington was criticising

Dr. Washington interviewing Mrs. Anna E. Williams regarding her remembrance of the writing of "Behind the Scenes."

Mrs. Mary Lincoln—from an old photograph, one of many circulated by the New York Photographic Co.

Mrs. Lincoln: newspapers were abusing her, and nearly every kind of a tale was put out about her actions in the White House after President Lincoln died. I cannot see why Mrs. Keckley was so criticised for writing in her book what had already appeared in the newspapers all over the country. Nobody spoke kindly about Mrs. Lincoln except Mrs. Keckley, who almost idolized her and made every sacrifice of her business for her. She always covered Mrs. Lincoln's faults. Why she wrote the book I can never understand.

Mrs. Keckley's book was suppressed. She made nothing from it, but lost most of her trade and some of her best friends of my race who thought the book did much harm to all colored persons similarly employed. My copy was misplaced years ago. I think she gave Mr. Slade a copy.

Mrs. Keckley whom I knew from childhood until her death at the Eighth Street house was a most charming person. Everybody delighted in her conversations and she could more than hold her own with Douglass, Highland Garnet, and other guests; men of the highest culture, attainment and education. She had a well modulated musical voice and refined manner of holding herself. She was at all times well-dressed, was very courteous, and had a broad knowledge of etiquette.

My husband, who knew Mrs. Keckley and my cousin, William Slade, was a sailor, had been with Admiral Dahlgren at the Washington Navy Yard and with Admiral Farragut in the battle of Mobile Bay. I first saw President Lincoln at the Washington Navy Yard when we were with Admiral Dahlgren. He bowed, saluted, and spoke to me when I spoke to him. When my cousin, Mr. Slade died, my husband acted as one of his executors.

June 11, 1938

Dr. John E. Washington has been an acquaintance of our family for many years, which accounts for mother's freedom in giving him the data as quoted.

She was born December 22, 1842 and was buried December 22, 1936 in Harmony Cemetery, not far from Mrs. Keckley's grave. Her mind was clear to the last and her memory of past events remarkable. She remembered dates and names perfectly.

On each of the several occasions that Dr. Washington consulted with her about Mrs. Keckley, she always repeated the same facts as if they had just happened.

As I was present at all of the interviews which Dr. Washington had with my mother, Mrs. John H. Brooks, whose maiden name was Hannah Frances Skinner, and have heard related to the family many times the story about Mrs. Keckley writing her book, "Behind the Scenes," I am delighted to verify the story as dictated by her.

Respectfully,

(Signed) Mary E. Brooks

1927–18th St. N. W.

During the Lincoln administration, James Redpath visited the White House quite often and it was through his advice, after he had studied conditions in Haiti, that Lincoln had Congress pass a bill for the recognition of the independence of this island. It was also upon facts presented by him that Lincoln received the first Haitian minister. Redpath was a friend of the colored people and as Mrs. Keckley seemed to know all of the really great men who visited the White House if only by name, it is natural that she should have trusted him to act as her literary adviser and ghost writer.

Redpath was one of the well-known literary writers of his day. He had supported Seward for President and was connected with the New York Radicals. Probably this is why the Radical papers of northern New York had so much in them about Mrs. Lincoln and even the extracts from *Behind the Scenes*. It is obvious that no ordinary man could have been the contact man for the Carlton Company. As the style of Redpath's book *John Brown* is identical with that of the Keckley book and the method of compiling it much the same, the evidence of Mrs. Brooks seems conclusive. Redpath had lived in Washington and New York, but after the war was over he made a trip through the South and became a great admirer of Jefferson Davis and assisted him to write his autobiography. Yet no one tried to take the credit from Davis because Redpath assisted him. Few men have written books of historical value without some assistance from research workers and others. It is no surprise that an expert should assist Mrs. Keckley to arrange her facts and make her book a good narrative.

To Mr. Anton Heitmuller of Washington, who visited her several times, Mrs. Keckley stated that Mrs. Lincoln's letters to her were never returned by Redpath and that the publishers printed them without her consent. To Mrs. Eliza Williams, her most confidential friend, she stated that what she did, she did to help Mrs. Lincoln, and that the publishers printed the letters without her consent.

Every unfavorable criticism possible was made against the book. It was said to be a book of scandal and trash, but now that nearly all celebrated Lincoln writers quote it, it is considered one of the greatest and most reliable source books.

In an appendix to *Behind the Scenes* are printed intimate personal letters from Mrs. Lincoln. These Mrs. Keckley entrusted to Mr. Redpath on his promise that nothing would be printed that would in any way injure Mrs. Lincoln. When the book appeared it was found that these letters had been included with but little editing. Robert Lincoln was furious. He was so enraged that he refused to listen to any explanation but roughly ordered Mrs. Keckley away from his door when she called to explain and apologize. He then prevailed on the publisher, G. W. Carlton & Co., to suppress the book.

Mrs. Lincoln never saw Elizabeth Keckley again although letters passed between them. As for Mrs. Keckley, the long remaining years were made doleful with the thought that what she had done to help her friend had only brought distress to both.

Newspaper men who sought interviews with Mrs. Keckley without success wrote what they imagined she would have said, had they been able to get her to talk.

There is nothing in the book that can be construed as an attack against the man who freed the colored people. There is not one word against Lincoln, Stevens, Sumner and many others. Only Seward is attacked by Mrs. Lincoln, and uncomplimentary remarks are made against other leaders whom Mrs. Lincoln thought were not doing all they could to bring the war to an end, or else were using Mr. Lincoln for what they could personally get out of the war, or else they had political ambitions and were trying in an underhand manner to cause Lincoln's defeat for a second administration.

Regardless of what the book reveals, nearly all authorities agree that had it not been published, the public would never have known about the family life of the martyred President and the heart throbs of the devoted woman who loved him more than words can ever tell. Even the letters which were printed without Mrs. Keckley's consent, give us a better picture of the real Mary Todd Lincoln and her troubles than any others yet discovered.

For many years after the publishing of the book, Mrs. Keckley continued to sew for the best families in Washington, and lived in the best colored homes. Like Mrs. Lincoln she suffered greatly from headaches and crying spells nearly all the time. She would never tell anyone what she grieved about. All day long she looked at Mrs. Lincoln's picture above the dresser, and seldom left her room for meals. She shunned everybody, and would never talk to a soul except to Mrs. Eliza Williams whom she had known since she lived on 12th Street.

Mrs. Williams, being well educated and a teacher of children in the Institute, came often during the day to see Mrs. Keckley, talk of old times and read the daily papers. She said to me that Mrs. Keckley never liked to talk about her book, but would always say it was a "sad memory," and that she "wrote it to help Mrs. Lincoln," "what was in the book was true" and "Mrs. Lincoln knew it all," that "she had tried many times to talk to Robert Lincoln, but he would never see her after he rebuked her for publishing his mother's letters." Mrs. Williams also said in her interview that Mrs. Keckley heard from her friend many times in a roundabout way after they were separated, and that she knew Mrs. Lincoln never had any hard feelings against her for the book. Miss Loretta Simms, who was also an inmate of the Home and waited on Mrs. Keckley, supported Mrs. Williams' story. Both attended Mrs. Keckley in her last sufferings.

MARY TODD LINCOLN

Love of the Negro for Lincoln's Wife

An intimate picture of the simple home life of the woman who was to become the First Lady and how she appeared in the eyes of her servant was given by Aunt Ruth Stanton, an old colored woman who was a nurse in the Lincoln family and who remembered back to 1848 when Robert Lincoln was five years old.

Aunt Ruth's story was printed in the *Illinois State Journal* in Springfield, February 12, 1895 when she was a janitress in St. Louis.

This is the story told by the old colored woman, minus the quaint dialect:

> The Lincolns were poor then and lived in a frame house with six rooms. Mrs. Lincoln belonged to the Episcopal church, and so did the Bradfords. I used to take the Bradford children to Sunday school, and on the way we would sometimes see Mr. Robert Lincoln, who was only 5 years old. He was going to Sunday school, too, and the Bradford children would say: "Oh, Ruth, there's that Bobby Lincoln with his patched pants! Let's go the other way, so as we won't meet him." Then we would go by a roundabout way to church to get away from Bobby Lincoln because he used to wear blue jean pants which his mother made for him and patched for him when he wore a hole in them. After awhile Mrs. Bradford

sent me over to help Mrs. Lincoln every Saturday, for she had no servant and had to do her own housework. Then Mrs. Bradford sent me to live with the Lincolns.

I scrubbed the floors and waited on the table and helped Mrs. Lincoln to clean the dishes and do the washing. She did all the upstairs work, made clothes for the boys, Robert and Willie, and cooked the meals. Mr. Lincoln was a very good and kind man, but I don't remember anything particular about him, for I was very young. He was a very tall man. That's all I can remember of him. He used to be at his office all the day long, and I did not see much of him, but I never expected to see him President of the United States.

Mrs. Lincoln was a very nice lady. She worked hard and was a good church member. Every Thursday the sewing society of the Episcopal church would meet at Mrs. Lincoln's house and make clothes for the very poor people. She was very plain in her ways, and I remember that she used to go to church wearing a cheap calico dress and a sun bonnet. She didn't have silk or satin dresses. The children, Robert, 5 years old, and Willie, a few years younger, were very good boys. I used to take care of them, for they were too small to go to school. We would play around the streets of Springfield, and the white children would throw stones at the colored children.

After I left, Mrs. Lincoln had to do all of her own housework, for she could not afford to get another servant. I have never seen any of the family since, but of course I have heard a great deal about them. I guess that Mr. Robert Lincoln does not remember when he used to wear patched jean pants since he has become a big man.

Mrs. Lincoln's tragedy interested me because I have always felt there is no character in American history who is more in need of a champion. From my interviews with the old folks I found that she was beloved as no other white woman in public life and that they thought of her as their earthly Holy Mary.

I learned that no colored servant who knew her ever thought her actions crazy or that she had a mean disposition. They knew that Mrs. Lincoln not only gave $200 to start the first Contraband Society, which was founded by Elizabeth Keckley, but that she sent from the White House for distribution among the poor old exslaves, many loads of presents which had been sent her, and that she visited these places regularly with her husband.

I found that the old people believe that because of attacks from without and trouble from within Mrs. Lincoln sought Mrs. Keckley as a friend to look out for her comfort and sympathize with her, and that she relied upon her more than upon her family.

The old folks loved Mary Lincoln with a love that went with them to the tomb, and they thought of her as second only to the Emancipator.

THE END

APPENDIX

To Whom It May Concern:

I recognize this portrait which my husband the late Richard Jones permitted Dr. John E. Washington to photograph from the original painting as an excellent reproduction of the portrait of President Lincoln. I was told that it was painted from life and presented to General Philip Sheridan by President Lincoln. In one corner it was signed R. Clague 1865.

Many years later, it was given to my husband who served the General for many years.

After his death, being so worked up at my loss, and the breaking up of my home, and thinking that the little cracks in the canvass, and the torn places in the canvass around the sides of the stretcher had ruined it, I threw the old painting out into the trash and ashes which destroyed it.

Several years ago when Dr. Washington asked for the painting, I told him the above story and said I would gladly have given it to him for his Lincoln collection.

My husband and the doctor were great friends and they often went over stories about Lincoln, the General and the Civil War. He gave Dr. Washington some autographed checks of General Sheridan. We lived in the same neighborhood for many years, and I am glad to state that the statement about the painting and my husband as written by Dr. Washington are true.

Dr. Washington gave me a photograph similar to this one and I shall prize it highly.

Respectfully,

Anna W. Jones.

Letter from Mrs. Richard Jones authenticating the photograph of the Sheridan-Lincoln portrait reproduced as frontispiece.

Reproduction of one of the Sheridan checks mentioned in the letter. Richard Jones was the orderly and servant of General Sheridan. The original check endorsed by Richard Jones is in the author's collection.

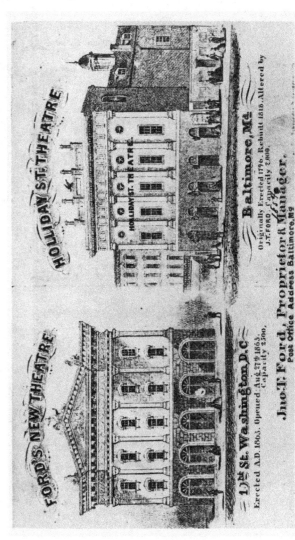

FORD'S THEATERS.

*Rare lithograph of earliest drawing of Ford's New Theater, issued
to celebrate its opening.
Obtained by author from the scrap-book of Joseph Sessford, Manager and ticket seller of Ford's Theater. Now in author's collection.*

Washington, D.C., March 8/16.

Dr. J. E. Washington,
    Washington, D.C.

Dear Sir:-

    This piece of black silk with little
white flowers in it, was taken from the
dress worn by Mrs. Mary Lincoln, Friday
evening, April 14, 1865 at Ford's Theatre.

    It is stained with the blood of
President Abraham Lincoln, and was given to
my father, Major C. A. Fleetwood by Mrs.
Slade to whom it was given by Mrs. Mary
Lincoln as a souvenir of the assassination.

        Respectfully,
                        Edith Fleetwood

P.S. Mrs. Slade was the wife of Mr. Wm.
Slade who was messenger to President Lincoln.

                Edith Fleetwood

*Letter from Miss Edith Fleetwood authenticating the piece of the
dress Mrs. Lincoln wore on the night of the assassination. This piece
of dress is in the author's collection.*

Statement of Elizabeth Keckley applying for a pension.

Statement of (Mrs.) Alberta Elizabeth Lewis-Savoy
Born - June 10th, 1863 at premises No. 388 Twelfth Street,
Northwest (now known as premises #1017 - 12th St. N.W.)

*****   Mrs. Elizabeth Keckley lived with my parents Mr. and Mrs.
WALKER LEWIS at 388   12th Street, Northwest, this city on three
different occasions.

She carried on an extensive dressmaking business and taught
young girls how to sew, fit and design pretty dresses. She had a
figure on which she draped the dresses. I forget the name she
called the figure; but she taught the S. T. TAYLOR system of
cutting and she set out from her dressmaking establishment finished
dressmakers.   Many seamstresses owe their success in life to the
thorough, painstaking instruction given by Mrs. Keckley.

If I were fifteen years of age when Mrs. Keckley moved to
our home at 1752 Pea Street, N. W., it would be 1878 A. D., and
she did not have any helpers at that time.   While living with us
on Pea Street, Mrs. Keckley gave me a piece of black thread and told
me that it came off of a dress of Mrs. Abraham Lincoln's; and she
also gave me a little piece of Valenciennes lace that came off of a
white linen cambric dress worn by her.

Respectfully submitted,

Alberta Elizabeth Lewis Savoy

Note:-Mrs. Keckley was living at our house 1017-12th St., n. w.,
in 1874...
*****   *A.E.L.S*

Note:- for verification, see Behind the Scenes by Elizabeth Keckley, Page 182.

Statement of Mrs. Lewis-Savoy with photograph of lace worn by
Mrs. Lincoln on a dress made by Mrs. Keckley.

*Copyright notice on back of the title page of "Behind the Scenes"
showing the mistake in stating that application for copyright was filed
in the Southern District of Pennsylvania instead of New York.*

*Application for copyright was at that time filed in the District in
which the Author lived. This mistake was one of the reasons for doubting that Mrs. Keckley was the real author.*

I, *Elizabeth Keckley* declare and
publish this to be my last will and testament.

I give, bequeath and devise to the National Association for the Relief of Destitute Colored Women and
Children all the property of which I am possessed.

I appoint Rebecca J. Cole to be executrix of
this my last will and testament, and request that she be
not required to give bond for the performance of this duty.

Elizabeth Keckley.

Attested and subscribed in the presence of the
testatrix, and of each other in the city of Washington,
District of Columbia, this *fourteenth* day of November, 1905.

Sara F Bullard.
La Fayette M. Hershaw.

The Will of Elizabeth Keckley.

Executive Mansion

Washington *April 5* 186*4*

Mrs ———————— (of Concord Mass)

Madam

The petition of persons under eighteen, praying that I would free all slave children, and the heading of which petition it appears you wrote, was handed me a few days since by Senator Sumner. Please tell these little people I am very glad their young hearts are so full of just and generous sympathy, and that, while I have not the power to grant all they ask, I trust they will remember that God has, and that, as it seems, He will to do it.

Yours truly
A. Lincoln

Letter from Lincoln to Mrs. Horace Mann.

This letter of President Lincoln to Mrs. Horace Mann of Massachusetts acknowledges a petition by persons under 18 years of age praying that he free all slave children. It is of great importance.

January 1, 1863 the President issued his celebrated proclamation which declared all slaves in states then in rebellion against the Union, and also in the District of Columbia, forever free. There were other slave states that were not in rebellion against the Union, and in these slavery was permitted to exist. Slaves in rebellious states only became free when the Union Army captured the Confederate Army in that state and carried out the provision of the Emancipation Proclamation.

It was not until February 1, 1865, two years after the issuing of the Emancipation Proclamation, that Congress passed and the President signed the 13th Amendment to the Constitution which forever abolished slavery in the United States.

In his letter written between the passing of these two important documents, Lincoln, as often before stated, claimed that he did not have the power to free the slaves but God had, and that he felt God would do so.

(Letter reproduced through the courtesy of the Library of Congress.)

PROCEEDINGS

OF THE

FORTY-EIGHTH ANNUAL SESSION

OF THE

BALTIMORE CONFERENCE

OF THE

African Methodist Episcopal Church,

April 13th, 1865.

BENJ. T. TANNER, Secretary,   J. D. S. HALL, Assistant.

PRICE FIFTEEN CENTS.

BALTIMORE:
PRINTED BY JAMES YOUNG,
114 West Baltimore street.
1865.

Reproduction of cover-title of the "Proceedings" of the Baltimore Conference and copy of the Resolution. This is the first formal resolution adopted relative to the assassination of Lincoln.
The original pamphlet is in the collection of the author.

PROCEEDINGS
of the
FORTY-EIGHTH ANNUAL SESSION
of the
African Methodist Episcopal Church
April 13th, 1865.

April 15, 1865.

"Conference met. Bishop Payne in the chair.

Bishop Payne here arose and gave notice of the terrible assassination of President Lincoln. He said it was a most painful duty, and the pain was increased from knowing he fell by the hand of a cowardly assassin, and not rather by a magnificent foe. He advised the appointment of a committee to draft resolutions expressive of the sentiments of the Conference.

The committee withdrew, and in a few minutes reported the following:—

Whereas, We the members of the Baltimore Annual Conference of the African M. E. Church have heard with most profound regret, and not unmingled with indignation, of the cowardly assassination on the 14th day of April, in the City of Washington, of the Chief Magistrate of the Republic, the great and good Abraham Lincoln, therefore,

Resolved, by the Baltimore Annual Conference of the African M. E. Church, in Conference assembled, that while we bow in submission to the event that has transpired, we can but shed tears at the cruel act of the assassin.

Resolved, That while the blood of John Brown was shed to inaugurate the meting out of justice to those who had long oppressed the Savior in the person of the bondmen, the death of the great President will be made the occasion of continuing the work until the divine mandate which awards death to men-stealers, be fully and literally accomplished.

Resolved, That we extend to his successor, President Johnson, our hands and hearts, together with the two hundred thousand muskets in the hands of our brethren to protect the flag of our country.

Resolved, That we tender to the estimable Lady of the White House our profoundest condolence. And be it further

Resolved, That we tender our sympathies to the Hon. W. H. Seward, Secretary of State, who has been inhumanly assaulted."

Fourth Day's Proceedings

April 17, 1865

On motion the Finance Committee were ordered to pay $17 for placing the Church in mourning in memory of the illustrous President deceased. Benediction by Bishop Wayman.

Fifth Day's Proceedings.

April 18th, 1865

The conference in a body, and headed by Bishops D. A. Payne and A. W. Wayman, and also accompanied by several visiting brethren from the Eastern Conferences, proceeded in order to the depot, and took a special train which had been provided, and at 8 o'clock started for Washington to take part in the burial services of our late illustrous President, Abraham Lincoln.

GENERAL HANCOCK'S APPEAL TO THE COLORED PEOPLE

———◆◆◆———

Headquarters Middle Military Division,
Washington, D. C., April 24, 1865.

To the Colored People of the District of Columbia and of Maryland, of Alexandria and the Border Counties of Virginia:

Your President has been murdered! He has fallen by the assassin, and without a moment's warning, simply and solely because he was your friend and the friend of our country. Had he been unfaithful to you and to the great cause of human freedom he might have lived. The pistol from which he met his death, though held by Booth, was fired by the hands of treason and slavery. Think of this, and remember how long and how anxiously this good man labored to break your chains and to make you happy. I now appeal to you, by every consideration which can move loyal and grateful hearts, to aid in discovering and arresting his murderer. Concealed by traitors, he is believed to be lurking somewhere within the limits of the District of Columbia, or the States of Maryland and Virginia. Go forth, then, and watch, and listen, and inquire, and search, and pray, by day and by night, until you have succeeded in dragging this monstrous and bloody criminal from his hiding place. You can do much; even the humblest and feeblest among you, by patience and unwearied vigilance, may render the most important assistance. Large rewards have been offered by the government, and by municipal authorities, and they will be paid for the apprehension of the murderer, or for any information which will aid in his arrest. But I feel that you need no such stimulus as this. You will hunt down this cowardly assassin of your best friend as you would the murderer of your own father. Do this, and God, whose servant has been slain, and the country which has given you freedom, will bless you for this noble act of duty.

All information which will lead to the arrest of Booth, or Surratt, or Herold, should be communicated to these headquarters, or to General Holt, Judge Advocate General, at Washington, or, if immediate action is required, then to the nearest military authorities.

All officers and soldiers in this command, and all loyal people, are enjoined to increase vigilance.

W. S. Hancock,

Major General U. S. Volunteers, Com'dg Middle
Military Division.

63D CONGRESS,
2D SESSION.

S. 4307.

IN THE SENATE OF THE UNITED STATES.

FEBRUARY 2, 1914.

Mr. MARTINE of New Jersey introduced the following bill; which was read twice and referred to the Committee on Claims.

A BILL

For the relief of Elizabeth Thomas.

1   *Be it enacted by the Senate and House of Representa-*

2 *tives of the United States of America in Congress assembled,*

3 That the Secretary of the Treasury be, and he is hereby,

4 authorized and directed to pay to Elizabeth Thomas, out of

5 any money in the Treasury not otherwise appropriated, the

6 sum of $10,000, the same being due her at the close of the

7 Civil War.

    Bill for the relief of Elizabeth Thomas, heroine of the battle of Fort Stevens.

    For fifty years Mrs. Thomas sought payment by the Government for the destruction of her home by the soldiers. President Lincoln promised that she would be paid.

    A search of the records reveals no payment to Mrs. Thomas. In 1914 Senator Martine of New Jersey introduced the bill reproduced here. It was apparently never reported out by the Committee.

    This treatment of Elizabeth Thomas is a monument to the ingratitude of Government and its disregard of a citizen without influence.

Lincoln-Thomas Day Celebration

SEPTEMBER 22ND was designated by the National Federation of Colored Women's Club of America, in session August 1-6, 1924 at Chicago, Illinois, as Memorial Day in honor of Abraham Lincoln and Elizabeth Thomas. In all colored Churches a fitting tribute will be paid these memorable characters Sunday, September 21st. Lincoln's Gettysburg speech will be read in school rooms where colored children assemble throughout the land as well as in the homes of thousands of patriotic colored American citizens.

LOCAL PROGRAM SEPTEMBER 22, 1924

At 12 o'clock noon a wreath will be placed at the Lincoln statue at Lincoln Park. At 12:30 o'clock another wreath will be placed at the Lincoln statue in front of the court house after which the members of the Federation will visit the Lincoln Memorial.

At 4 p. m. the entire Federation will make a pilgrimage to Fort Stephens where it is expected hundreds of the colored citizens will also assemble.

Program at Fort Stephens

4 P. M. SEPTEMBER 22ND

To reach Fort Stephens, take the Georgia Ave. car, get off at Power House. Committee will meet cars and direct to grounds.

PRESIDING OFFICER, MRS. JULIA MASON LAYTON

SPEAKERS—Ten minutes.

Mrs. Virginia White Speel, Chairman of Women's work in and for the District of Columbia.

Mrs. M. C. Lawton, Chairman of Eastern Division Colored Section.

Miss Hallie Q. Brown, Director of Colored Women's activities at National Republican Headquarters.

Mrs. M. C. Terrell, President of the Women's Republican League.

Chorus—"Coolidge and Dawes". Composed by E. M. Boston and led by Mrs Mae Richardson and descendants of Elizabeth Thomas.

ELIZABETH THOMAS

Generally referred to as the "Heroine of Fort Stephens," as she appeared two years before her death at the Civil War Veterans Reunion, May 30th 1924.

PROGRAM AT FORT STEPHENS—Continued

SPEAKERS—five minutes.
Miss R. E. Bell, President of the Elizabeth Thomas Citizens' Association.
Mr. Harry Clarke.
Mr. Perri W. Frisby.
Mr. Jesse Foster.
Mr. Thomas L. Jones, D. C. Delegate.
Mr. Phoenix.

Music under the direction of Mrs. Richardson.

Julia Mason Layton, President of Federated League of Women's Political Clubs
Eva A. Ghass, Organizer
Gabrielle Pelham, Chairman, Committee of Arrangements.

PROGRAM OF LINCOLN-THOMAS DAY CELEBRATION—From the original in the author's collection. He secured it from Miss R. E. Bell, President of the Elizabeth Thomas Citizen's Association.

Peter Brown's story regarding the Battle of Fort Stevens, which appeared in the Washington Evening Star, *and which is reprinted here by courtesy of the* Evening Star.

"The stone spring-house is the only building on the Lay premises, in front of Fort Stevens (Brightwood Ave, Washington, D.C.) that survived the terrific cannonade, on the afternoon of July 12, 1864. The fine Mansion house, with all its valuable contents, the barn and other structures were destroyed by the exploding shells. These buildings, and the available trees that surrounded them, were occupied by Confederate sharp-shooters, who were killing and wounding the pickets in front of the Fort,—and taking long range

shots at the officers, who were standing on the parapet. A shot aimed at Gen. Wright, who was using a field-glass, struck Surgeon Crawford of the 102 Penna. reg't inflicting a severe wound. President Lincoln was standing on the parapet when this shot was fired. The guns of the Fort opened on the buildings and trees, to dislodge the sharp-shooters and this brought on the engagement, known in history, as the Battle of Fort Stevens."

REWARD FOR THE CAPTURE OF BOOTH.

[To accompany bill H. R. No. 801.]

Mr. HOTCHKISS, from the Committee of Claims, made the following

REPORT.

The Committee of Claims, pursuant to the resolution of the House of Representatives of May 7, 1866, which was in these words—

On motion of Mr. Kelley,

Resolved, That the Committee of Claims be instructed to inquire into the fairness and propriety of the distribution of the rewards offered for the arrest of Jefferson Davis and the conspirators to murder President Lincoln.

submit the following report:

Your committee have carefully considered the claims of the parties presenting evidence to them, or as to the merits of whose claims they have been able to procure evidence, and the terms of the several offers of reward, and the circumstances under which they were made, and they respectfully report, that, in their judgment, a liberal construction of such offers authorizes the award of five thousand dollars to the parties engaged in the arrest of Payne, who attempted the assassination of the Secretary of State, which sum is, in the opinion of the committee, amply sufficient to compensate the parties who effected such arrest for the time and efforts devoted to that end. The circumstances attending such arrest were, to state them briefly, as follows:

On Saturday night, the 15th April, 1866, Susan Mahony, now Susan Jackson, a colored servant girl of Mrs. Surratt, by feigning sleep, overheard disclosures and witnessed transactions, at Mrs. Surratt's house, showing that the inmates of, and the visitors at, that house were connected with the assassination plot. On the next day she made haste to communicate these facts to her aunt, Mary Ann Griffin, a colored woman of this city in the employ of John H. Kimball. This woman on the next day communicated the same to Mr. Kimball, who acted upon this information. These colored women were somewhat tardy in their movements, but it should be borne in mind that they were under the restraints incident to their life-long position of servitude and assumed inferiority; and fears for their personal safety, with a certain prospect of loss of place and employment, to say nothing of persecution in case they should be suspected of being informers against their employers. Under these circumstances the committee regard their conduct as highly commendable, and their acts as coming within the spirit and letter of the offers of reward for the arrest of Payne.

It has been further shown to the committee that the said Kimball, immediately upon receiving the aforesaid information, started for General Augur's headquarters: that on the way he was joined by Mr. P. M. Clark, who was making voluntary efforts to discover the assassins; that the two were instrumental in setting the force in motion for taking possession of the Surratt house.

The committee, therefore, regard the said Kimball and Clark as parties to the proceedings which, as hereinafter shown, resulted in the capture of Payne.

Immediately upon the examination of Kimball, at General Augur's headquarters, a force of five detectives, commanded by Major H. W. Smith, took possession of Mrs. Surratt's house, and in a short time thereafter Payne came there and fell into their hands.

And the committee further report that in their opinion the sum to be awarded should be distributed as follows:

To Major H. W. Smith who had charge of, and commanded the force,

the sum of	$1,000
Richard C. Morgan, detective	500
Eli Devore, detective	500
Charles H. Rosch, detective	500
Thomas Sampson, detective	500
William M. Wernerkirch, detective	500
John H. Kimball, citizen	500
P. M. Clark, citizen	500
Susan Jackson, colored	250
Mary Ann Griffin	250

Official report on the part played by Susan Jackson in the arrest of the conspirators. (Ordered printed July 24, 1866.)

The old colored people believe that Susan knew of the plot before the assassination for she was the servant of Mrs. Surratt and was in the house during the meetings when the assassination was planned.

I Saw Lincoln Shot!

And here is my story—told now for the first time

By William J. Ferguson

THIS is the fourteenth of April, 1920. It is exactly fifty-five years since I stood in the wings of Ford's Theatre—waiting for my cue to go on the stage—and saw the murder of Abraham Lincoln and the flight of John Wilkes Booth, his assassin.

No other person witnessed the whole of that tragic event. From the moment he fired the death dealing shot until he had leaped to the back of his horse in the alley behind the theatre, Booth was never out of my sight.

I was standing in the first entrance at the time, just off stage to the left of the audience. The President and Mrs. Lincoln, together with a young woman and an army officer whom I did not recognize, were sitting in the balcony box on the right, which was almost directly opposite me and about thirty feet away. At my side was Miss Laura Keene, star of "Our American Cousin"—the comedy that had reached the second scene of its third act when the assassination took place. It was a few minutes before ten o'clock.

Miss Keene had been rehearsing with me the lines I was about to speak. Harry Hawk, the "Asa Trenchard" of the piece, had just finished a soliloquy and had turned toward the rear to make his exit.

Suddenly a shot rang out close to where the President was sitting in a rocking chair, hidden from the audience by a draped lace curtain and the wooden wall that shut off his box from the balcony. I saw a puff of smoke. Mr. Lincoln's head sagged forward. At the same instant a man sprang to the front of the box. He grasped the rail with his right hand. His left hand held a bowie knife. I recognized him as John Wilkes Booth, an actor whom I had seen fre-

quently in the course of my season's work as call boy, amanuensis, and filler of utility parts.

From the balcony box to the stage was a direct drop of twelve feet. As Booth was about to spring over the rail, the army officer, who, I learned later, was

William J. Ferguson

Major H. R. Rathbone, rushed forward and grabbed him by his coat tails. The assassin lunged back viciously with his knife. The weapon entered Major Rathbone's left upper arm and broke his hold.

As Booth vaulted over the rail one of his spurs caught in the folds of an American flag, with which the box had been

draped to celebrate the fall of Richmond and the reoccupation of Fort Sumter. He whirled around in the air and fell to the stage heavily on his right knee.

Almost instantly, however, the assassin was on his feet, and rushing across the front of the stage directly toward the entrance where Miss Keene and I were standing. Dimly I realized that Mr. Lincoln had been shot—for I had seen his head, the face still lit by a tender half smile, sink forward to his chest. And I knew that Booth—a man with whom I had been talking that very afternoon—must have committed the deed. But the whole thing was too monstrous, too incredible!

I shall never forget the assassin's appearance as he leaped toward us. The usual olive complexion of his handsome oval face was blanched to a deathly white. His black eyes were blazing. His lips were drawn against his teeth and he was panting in pain, for the fall had fractured his leg. How he was able, with a broken leg, to make those swift five-foot strides, I shall never be able to understand.

In another moment Booth had run between Miss Keene and myself, pushing us apart and back against the two walls of the entrance. I felt his hot breath upon my face. As he shoved me with his left hand, the knife flashed before my eyes.

Back of the wings was a narrow passage which led to a door in the rear wall opening into an alley. Miss Jenny Gourlay, one of the players, and William Withers, leader of the orchestra, were talking together in the passage. They had been so intent in the conversation that they knew nothing about the crime. Unconsciously, however, they blocked the path of Booth's escape.

As the assassin rushed down this

15

Sample pages from an article by William J. Ferguson on the assassination of Lincoln which appeared originally in the August 1920 issue of the American Magazine *and which is reprinted here by permission of the magazine.*

passage, Withers turned around in surprise at the commotion. Booth struck at him with the knife and slashed the cloth up his coat for ten or twelve inches.

By this time I had partly recovered from my daze. Following after Booth, I had got as far as the angle of the wall when he dashed through the rear door, leaving it open behind him.

Little John Burroughs, who was bundle boy for the actors at the theatre, was holding by the bridle the bay mare which Booth had left in the alley a little earlier in the evening. Booth shoved the boy to the ground, vaulted on his mount, and dug his left spur in her flank. The mare leaped forward, her hoofs striking sparks from the cobblestones into

the murky April night. An instant later they were galloping madly down the alley to the angle of another small alley which led into F Street.

All these events had passed with incredible swiftness. I suppose not more than forty seconds had elapsed between the firing of the shot and Booth's disappearance.　　　*(Continued on page 82)*

Ferguson—Who Saw the Greatest Murder in Modern History

Still an important actor on Broadway, where he has been playing for forty-seven years

By Merle Crowell

FORD'S THEATRE

Friday Evening April 14th, 1865.

THIS EVENING
PRESIDENT LINCOLN

BENEFIT
AND
LAST NIGHT
OF MISS
LAURA KEENE

MR JOHN DYOTT
AND
MR HARRY HAWK

TOM TAYLOR'S CELEBRATED ECCENTRIC COMEDY

ONE THOUSAND NIGHTS,
ENTITLED
OUR AMERICAN
COUSIN

BENEFIT OF MISS JENNIE GOURLAY
THE OCTOROON.

EDWIN ADAMS

From the collection of Judd Stewart. Facsimile of the program used in Ford's Theatre the night of the assassination

IT WAS hard to believe that William J. Ferguson—one of the actors at Ford's Theatre on the night of Lincoln's assassination—was still playing on Broadway.

"There must be some mistake," I protested. "Where is he?"

"Up at the Casino. Drop around and see for yourself?"

I did see for myself—and rubbed my eyes to look at the program again. For in the rôle of Oliver Butts, a sentimental butler, Ferguson was leading several of the funniest numbers in "The Little Whopper," a girl-and-music comedy. His work included bits of eccentric dancing and snatches of song. To me it was the comedy hit of the whole performance.

Between acts I went back-stage.

"You'd like to have a chat with me!" repeated Ferguson. "Well, I'm pretty busy these days, but—"

"Oh, any time will do, Mr. Ferguson," I hastened to assure him. "Forenoon, afternoon, or evening."

A smile came into Ferguson's deep blue eyes and broke out a moment later on his lips.

"Suppose you listen to my daily program, young man," he remarked. "My home is out in the other end of Brooklyn. I get up every morning before seven o'clock, ride for half an hour on the trolley to the nearest subway station, travel about ten miles in the tube, cross the Hudson River on a ferry, and then take another trolley to the studio in Jersey where I am kept busy at the 'movies' all day. I arrive back here at the theatre in time for the evening performance, and when I get home again it is one o'clock in the morning. Really, the only spare time I seem to have"—and the smile grew broader—"are the six hours that I waste in sleep."

"How long have you been keeping this up?"

"Oh, for three months," he replied—and dodged back onto the stage.

Ferguson has been playing before Broadway audiences for half a century. All the stage folk look on him as a sort of "miracle man;" and they were not at all

surprised, two years ago, when he decided to break into motion pictures—where he scored an immediate success.

"I wasn't going to let a lot of youngsters get the jump on me in an entirely new field," he declared.

Grant's guns were still hammering the walls of Vicksburg when Ferguson first faced an audience across the footlights. Since then he has appeared before millions of people in hundreds of characters. He has taken all the male rôles in every one of Shakespeare's popularly acted dramas. With the adaptability of the true craftsman, he has played leading, comedy, heavy and juvenile parts at will. He has trod the boards with practically every great figure in American dramatic history since the Civil War. And to-day—with the Psalmist's three score years and ten well behind him—he is actually busier than ever before. Richard Mansfield, Edwin Booth, Joe Jefferson, Mary Anderson, Madame Modjeska, and Clara Morris are among the great actors and actresses with whom his name has at times been billed.

FERGUSON was born in Baltimore, Maryland. At the age of eleven he became a printer's devil on the Baltimore "Clipper." Although he soon learned how to arrange and set type he found little fascination in newspaper work. Already the theatre was beginning to beckon.

An opening came when he was sixteen years old. John T. Ford—a fellow elder with Ferguson's father in the Third Presbyterian Church of Baltimore—needed a call boy in his Washington theatre. Young Ferguson was offered the job at five dollars a week, plus what money he could pick up by serving as amanuensis to the actors. This latter work consisted in copying individual parts from manuscripts at the rate of eight cents for forty-two handwritten lines.

The double duties kept the youth occupied from nine in the morning until eleven in the evening. During every performance he watched *(Continued on page 86)*

Sample page from an article by Merle Crowell about William Ferguson which also appeared in the American Magazine and is reprinted here by permission of the author.

Springfield, Ills. Aug: 15. 1855

Hon: Geo. Robertson
        Lexington, Ky.
                My dear Sir:

                        The volume you
left for me has been received— I am really
grateful for the honor of your kind remem=
brance, as well as for the book— The partial
reading I have already given it, has afforded
me much of both pleasure and instruction—
It was new to me that the exact question
which led to the Missouri compromise, had
arisen before it arose in regard to Missouri;
and that you had taken so prominent a
part in it— Your short, but able and pat=
riotic speech upon that occasion, has not
been improved upon since, by those hold=
ing the same views; and, with all the lights
you then had, the views you took appear
to me as very reasonable—

You are not a friend of slavery in the ab=
stract— In that speech you spoke of "the
~~peaceful extinction of slavery~~" and used oth=
er ~~expressions~~ indicating your belief that
the thing was, at some time, to have an end—
Since then we have had thirty six years of

experience; and this experience has demonstrated, I think, that there is no peaceful extinction of slavery in prospect for us—The signal failure of Henry Clay, and other good and great men, in 1849, to effect any thing in favor of gradual emancipation in Kentucky, together with a thousand other signs, extinguishes that hope utterly. On the question of liberty, as a principle, we are not what we have been—When we were the political slaves of King George, and wanted to be free, we called the maxim that "all men are created equal" a self evident truth; but now when we have grown fat, and have lost all dread of being slaves ourselves, we have become so greedy to be *masters* that we call the same maxim "a self: evident lie" The fourth of July has not quite dwindled away; it is still a great day — *for burning fire-crackers*!!!.

That spirit which desired the peaceful extinction of slavery, has itself become extinct, with the *occasion*, and *the men* of the Revolution—Under the impulse of that occasion, nearly half the

State, adoption systems of emancipation at once; and it is a significant fact, that not a single state has done the like since—

So far as peaceful, voluntary emancipation is concerned, the condition of the negro slave in America, scarcely less terrible to the contemplation of a free mind, is now as fixed, and as hopeless of change for the better, as that of the lost souls of the finally impenitent— The Autocrat of all the Russias will resign his crown, and proclaim his subjects free republicans, sooner than will our American masters voluntarily give up their slaves—

Our political problem now is "Can we, as a nation, continue together permanently—forever—— half slave, and half free?" The problem is too mighty for me— May God, in his mercy, superintend the solution—

Your much obliged friend
and humble servant
A. Lincoln—